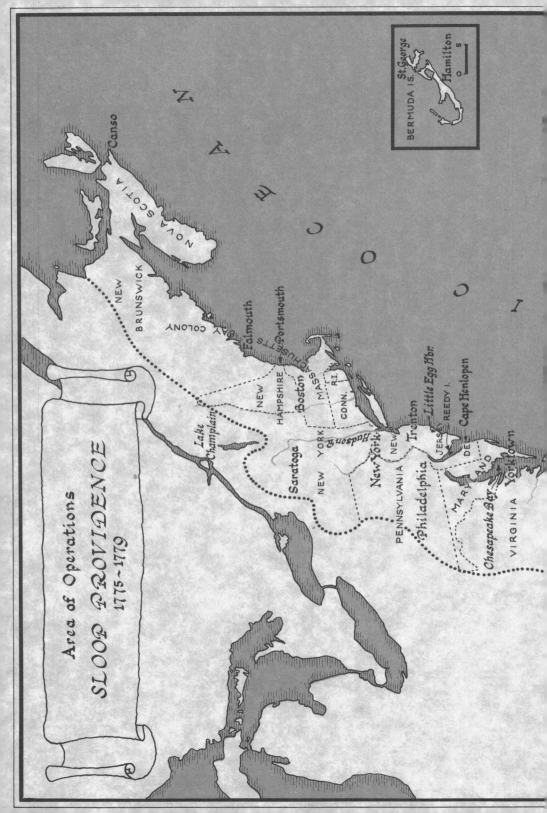

Area of Operations
SLOOP PROVIDENCE
1775~1779

N OCEAN

Canso

NOVA SCOTIA

NEW BRUNSWICK

MASSACHUSETTS BAY COLONY

Falmouth
Portsmouth

NEW HAMPSHIRE

Lake Champlain

Saratoga

NEW YORK

Boston
MASS.
R.I.
CONN.

Hudson R.

New York

NEW JERSEY

Trenton

Little Egg Hbr.
Reedy I.
Cape Henlopen

PENNSYLVANIA

Philadelphia

DEL.

MARYLAND

Chesapeake Bay

VIRGINIA

Yorktown

BERMUDA IS.
St. George
Hamilton

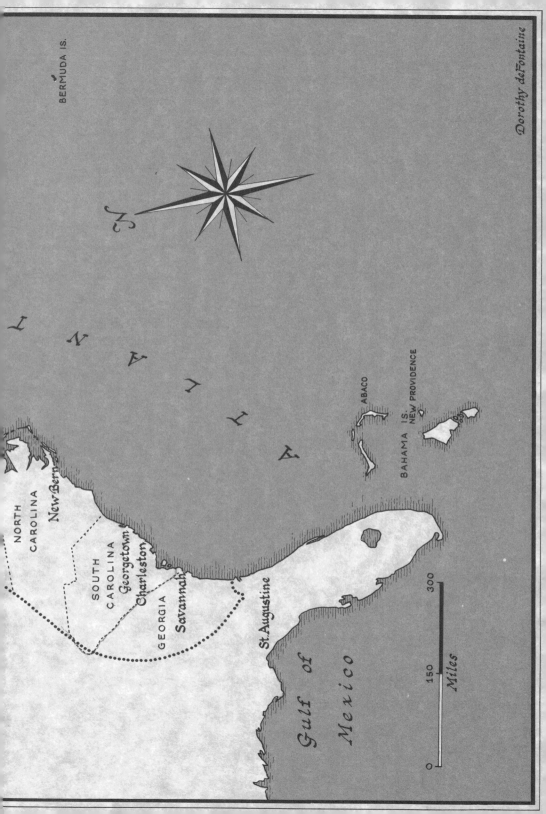

BERMUDA IS.

Dorothy deFontaine

ATLANTIC

ABACO

BAHAMA IS.
NEW PROVIDENCE

NORTH
CAROLINA

New Bern

SOUTH
CAROLINA
Georgetown
Charleston

GEORGIA
Savannah

St. Augustine

Gulf of Mexico

0   150   300
Miles

Valour Fore & Aft

HOPE S. RIDER

Valour Fore & Aft

BEING THE ADVENTURES OF
AMERICA'S FIRST NAVAL VESSEL

SEAPORT '76 FOUNDATION, LTD.
NEWPORT, RHODE ISLAND

Seaport '76 Foundation, Ltd., is a non-profit organization dedicated to preserving in vital, dynamic form the rich maritime heritage of 18th Century America. Its initial project, sending to sea a reproduction of sloop *Providence*, this country's first naval vessel, is one step in a program aimed at bringing to all our people a sense of the glory of our naval history, and the vigor and valour of the men who made it.

Membership in Seaport '76 is offered to anyone interested in American sailing history and its preservation. Inquiries are welcome at Box 76, Newport, Rhode Island 02840.

First edition published by United States Naval Institute, Annapolis, Maryland

Library of Congress Catalog Card Number: 76-17516
ISBN: 0-87021-744-5

Printed in the United States of America

To Two Great Rhode Island Mariners

John Peck Rathbun
who made this story worth telling

and

John Nicholas Brown
who made the telling possible

Foreword

creation of an 18th Century maritime museum complex in Rhode Island planned to complement 19th Century Mystic Seaport and 20th Century Southport.

Already sloop *Providence* is a familiar sight in Narragansett Bay, where she has taken part in historical reenactments of Revolution-ary events and visited several ports that welcomed her ancestor, including India Point in Providence, where the keel of John Brown's *Katy* was laid. Wherever she goes, she is a colorful spectacle, from her black hull, with its broad buff stripe and touches of red, blue and gold, to the Colonial flags whipping in the wind and the long pennant that streams from her masthead as defiantly as it did two centuries ago. Officers in Revolutionary uniform on the quarterdeck direct the acrobatic activities of the Sea Explorers, both boys and girls, who form her crew, and the marines manning the carriage guns that send out, if not cannon-balls, satisfying bangs and puffs of smoke. Nylon replaces canvas and hemp, and fiberglass some of the wood, but despite the modern compromises, the look, the feel, and the performance of this *Providence* are faithful to the original.

Seaport '76's plans for the sloop include using her extensively for sail training, and sending her to ports all over the United States as a visible symbol of the dauntless spirit that made this nation and its Navy great. She will take part in historical reenactments, among them her own single-handed capture of Nassau, and some of her crew may participate in underwater archeological opera-tions. Project Heritage Restored in Maine is now recovering valuable artifacts from the brig *Defence* in Penobscot Bay, and the University of Rhode Island has been exploring four British frigates scuttled off Portsmouth, R. I. The site of sunken sloop *Providence* in the Penobscot River just south of Bangor, Maine, has been located, and may itself become the object of archeological diving opera-tions.

Whatever the activities of the sloop, her chief aim will be education—to bring to as many people as possible, besides those lucky enough to sail on her, a sense of living history and the valour and endurance of the men who made it.

Several noted historians have written about the early Conti-nental Navy. This biography of a single sloop deals with other vessels in the fleet only when the *Providence* sailed with them, thus neglecting many that had interesting careers of their own. In recounting those fleet actions that did involve sloop *Providence*—the first expedition to the Bahamas, the ensuing battle with HMS

ONE PICTURE is said to be worth a thousand words, but the Holman painting reproduced at the front of this volume is worth a whole book. As John Nicholas Brown indicates, his acquisition of the canvas sparked this research, aimed mainly at furnishing documentary evidence of the identity of the painted sloop. John Millar of Newport, who had located the painting in Greenwich, England, had recognized the ensign (as the English had not) as the Grand Union flag, and the sloop flying it as the *Providence*. However, the painting, which was signed by Francis Holman and dated 1777, was designated simply as "An Armed Vessel Attacking an English Ship." "Maybe that's not the *Providence*," said Mr. Brown. "Could you find out?"

This volume contains the answer to that question—whether the "yes" is unequivocal or not is up to the reader to judge. The course of "finding out," like that of the *Providence* herself, was neither smooth nor straight, but it was incredibly rewarding. Sloop *Providence, ex-Katy,* was a most remarkable vessel, whose history is rooted in pre-revolutionary events and involves some of the prime movers of the rebellion. It also touches upon the careers of several naval captains, some of whose names are already well known, like John Paul Jones, and others, such as John Peck Rathbun and Jonathan Pitcher, who have only recently begun to receive long-overdue recognition. Under the command of such men, she earned a reputation as a "lucky sloop"—an epithet bestowed by no less august a body than the Marine Committee of the Continental Congress itself—and became noted for exploits that James Fenimore Cooper characterized as "greatly exceeding what might have been expected from her force."

Although as a result of those exploits she became famous in her own day, the full story of her adventures, together with her captains', has gone untold for a couple of centuries. If this volume succeeds in putting into sharper focus the somewhat blurred picture of the *Providence* and the valiant men who sailed her, it will have more than served its purpose.

Sloop *Providence* has attained national prominence in an even more tangible way. Although there are no plans of her construction extant, her type, the Rhode Island sloop, is well known, and several scale models of her have been built. Now a much more ambitious project is under way. Seaport '76 Foundation, Ltd., of Newport, R. I., a non-profit organization relying heavily on the continuing support of its membership, has completed a full-size, operational reproduction of the *Providence* as the first step in the

Preface

If one is fortunate enough to be a Rhode Islander, it is natural to be interested in nautical matters and especially in the early history of ships plying the waters of Narragansett Bay. So, when the marine scene painted by Francis Holman in 1777 came to my attention a year or so ago, I could not resist acquiring it. As can be seen from the reproduction of this painting used as a frontispiece to this book, the subject is an encounter between the USS *Providence* and a British full-rigged ship. The *Providence* had been acquired by the Continental Congress from the Colony of Rhode Island, which had recently purchased her for $1250 from my ancestor, John Brown of Providence, who had built and operated her as the *Katy*. There is a jaunty impertinence about this representation which shows her great courage and disregard of danger. I decided that I would like to know more about the *Katy* and asked the author of this book, Mrs. Hope Sisson Rider, to make some researches. The result is this volume. The story of this little sloop, which, by the way, was John Paul Jones' first command, has been based upon the most rigorous research of original eighteenth century documents. Yet the carefulness of Mrs. Rider's scholarship has only enhanced the dramatic story of a little ship fighting against the greatest naval power in the world.

This book describes in detail the background which produced Rhode Island's own navy and later provided ships when the Continental Congress decided to have a navy of its own. In all the ramifications the *Katy* stands out as a shining example of the way Americans braved hardships and the deep in order to pursue desperate adventures in the name of liberty.

Newport, Rhode Island   John Nicholas Brown

Glasgow, and the disastrous venture at the Penobscot—I have tried to stick as close to the *Providence* as possible, with apology for any inattention to the others. Also, in an attempt to convey some sense of what it was like to live and work aboard a small rebel vessel in the days of fighting sail, I have included some details of shipboard routine that must remain conjectural, although they are based on documented practice of the period.

Putting together this history of an indomitable sloop has been a source of such pleasure that I feel as lucky as the *Providence* to have been given the privilege of writing about her. For this I am inexpressibly grateful to John Nicholas Brown. Not only did he instigate the research, but his constant encouragement, enthusiasm, and editorial help turned it into a book which, without him, would not yet have been written.

The sense of vicariously enjoying the luck of the sloop is strengthened by the extraordinary number of people who have generously shared their own knowledge in support of this work. My particular thanks go to John Millar of Newport, R. I., Frank H. Rathbun of Alexandria, Va., Emil S. Guba of Waltham, Mass. and Henry Beetle Hough of Martha's Vineyard; to Louise Gerretson of the Naval Institute Press, Nat Shipton and Nancy Chudacoff of the R. I. Historical Society, Phyllis Peloquin of R. I. Archives, and Alan Perry of the National Archives. Staff members of the Providence Athenaeum, Mass. Archives, and the Historical Societies of Massachusetts and Maine have also been of great help. In addition, I am indebted to Dr. William James Morgan and his associates in the Naval History Division for the publication of *Naval Documents of the American Revolution,* an invaluable collection of original material from this country and abroad. Although wherever possible I have gone to the original manuscripts themselves, many of which are in New England, for less accessible material, such as British Public Record Office documents, I have relied heavily and gratefully on *Naval Documents.*

To all known and unknown benefactors who have contributed to the completion of *Valour Fore & Aft,* my profound thanks.

Providence, Rhode Island   Hope Sisson Rider

Contents

Illustrations

Valour Fore & Aft

CHAPTER I

Rhode Island Gets a Navy

JUNE 1772—JUNE 1775

RHODE ISLAND HAD the best of reasons in 1772 for becoming the first of the colonies to send a fleet to sea. Its very name—Rhode Island and Providence Plantations—reflected its maritime situation. Aquidneck Island, site of Newport, the largest and most prosperous town, was then known as Rhode Island. Providence, only half the size of Newport, lay 25 miles to the northwest up the Providence River, and the Plantations were a thin string of settlements, mostly along the edges of Narragansett Bay. Nearly all of the Colony's inhabitants earned their living in some way connected with the sea, and any interference with maritime commerce was a threat to their very existence. Consequently, British attempts to regulate and tax colonial trade were especially keenly felt and bitterly resented in this, the smallest of the colonies.

Newport, long the capital of the Colony and home of some of its most prosperous citizens, was a stronghold of Tory sympathy. Many townsmen were Quakers, more inclined to compromise with the King's officers than to defy them. Although there were loyalists on the mainland too, there the spirit of rebellion flourished. Prosperous Providence merchants, including Nicholas and John Brown, were particularly provoked at the imposition of what they considered unreasonable duties and restrictions on their trade. They were not disposed to take them lying down.

Three years before Rhode Island authorized its navy, an incident had taken place that may be said to be the real beginning of the Revolution. It not only antedated the Boston Tea Party, but comprised much more drastic action. In June 1772, a band of Providence patriots burned the British customs schooner *Gaspee*—an act of open hostility that was to lead directly, though not immediately, to the sailing of Flagship *Katy* in June 1775. The *Katy* took no part in the burning of the *Gaspee*, being out on an innocent whaling voyage at the time, but she was owned by John Brown. And he was involved in it up to his neck.

The story is familiar enough. Lieutenant William Dudingston, commander of the *Gaspee*, was, from the colonial viewpoint, excessively zealous in stopping and searching local vessels. Furthermore, his arrogant refusal to present his credentials to civil authority, in which Rhode Island's charter vested an unusual amount of power, rendered his activities illegal in their eyes. Bitter correspondence between the Governor and the British lieutenant produced nothing but rising tempers, but when the chance came for direct action, John Brown and his compatriots took it.

It was on 9 June 1772, that Captain Thomas Lindsey, returning from New York in his Providence packet *Hannah,* was chased by the *Gaspee.* Captain Lindsey ran up Narragansett Bay and, hoping the British ship with her deeper draft would follow, sailed through the shoal water off Namquit Point. There, sure enough, the *Gaspee* went aground. On reaching Providence, Captain Lindsey hurried to John Brown with the news that the hated schooner was stranded and could not be got off until high tide early the next morning. John Brown wasted no time. The rest is history—the summoning of Abraham Whipple, veteran captain of Brown ships, to make ready seven longboats; the drum beaten in the streets to convene volunteers at Sabin's tavern. There in the evening bullets were cast in the kitchen while out front final plans were laid. There was apparently small attempt at either secrecy or disguise, although it was prudently decided that the use of proper names should be avoided. Orders were to be given by John Brown and Captain Whipple, addressed respectively as "Head Sheriff" and "Captain." Near midnight the seven boats, oars muffled, pulled away from the dock for the row downriver to the stranded schooner. In the sternsheets of one of them sat John Brown, representing the flouted civil authority of the Colony.

An eyewitness account[1] of what followed describes the hail from the *Gaspee* as the longboats approached, now joined by one from Bristol, and the appearance of Lieutenant Dudingston on deck in his nightshirt to demand who went there. As Captain Whipple shouted in reply, "The High Sheriff of this colony, damn you!", an impetuous volunteer snatched up his neighbor's rifle and shot the British lieutenant in the groin. At sight of their fallen captain and the attackers swarming over the rail, the crew of the *Gaspee* promptly surrendered. Save for the wounding of Lieutenant Dudingston, whose wound was immediately dressed, the plans so hastily formulated had been carried out with incredible smoothness. The British seamen and their captain were speedily put ashore at Pawtuxet, while the firing party remained on board to put the *Gaspee* to the torch.

Great was the rejoicing in Providence the next morning as smoke from the fire could still be seen downriver, and the town buzzed with the news of the heroes who had rid them of the detested schooner. So little secrecy had been attempted that everyone knew who they were. Two young participants openly bragged of their exploit as they cavorted about in the street modeling Lieutenant Dudingston's cocked hat.

Unfortunately, the identities of the perpetrators were soon equally well known to the authorities representing the King at Newport. Understandably outraged, they sent off frantic reports to the Admiralty in London, and set out to bring the malefactors to justice. Governor Joseph Wanton promptly offered a reward of one hundred pounds for information leading to the conviction of the perpetrators, but none was forthcoming. British frustration and indignation found voice, when the news reached England, from no less a personage than his Britannic Majesty himself. In August 1772, John Brown and Abraham Whipple were distinguished by particular mention, though not by name, in a special proclamation by George III.

The King's proclamation (see Appendix A) announced the burning of "our vessel called the Gaspee schooner" between the hours of twelve and one in the morning on the tenth day of June last, by "a great number of persons, armed with guns and other offensive weapons, and led by two persons who were called the captain and head sheriff." In order to discover the "outrageous and heinous offenders," rewards were offered—£500 and amnesty for the informer for the conviction of any of the participants, and an extra £500 for conviction of the head sheriff or captain. There would be no amnesty for them.

To implement his proclamation, the King convened a Board of Inquiry at Newport, including his "trusty and beloved" chief justices of Rhode Island, Massachusetts, and New York. To this court he gave the broadest possible authority, including the extraordinary power to send suspects back to England for trial. This was a clear abrogation of the charter of the Colony. News of it caused consternation among all the colonial governments, expressed through those Committees of Correspondence that were the forerunners of the Continental Congress.

The Board sat, off and on, for ten months, hearing a long succession of witnesses and reading pages of sworn testimony. One of the more interesting depositions was made by an ex-midshipman of the *Gaspee,* to whom we are indebted for a rare contemporary description of John Brown and Abraham Whipple. "The head sheriff," he said, "was a tall, genteel man, dressed in blue clothes, his hair tied behind, and had on a ruffled shirt . . . . The captain . . . was a well set man of swarthy complexion, full face, hoarse voice, and wore a white cap, was well dressed, and appeared rather above the common rank of mankind."[2]

However, proclamations, rewards, and depositions were all in

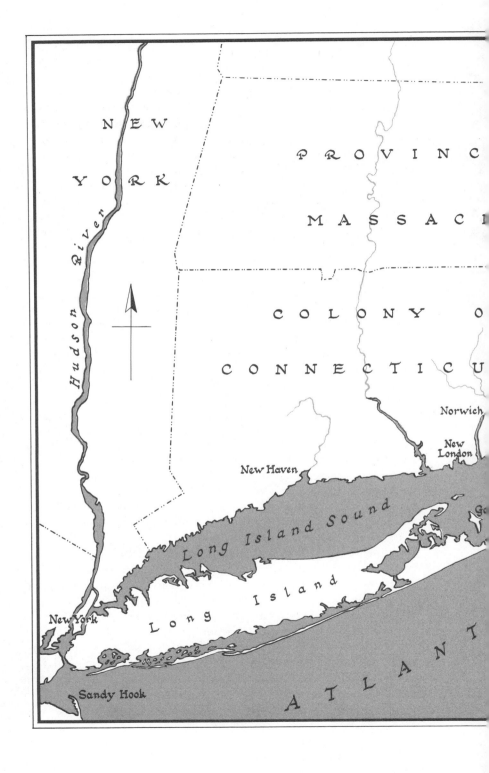

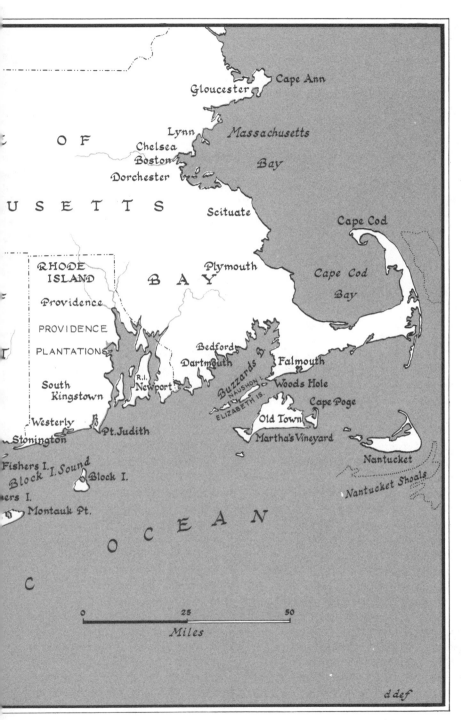

The colonies of Massachusetts, Rhode Island, and Connecticut, and surrounding waters.

vain, and it remains one of the most remarkable facts about the whole extraordinary affair that the Court was unable to return a single accusation. A negro slave, who did name a number of the participants, was later found to have been under coercion by the British, and his testimony was discredited. In his official report, the Chief Justice summed up the Court's incredible failure by saying, "My sentiments upon the whole are, that this daring insult was committed by a number of bold, daring, rash enterprising sailors, collected suddenly from the neighborhood, who banded themselves together, upon this bold enterprize; by whom stimulated for the purpose, I cannot conjecture . . . . "

So the malefactors, John Brown and Abraham Whipple at the forefront, went unapprehended but not unremembered by the British. Retaliatory measures were inevitable, and more import duties and stricter enforcement provoked further resentment on the part of colonials as opposition hardened on both sides. There was no immediate replacement of the *Gaspee,* however, and Narragansett Bay was more or less neglected by the British, whose attention in 1773 was directed toward Massachusetts. In the spring of 1774, Vice Admiral Samuel Graves was sent to help General Thomas Gage keep Boston in line and to blockade the harbor. There he sat in his flagship *Preston,* thinking up new schemes to harass colonial shipping and writing letters outlining them to the British Admiralty. In November 1774, the respite from surveillance that Newport and the Bay had enjoyed came to an end, when Admiral Graves sent the 20-gun frigate *Rose,* with Captain James Wallace commanding a crew of 130, to take up the station of the departed *Gaspee.*

Where the *Katy* was and what she was doing in the spring of 1774, we can only guess. Indeed, we have almost no information about her origins and early history. John Brown owned a shipyard at India Point in Providence, where he probably had her built by craftsmen skilled in the construction of Rhode Island sloops. Although no plans of the *Katy* exist, this type of vessel is still in use today and provides reliable data of her design. Possibly she was built before the end of the Seven Years War in 1763 to be used as a privateer. The earliest of her voyages for which there is record is a cruise to Surinam, the Dutch colony on the northern coast of South America, in 1769. The following year she went out as a whaler, and after another whaling voyage in 1772, the record is silent.

Built for speed as well as strength, she was designed to serve a number of useful purposes. Her hull, sixty-odd feet long with a twenty-foot beam, was heavily timbered. A high quarterdeck ran nearly half her length, giving ample room below for officers' sleeping quarters—captain on the starboard side, junior officers to port—the wardroom, and a great stern cabin lighted by five big windows. To compensate for her weight and beam, she was designed to carry a good bit of sail. Her single mast, towering more than eighty feet above the open gundeck, was crossed by two yards that swung in rope slings and were rigged to carry a big square topsail as well as studding sails for running before the wind. She carried an enormous gaff-headed mainsail, and on her 39-foot bowsprit and jib-boom could be rigged three headsails—fore staysail, jib, and flying jib. Thanks to the Holman painting, reproduced as the frontispiece of this book, we have a good idea of what the *Katy* looked like in action, although there is reason to suppose that in her early days her sides were painted black rather than scraped as they appear in the painting.

We can only speculate about the time and manner of her armament. If she was designed as a privateer or armed merchantman from the beginning, as seems likely, then at least some of her ten carriage guns would have been part of her original equipment. The *Katy*'s cannon, named for the weight of the shot they threw, were four-pounders. She certainly carried some of them— probably six, mounted on the main deck—before her appointment as flagship in 1775, but just how long before and how many, we cannot be certain.

Some clue may be provided by Captain Wallace soon after his arrival at Newport in the *Rose*. Having dropped her hook in the harbor on 27 November 1774, he almost immediately took the *Rose* out again on a two-week scouting cruise in Long Island Sound. Upon his return, he discovered that a number of cannon had, during his absence, been removed from Fort (now Goat) Island, and carried off up the Bay to Providence. In an indignant report sent to Admiral Graves in Boston, he listed among the ordnance seized by the inhabitants, "they say here of Providence," six four-pounders which "formerly belonged to a Province Sloop they had here."[3] It is quite possible that that sloop was the *Katy*, whose cannon, once her privateering days were over, had been dismounted and stored in the fort when she became a merchantman and whaler. When a British warship once again appeared in Newport Harbor, John

Brown would have certainly felt that those guns would be a lot safer back on board his sloop. The fact that the first account of the *Katy* in action described her as mounting six carriage guns lends strength to this speculation. After communicating with the General Assembly, on whose order the cannon evacuation was carried out, John Brown would have despatched the *Katy* to do the job. It needed a vessel of her size and strength for, besides her own old guns, the ordnance removed consisted of six twenty-four pounders, eighteen eighteen-pounders, and fourteen six-pounders—a pretty heavy cargo. The supposition that it was the *Katy* who did the transporting is further bolstered by the fact that a few months later, as Rhode Island's flagship, she paid the fort another visit, stripping it of all the remaining cannon.

The early months of 1775 brought no easing of tension in the Colony. Captain Wallace, like Admiral Graves a believer in the theory that more repressive measures would bring the rebels to heel, assiduously employed the *Rose* in the same unpopular service as the late unlamented *Gaspee*. In addition, he brought to his job certain knowledge of which men were responsible for the destruction of the British schooner. Although he had no immediate means of bringing the perpetrators to justice, he was in no way kindly disposed toward John Brown or Abraham Whipple. His high-handed behavior in stopping and seizing ships did nothing to endear him to Rhode Islanders. Even Newport, generally more sympathetic to the British cause than Providence, began to show annoyance.

All during the winter and early spring of 1775, the *Providence Gazette* and the *Newport Mercury* printed frequent reports of harassment. A Salem captain "was treated very rudely by the officer and people of the *Rose* . . . who insisted on going into the hold among his hemp with a light." A sloop from Nantucket was fired on three times off Sakonnet Point, one shot whistling close between two of her men. A threat to tar and feather Captain Wallace came to nothing, and a plot to seize him and his ship was frustrated when word of it leaked out. Admiral Graves nonetheless saw fit to send reinforcement, and the sloop *Swan,* carrying 14 guns and 100 men, came to join the *Rose* in Newport Harbor. On 25 February, the *Gazette* reported that the two vessels "are very vigilant in searching

HMS Rose, *Flagship* Katy's *adversary before the Revolutionary War. Detail from an aquatint by Dominic Serres, after a sketch by Sir James Wallace. Courtesy, The Mariners Museum, Newport News, Virginia.*

almost every Vessel that arrives in the River.—Three Seizures have been made by them within a few Days past." No boat, however innocent, was apparently immune—on 19 April, according to the *Gazette*, "the point ferryboat had two shot fired at her from the tender of the ship *Rose* in this harbor, one of which went between the post-rider and the ferryman."

Throughout the spring of '75, patriotic sentiment and resentment of Captain Wallace's actions had prompted the General Assembly to make preparations for war. Orders were given for troops to be raised, and officers commissioned. When newly re-elected Governor Wanton of Newport refused to sign the commissions, the Legislature refused to let him take the oath of office. To

Deputy Governor Nicholas Cooke, a bold and able patriot from Providence, fell the task of directing the affairs of the Colony.

News of the Battle of Lexington did nothing to soothe Captain Wallace's irascible temper, which led him, a week afterward, to commit an act unprecedented in British-colonial relations. It was to have far-reaching repercussions throughout the colonies and for the *Katy* as well.

On 26 April 1775, Captain Wallace kidnaped John Brown. Public records of this extraordinary act are meager, but the circumstances are well documented. John Brown, already at the top of Captain Wallace's wanted list as "head sheriff" of the *Gaspee* affair, had been secretly appointed by the General Assembly as its agent to procure flour for the rebel forces. Captain Wallace, whose sources of intelligence included, incredibly, Metcalf Bowler of Newport, Speaker of the House, had learned of this appointment almost as soon as it was made. When John Brown went down to Newport to claim his flour, Captain Wallace was ready for him. The flour had been duly cleared at customs and loaded aboard two sloops, the *Diana*, owned by the Lindsey of *Gaspee* fame, and the *Abigail*, belonging to the Hacker family of Providence. Mr. Brown was a passenger aboard the *Diana*, bound for Providence, when Captain Wallace snatched the chance to repay old scores. He seized the flour, the sloops, and John Brown.

The log of the *Rose* noted laconically, "Seized the Sloops Diana and Abigal with 300 Barrels of flour bound to Providence for the Rebel Army, sent an Officer and 10 Men on board the Diana."[4] No mention was made of Mr. Brown or the fact that he was detained overnight and sent off to Boston in the morning.

The *Newport Mercury* of 1 May was more explicit. "Last Wednesday, as Mr. John Brown, of Providence, merchant, was going from this town to Providence, in one of the Packets, the Packet was stopped, by order of Capt. Wallace, of the ship Rose, and Mr. Brown taken on board the ship Swan: soon after which another packet was stopped as she was going up. These Packets had on board a quantity of flour, which Mr. Brown had purchased for a number of vessels he was fitting out. Part, or all, of the flour was taken on board the ships; and the next day Mr. Brown was sent off in one of the packets, to be carried to Admiral Graves, at Boston, without having a single reason given for his being thus violently seized and carried out of this colony, contrary to all law, equity and justice."

Aboard the British man-of-war *Swan* in Newport Harbor, on 26 April, John Brown spent an uncomfortable night, while family, friends, and assorted dignitaries frantically but unsuccessfully sought his release. One prominent Newporter managed to get to see him, and wrote to John's brother, Nicholas Brown, that "On seeing him the Sympathising Tear trickled on my Cheek. I was from four o'clock in the morning till 10 or 11 in Soliciting and taking every method to effect [his release] but in vain."[5]

Captain Wallace remained adamant and the next morning, disregarding all protests, loaded the flour and his prisoner into the *Abigail* and sent her off for Boston. For the *Diana* he had other plans—to arm her for use as a tender to the *Rose*.

John Brown's state of mind as Newport fell away astern can well be imagined. Facing the possibility of being sent to England for trial, either as ringleader of the *Gaspee* affair or agent of the rebels of Rhode Island, he could look forward to little mercy at the hands of a hostile jury.

During the five days that it took *Abigail* to get to Boston, news of the seizure roused the neighboring colonies, and letters of protest poured into the Massachusetts capital. Governor Wanton wrote to General Gage that "Yesterday, Capt. Wallis . . . stopped a small Sloop, bound to Providence with a Quantity of Flour, consigned to Mr. John Brown, Merchant in that Town, who was a Passenger on board said Sloop, with a regular Sufferance from the Custom House for the Flour; notwithstanding which, Capt. Wallis detained Mr. Brown on board His Majesty's Ship *Swan*, and contrary to my Request for his dismission has sent him round to Boston, to the very great Distress of his Family and numerous connexions . . . . "[6]

Ex-Governor Stephen Hopkins, soon to become a Rhode Island delegate to the First Continental Congress, reported the seizure to the Provincial Congress of Massachusetts. He was more candid about the flour, noting that John Brown had been appointed "to purchase Provisions, for the Use of this and your Government," and strongly urging reprisal. "We have thought Proper to send you this Notice, to the End that you may detain all such of the King's Officers . . . as may be in your Hands, to answer and be accountable for the Conduct and Treatment, which may be had and acted to Mr. Brown." Recognition of the fact that the intelligence leak came from a high source was expressed in Hopkins' admission that "the first Struggle, which hath happened

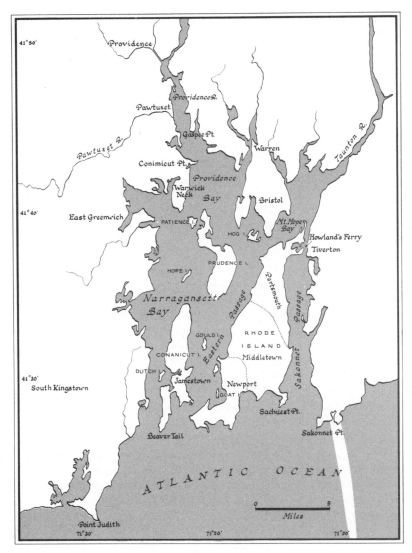

Scene of Katy—Providence*'s adventures in Narragansett Bay.*

in our Colony, hath been unfavorable; an Event which could not
have come to pass, but by the Faithlessness of some of the Members
of our Assembly, who must have revealed their Proceedings,
although the Oath of GOD was upon them to Secrecy . . . "[7]

As news of the seizure of one of Providence's most prominent
citizens spread, repercussions began to be felt in the neighboring
colonies. In response to Hopkins' letter, the Massachusetts Congress offered to provide prisoners of war for Mr. Brown's
exchange. From Fort Ticonderoga, General Ethan Allen wrote to
Governor Trumbull of Connecticut, "I make you a Present of a
Major a Captain and two Lieuts in the regular establishment of
George the Third I hope they may serve as ransoms for Some of
our Friends at Boston and particularly for Capt. Brown of Rhodeisland."[8]

The affair had reached the proportions of a cause célèbre by the
time the *Abigail* arrived in Boston with her unhappy, though celebrated, passenger. John Brown's brothers Moses and Joseph had
been busy for several days in Boston, petitioning the Massachusetts
Congress, General Gage, and Vice Admiral Graves, and doubtless
when the *Abigail* finally arrived, the British authorities were as anxious as they to smooth things over. There was no need for an
exchange of prisoners. John Brown was taken aboard HMS *Preston*,
and then, in company with both the Admiral and Moses Brown, to
appear before General Gage. In a conciliatory atmosphere, both
brothers signed a solemn pledge to urge cooperation between British and colonial authorities, and were dismissed—to ride back to
Providence, tradition has it, on a single horse.

The *Newport Mercury* commented with feeling, "Mr. John
Brown, merchant, whom we mentioned in our last to have been
illegally seized and sent to Admiral Graves, at Boston, by order of
Capt. Wallace, of the ship Rose, on this station for the *protection* of
trade, was there honorably discharged, and his Flour, which was
unrighteously taken from him, ordered to be paid for, with dam-
ages etc. for the detention of the two packets . . . . Several thousands, sterling, have been recovered in England, for a less violence
than that committed on the person and liberty of Mr. Brown."[9]

The diary of Newporter Ezra Stiles confirmed the *Mercury*
report and included mention of the burning of the *Gaspee*, which
was tactfully omitted from the public record. Under date of 4 May
1775, Dr. Stiles wrote, "A little before sunset Mr. Russel of Providence came to town and informs that Mr. Jno. Brown was dismissed and came home to Providence last night about XI h at

night. That he was first put on board Adm. Graves, then bro't before Gen. Gage. Capt. Wallace's pretence for apprehending him was that he was concerned in burning the *Gaspee* Schooner. Application was made to Judge Oliver of the Commissioners that sat on that Affair at Newport and he testified that no Accusation was exhibited against Mr. Brown, upon which Gen. Gage dismissed him, paid him for his flour, ordered the Packets to be returned to Providence and to be paid Demurage, and has sent off a Reprimand to Capt. Wallace of the *Rose* Man o' War here—A humbling stroke to the Tories! The General and Admiral treated Mr. Brown politely and dismissed him with Honor."[10]

It appeared that the crisis was over and, with a conciliatory attitude demonstrated by both sides, that further hostility might be avoided. On 7 May, John Brown appeared before the Rhode Island General Assembly to deliver an appeal for negotiation with General Gage and moderation in dealings with the British. The ensuing motion passed the Lower House, but was defeated in the Upper. Mr. Brown had acted in good faith with his contract with the General in Boston; had Captain Wallace done likewise, the course of Rhode Island, and perhaps United States, history might have been a bit different. However, Captain Wallace, frustrated, resentful, and still angry, was in no frame of mind to make peace. Threats by him and his officers against John Brown and his vessels were reported and, more important, he showed no slightest inclination to return the seized packets to their owners. On the contrary, Lindsey's *Diana* had already been armed and manned, to serve as a tender to the *Rose,* and the *Abigail,* on her return from Boston, awaited a similar fate. Whether or not Captain Wallace had Vice Admiral Graves' tacit consent to this course, we can only guess. It is unlikely that he would have disobeyed direct orders from his superior to return the packets, and there is no record that he was reprimanded for failing to do so.

The continued detention of the packets would have been galling enough to Rhode Islanders; their use against the Colony's own boats was nothing short of infuriating. One of the biggest problems for shipowners was to warn their incoming vessels, which, back from long voyages and ignorant of Captain Wallace's activities, might fall easily into his hands. While their suspicions would be aroused at the sight of a British ship of war, nothing could be more reassuring than the appearance of their own familiar packets. These, like wolves in sheep's clothing, were thus doubly dangerous.

The patriots in the Colony were understandably outraged at Captain Wallace's abrogation of the agreement with General Gage—none more so than John Brown, who felt a special sense of responsibility for the loss of the two boats, not to mention justifiable indignation at his own treatment. In an effort to force Captain Wallace's hand, he instigated a suit against him for £10,000. This action came to nothing when it was learned that under the law the writ could not be served on the British captain.

Legal redress had failed, but something had to be done— especially when the *Diana* on 6 June made seizure of a schooner loaded with provisions belonging, according to the *Mercury*, to "near 70 poor men at Nantucket, and the chief [supplies] their families had to depend on for a considerable time to come." That was too much for outraged Rhode Islanders in general and John Brown in particular. Their patience had run out, but their determination to get the packets back had not. With legal relief unavailable, there remained but one way to do it: to take them by force.

It cannot have taken long to determine that the best way to exert that force would be to arm and man a vessel of sufficient speed and strength to recapture the packets. The choice of a ship suitable to undertake the mission was a foregone conclusion. John Brown's *Katy*, which had already sailed in the service of the Colony, was both ready and available. She was equipped to mount ten carriage guns, of which six were already mounted on the gundeck, and had plenty of room for portable swivel guns to be used on the bulwarks, on the quarterdeck, or as bow or stern guns as needed. Her wide beam gave ample space below for enough crewmen to sail the sloop and man the guns. That great spread of canvas made her a fast sailer, and her shallow draft of less than ten feet, together with the agility afforded by her fore-and-aft rig, suited her perfectly for hit-and-run operations in Narragansett Bay.

The question of who would command her presented equally little difficulty. Captain Abraham Whipple, already in as much trouble with the British as he could get, had nothing to lose by fighting them openly. The courage and seamanship that had made him one of the Browns' most successful captains and that had been so apparent at the burning of the *Gaspee* were just the qualities needed for this assignment.

John Brown thus stood ready to furnish both vessel and captain, but he had one grave reservation about sending them out. He didn't want to go it alone. Accordingly, when the General Assembly met in East Greenwich on 12 June 1775, he addressed to its secretary and Deputy Governor Cooke a private and most illuminating letter. It deserves quotation in full.

> Gentlemen   Providence, June 12th 1775
>   Applycation havg this Day bin Made to persons here to Risque Mr Hackers Boat, he being gone to the Camp, his Son was in Doubt wiether he Could Concent for her to go for fear his father mought Loose her as well as the one now in the hands of the men of warr, and as both the Boats now held by the men of warr are said to be Detained on Account of their haveing bin Imployd in the Colonys Service in bringing up the Guns Flour &c. it is Requested that You use your Interest in the Assembly that Sum Effectual Method be Immediately Tacon in Order that the Said Boats be forthwith Delivered up or Tacon, Sum principle people proposes that if Capt Wallace will not Deliver them up the Sherriff of the County of Newport be Orderd by the Assembly to take him and Committ him to Jail till said Packetts are Delivered, Others thinks that if the Sloop *Catey* goes out as my Property that it will make me so much more Obnoctious then Any Other person to Capt Wallace &c that my Vessills and Cargoes will be all tacon as they Came in, and I now having 10 Sail out, that its unreasonable that the publick Should Desire me to Sacrifise all my privit Interest for the Bennifitt of the Common Cause, Its therefore proposd that the Colony purchass Sum proper Vessill to be used in Garding the Coast, procureing powder or aney Other use they please I Expect the *Catey* under the Command of Capt Whipple will go Down with Hackers Boat tomorrow to meet Collo Vernon with his men so as to be Reddy to go out tomorrow nite I mention this that the General Assembly may if they think it worthy of Notice take the Same in to Consideration and Give Such Directions in this Matter as they in their Wisdom may think proper
>   I am Gentlemen
>
>   John Brown
>
> P.S. if the Colony will purchase the *Catey* I will agree to Leave it to aney three persons acquainted with navigation to Fix her Value
>
>   as I Faired so badly by Means of Undertaking to purchass the Flour for the Government, I Chuse you should keep my name Concealed from the House. Perhaps the Assembly may agree to hire and Resque both Vessills that goes to Retaik the packetts and to be at the Expense of fixing them weither they purchass or not which Countenence is Absolutely Necessary for the Incoragement of those who may go that doeth not allready belong to the Armey—[11]

This letter, with the General Assembly resolution that followed it, makes perfectly clear John Brown's role as prime mover in the creation of the first colonial navy, and hence the direct connection between the formation of that navy and the burning of the *Gaspee* almost exactly three years earlier. The General Assembly on 12 June 1775, Nicholas Cooke presiding, lost no time in taking "this matter into consideration," and in its wisdom passed the following historic resolution:

> It is voted and resolved that his Honor the Deputy Governor be, and he is hereby requested to write to James Wallace, Esq., commander of His Majesty's ship *Rose*, now in the harbor of Newport, and demand of him the reason of his conduct towards the inhabitants of this colony in stopping and detaining their vessels; and also to demand of him the packets he detains. [See Appendix B.]
>
> It is voted and resolved that the committee of safety be, and they are hereby directed to charter two suitable vessels, for the use of the colony, and fit out the same in the best manner to protect the trade of this colony . . . .
>
> That the largest of the said vessels be manned with eighty men, exclusive of officers; and be equipped with ten guns, four-pounders; fourteen swivel guns, a sufficient number of small arms, and all necessary warlike stores.
>
> That the small vessel be manned with a number not exceeding thirty men.
>
> That the whole be included in the number of fifteen hundred men, ordered to be raised in this colony . . . .
>
> That they receive the same bounty and pay as the land forces . . . .
>
> That the following officers be, and are hereby, appointed . . . to wit: of the largest vessel, Abraham Whipple, commander, with the rank and power of commodore of both vessels . . . . [12]

This pioneer naval resolution, with its preliminary stipulation of a last-ditch appeal to Captain Wallace, makes it clear that recapture of the seized packets was the raison-d'être of America's first navy. Although the name of John Brown's *Katy* does not appear, the orders shortly handed to Captain Whipple were addressed to "Captain Abraham Whipple, Commander of the Sloop *Katy*." Thus the relationship between the sequence of events from the burning of the *Gaspee* to the creation of Rhode Island's navy is easily traced. The key role of John Brown in the formation of that navy is as indisputable as the selection of his *Katy* for its flagship was inevitable.

The first naval orders ever issued to an American captain were handed to Abraham Whipple on 12 June 1775. (See Appendix C.) Although they made no direct mention of packets, they gave him plenty of leeway. They enjoined him, together with all others on board his said vessel, to "encounter expunge expel and resist by Force of Arms, as well by Land as Sea, and also to kill, slay and destroy . . . every such Person as shall attempt . . . the Destruction Invasion, Detriment or Annoyance of the Inhabitants of this Colony . . . and to take by all Ways and Means such Persons, with their ships, Vessels, Armour, Ammunition or other Goods as shall in hostile Manner invade or attempt the Hurt of this Plantation . . . . " All vessels carrying "Soldiers, Arms, Powder, Ammunition, Horses, Provisions, Cloathing, or anything else for the use of the Armies of Enemies of the united American Colonies shall be seized as Prizes." Following some regulations as to prizes came an injunction against captives' being "killed in Cold Blood, wounded, hurt, or inhumanly treated," and a warning that "no female Prisoner shall be in any manner abused under great and high Penalties . . . ."[13]

In addition to these orders, Captain Whipple was honored by a cryptic note from Captain Wallace, informing him that "You, Abraham Whipple, on the 10th June, 1772, burned His Majesty's vessel, the Gaspee, and I will hang you at the yard-arm."

To which Captain Whipple replied with some brief but sound advice.

Sir—Always catch a man before you hang him.
Abraham Whipple.[14]

CHAPTER II

Flagship Katy in Action

JUNE—NOVEMBER 1775

SUCH WAS THE TRAIN of events that led from the burning of the *Gaspee* in 1772 to the seizure of John Brown and the sailing of the *Katy* as Rhode Island's flagship in 1775. The exact extent of her armament at this time is not known. Her cannon were four-pounders, so rated by the weight of the balls they threw, mounted on movable carriages on the gundeck. Apparently *Katy* carried six of these so-called carriage guns—perhaps those taken from Newport a few months earlier—and four more would be added later in accordance with General Assembly instructions. Next in size were smaller, more flexible cannon known as swivel guns; these could be used as bow guns or stern chasers, or mounted on bulwarks as desired.

Gulls screamed and wheeled overhead as the *Katy* moved easily down the Providence River in a light following breeze on 15 June 1775. From her quarterdeck Captain Abraham Whipple surveyed his command. Running sails and the huge main bellied gently in the light air, and water lisped quietly along her bow. Men stood ready to man the swivels on the quarterdeck bulwarks, while on the gundeck below, crews waited at the cannon with shot, wadding, and slow-matches at hand. If the order to clear for action were given, the guns would be run out, and ship's boys would bring cartridges (cloth bags stuffed with gunpowder) up from the magazine to the gunners. Astern of the *Katy* sailed the little sloop *Washington*, Lieutenant John Grimes commanding, prepared to follow the flagship wherever she led.

The primary target of the infant navy was the recapture of the seized flour packets, Lindsey's *Diana* and Hacker's *Abigail*, still armed and serving as tenders to the *Rose* despite General Gage's orders for them to be returned to their owners. For once, Captain Wallace proved remarkably cooperative. Having that morning received intelligence of "armed vessels being fitted out by the rebels at Providence," he had sent the *Diana* under Master Savage Gardner with a petty officer and eleven men "to reconitre the different passages up the River."[1] In pursuance of this mission, the *Diana* was standing on and off between the north end of Conanicut (now Jamestown) and Gould islands. She was within sight of the *Rose* when, according to Master Gardner's report to Captain Wallace,

> a Sloop coming before the Wind, I lay'd too to speak her—a little after six being within hail, She hail'd Us and told Us to bring too or she would sink Us immediately . . . and directly fired a shot which we returned with our Small Arms and Swivels and kept a smart fire on both Sides for near half an hour, till by accident the Powder Chest with the remainder of the Swivel Cartridges blew up—in this Sloop

we saw six Carriage Guns mounted and a great number of Men Onboard—The Ammunition for the Small Arms being near expended and another Armed Vessel with Carriage Guns belonging to the Rebels joining and bringing Us between two fires, so that there was no possibility of saving the Vessel—I thought it prudent to run her ashore which I accordingly accomplished near the North end of [Conanicut] and got onshore with the People and part of the Small Arms. They immediately landed a number of Men from the Vessels in whale Boats who closely pursued and fired at Us—being so closely pursued and night coming on thought it necessary to separate and conceal Ourselves till a proper Opportunity offered of joining the Ship which was accomplished the next day without the loss of one Man . . . .[2]

While the Britishers looked for hiding places on Jamestown, the *Washington,* with *Katy* standing guard, quickly got the *Diana* afloat again, and "carried her off in Triumph, the 3 Vessels all sailing off Northward together."[3]

Such was the happy outcome of *Katy*'s first military assignment, and the historic exchange of shots between American and British naval forces. The war at sea had begun. *Katy*'s broadside of four-pounders had done its work without damaging the *Diana* and had secured for the rebel forces a good supply of sorely needed weapons—18 bright muskets, 17 cutlasses, 16 bayonets with scabbards, 12 pistols, 4 swivel guns and an assortment of powder and shot.

The British seamen stranded on Jamestown managed to get safely back to the *Rose* the next day, some of them by commandeering the ferry to Newport, but Captain Wallace was exceedingly irritated. On 17 June he planned his revenge. Hearing that the *Katy* and *Washington* were at anchor about twelve miles away, he got the *Rose* and the *Swan* under way "as secret as possible, expecting to fall upon them by Surprize. However they got Intelligence and moved higher up toward Providence in shallow Water, where it was not proper for us to pursue them." Still further frustration was in store. Upon his return to Newport, where he had left five vessels loaded with supplies to be sent to the fleet at Boston, Captain Wallace found that "a great number of the Towns People had taken advantage of our absence, Arm'd a number of Boats and Vessels—taken the Victuallers, carried them to Town, dismantled and unloaded them, and this done in the space of two or three hours."[4]

Altogether the initial action of the first American navy could be hailed as a signal success. However slight this twisting of the

British lion's tail, it must have been a marvelous satisfaction to the patriots to know that they were no longer helplessly watching their ships being snapped up by the enemy. Resistance on the water as well as on land had started.

After this auspicious beginning, reports of the *Katy's* activities are meager and tantalizingly vague. From them we glean that her first action was also her most dramatic, but it is difficult to make an accurate assessment of what she actually accomplished. Captain Whipple's recollection, expressed in a report to Congress several years later, was of having made a significant achievement. Explaining his appointment as Commodore "in order to clear the Bay of the enemy's tenders, and open a communication to the sea for the

Commodore Abraham Wipple, captain of Flagship Katy *of Rhode Island's Navy. From a painting by Edward Savage. Courtesy, U.S. Naval Academy Museum.*

numerous vessels which had been blocked up in our harbors and rivers," he went on to cite his accomplishments.

> By my exertions on the first day of my command I had the good fortune to take one of the British tendrs; and cleared the Bay of the remainder, whereby the principal part of the homeward bound ves- sels arrived safe without opposition, and the day became memorable for the first shot on Water in defiance of the British flag, which I ventured to do at no small hazard, from a sense of my country's wrongs, and at the same time when no man in the colony would undertake the hazardous business, lest he should be destined to the threatened cord. I continued cruising in our Bay until the 12th day of September 1775, during which period I had a number of actions with vessels of superior force, which were productive of advantage to America, and served to convince our enemies that their sons wanted not spirit to defend their just rights, even against a formidable power and almost under every discouragement.[5]

A somewhat less sanguine appraisal was made by Nicholas Cooke in a letter to Samuel Ward and Stephen Hopkins, the Rhode Island delegates to the Congress at Philadelphia. On 18 July he wrote that "We have three men of War and one packet that are constantly aRobing and plundering allmost all the Vessels that comes in Especially those that belong to providence none Escape that they can get in their power . . . . "[6]

It is easy to see that only limited success could be expected of the *Katy*, whose armament had been increased to 10 guns, probably by mounting four carriage guns on the quarterdeck, and 6-gun *Washington* against Captain Wallace's frigates and their tenders, particularly as the British captain enjoyed a considerable amount of support from Newporters. Governor Wanton, who had been denied his office by the Legislature because of his Tory sympa- thies, frequently invited Captain Wallace to dinner at his house. However, the mere presence of the two armed sloops was a con- stant annoyance to the British. Captain Whipple's strategy was to stay up in the Providence River in water too shallow for the fri- gates, action with whom he must at all costs avoid, and to be ready to dash down the Bay on the smaller vessels whenever opportunity offered. One of these was the flour packet *Abigail*, belonging to the Hackers, but still retained by Captain Wallace as a tender to the *Rose*. Concerning her, Captain Whipple had some specific instruc- tions from the Committee of Safety of the Rhode Island Assembly, which had received "certain advice" that all the men-of-war had sailed from Newport on 23 July, having left the packet in the possession of a prize schooner. Captain Whipple was requested to "sail as early tomorrow morning as you can, and go down the bay till you are certain whether the ships are in Newport or not. If they are not we advise your going out on the west side on Conannicutt, go round the Light house and run into Newport harbor and go directly alongside of Hackers Packet now in the hands of our Enemies and bring her directly to Providence. You'll order Capt Grimes either to be beating down to Newport as you run in or to go out before you or any other way as you may think will be best to accomplish the taking said packet." A postscript added, "If the Ships should be in tomorrow, perhaps they may soon go out again & leave the Packet in possession of said schooner. Therefore we hope you'll keep so good a lookout that you'll have possession of said Packet very soon."[7]

The British ships did indeed go out as scheduled, but there is no record that the *Katy* managed to retake the *Abigail* during their absence. A possible explanation is that on the Committee of Safety, which was charged with emergency action during recess of the Assembly and specifically empowered to direct the little navy, was Metcalf Bowler of Newport, Speaker of the House and spy for the British. Consequently these orders, as well as any other action taken by the Legislature, were promptly transmitted to Captain Wallace at Newport, where he could take precautions to forestall any Rebel raids.

Throughout the summer of 1775 military preparations on both sides were stepped up. Captain Wallace stopped colonial vessels with increasing zeal and diminishing pretext of protecting trade. One seizure that gave him particular satisfaction was that of "Sloop Victory from whaling . . . belongg to John Brown of Providence."[8] She was sent to Admiral Graves in Boston with 47 hogsheads of rum. The loss of his vessel on 22 June coincided, ironically enough, with the Assembly's formal contract with John Brown to hire the *Katy* for $90 a month.

Captain Wallace's vigor earned high praise from his admiral, who rewarded him with reinforcements. On 14 August the frigate *Glasgow*, sister ship to the *Rose*, arrived in Newport Harbor. The *Mercury* commented dryly, "We are now *protected* by two ships of 20 guns and one of 16, which is very lucky, as a Spanish war seems so very near, we having never before had any ship stationed here, for our protection, in time of war."[9] When a month later the bomb brig *Bol-*

ton (a vessel especially designed to mount a heavy mortar) joined the three men-of-war and their several tenders, Captain Wallace was in command of quite a respectable squadron.

The *Katy* enjoyed considerable variety in her activities that summer. Besides skirmishing with the smaller British boats, she served briefly as a prison ship. On 5 August the *Providence Gazette* told its readers that "The beginning of last week a Sailor, Name unknown, supposed to be a Spy from the Rose Man of War, was apprehended at East Greenwich, and put on board the private Sloop of War Caty, in the Service of this Colony, then riding at Anchor in the Harbour of East Greenwich, where, on the Wednesday following, he died by excessive Drinking."[10]

Another type of assignment was carried out on 10 August. While the British ships were out cruising in the sound, the *Katy* sailed into Newport, where the last cannon left on Fort Island, including a couple of 18-pounders, were loaded aboard and carried upriver to fortifications below Providence.[11]

Captain Wallace cannot have been pleased to learn of this second removal of cannon, and it must have been his mounting irritation at the temerity of the "Providence privateers" that provoked him into retaliatory action. The *New York Journal* of 31 August reported,

> We hear from Providence, that on Tuesday the 22nd instant his Majesty's ships the Rose, Swan and Glasgow, attempted to go to Providence, and got within 8 miles of the town, when two of them ran ashore and the other came to an anchor. Soon after arrived a brig and a sloop inward bound from the West-Indies, these were immediately chased by the men of war's barges and 3 cutters, till they ran ashore at Warwick, where they were boarded by the man of war's men in sight of a great number of people who had assembled on the shore. There were in the harbour 2 armed schooners [sic] fitted out by the town of Providence for the protection of their trade, and were going to convoy a small fleet down the river. A smart engagement then began and lasted 3 hours and an half, during which, an incessant fire was kept up between the 2 schooners and the brig and sloop, which the people on board often attempted to get off, but as often were driven from the windlasses. But at last they cut the brig's cable and carried her off, with the Captain on board, who refused to quit her; the sloop we retook and brought into the harbour, tho' fired upon by the man of war as we passed them. We had not a man killed or wounded, which is surprising. Upwards of 30 cannon ball were picked up on the shore. It is supposed many of the enemy are killed.[12]

Another encounter that took place a week later annoyed Captain Wallace still further. He sent "a Sloop with a petty Officer and 6 Men to weigh the stream Anchor, at 10 weigh'd and came to sail. 4 PM Anchd in Rhode Isld Harbour at 7 return'd the Sloop with our Petty Officer & Men but was oblig'd to leave our Stream Anchor and Cable being Chac'd by the rebel Privateers."[13] It was to be quite a while before the *Rose* was to get that cable and stream anchor replaced.

As the summer wore on, Captain Wallace's major problem became that of finding provisions for his own ships as well as Admiral Graves' squadron in Boston Harbor. General Washington's arrival at Cambridge in the middle of July 1775, to take over command of the colonial army, including the Rhode Island camp at Jamaica Plain, had effectively prevented the British from making any forward progress. Soldiers and sailors alike had to be supplied by sea. On the several islands scattered throughout Narragansett Bay were grazing a tempting array of cattle and sheep, which Captain Wallace viewed as fresh meat for the British forces. Since the General Assembly had forbidden selling to the enemy, he felt justified in taking the stock by force, while the patriots tried to beat him to it by removing the animals before he got there. The cat-and-mouse game that developed was the source of several bloody incidents—the firing on Stonington and Bristol and the burning of Jamestown. Captain Wallace's threats to destroy Newport were so terrifying that, on appeal from the inhabitants, town merchants were allowed to supply him with certain items.

On 26 August the General Assembly, in a historic session that extolled the virtues of a navy and incidentally gave Captain Whipple a retroactive pay raise from £7.10 to £9 a month, voted and resolved that a committee be appointed to cause "all the cattle and sheep, that are fit to be killed, to be forthwith removed and carried off all the islands in this colony, Rhode Island excepted; and Block Island for which provision hath already been made . . . . And the said Committee are also empowered to order the two armed vessels belonging to the colony, to assist in removing said cattle and sheep."[14]

Katy's hold resounded with baa's and moo's as she served as transport for her four-legged passengers. The removal of the animals to the mainland infuriated Captain Wallace. He wrote to his friend Governor Wanton, "I am informed the Assembly of your Colony among many extraordinary Treasonable Acts have passed one for Striping the Islands of their Stock with intent to destroy the Kings Service and his faithful Subjects—If in their Madness and Infatuation they should attempt this, it will become my duty to destroy every Vessel and Craft we can meet upon the Water . . . . "[15]

The mad, infatuated patriots nonetheless continued to do their utmost to deprive the British of fresh meat. It was not Captain Wallace's threats but an idea of General George Washington's that was to put an end to the *Katy*'s stocktaking service and her vigil in the Bay.

The Bermuda Venture

General Washington, encamped at Cambridge, was increasingly plagued by a shortage of military supplies, not least of which was a desperate lack of gunpowder. He was also a firm believer in the value of sea power; in fact, he was soon to send to sea on his own initiative a small fleet of schooners to intercept British supply ships. His first move in this direction appears to be a letter to Deputy Governor Nicholas Cooke, in which he delicately broached a scheme to relieve the powder shortage. "I am now Sir," he wrote from the camp at Cambridge on 4 August, "in strict Confidence to acquaint you that our Necessities in the Articles of Powder and Lead are so great as to require an immediate Supply . . . " Various projects for obtaining this supply had been suggested, among them one which had "some Weight" with the General. He had learned that in Bermuda, "there is a very considerable Magazine of Powder in a remote Part of the Island and the Inhabitants well disposed not only to our Cause in General, but to assist in this Enterprize in particular; we understand there are two Armed Vessels in your Province commanded by Men of known Activity and Spirit; one of which it is proposed to despatch on this Errand . . . I am very sensible that at first view the project may appear hazardous and its Success must depend on the Concurrence of many Circumstances; but we are in a Situation which requires us to run all Risques . . . ."[16]

Deputy Governor Cooke's reply on 8 August was discouraging. Two vessels carrying powder for Massachusetts and Providence were, he said, "hourly expected." The British had gained intelligence (doubtless from Metcalf Bowler) of their imminent arrival and were cruising for them off Block Island. The *Washington* would "sail this day" on a dangerous mission to reach the powder ships before they fell into the hands of the British and to divert them to another port. "The other armed Sloop," he added, "by her being within the river, prevents the Cutters and Barges from committing Depredations; so that she cannot be spared . . . . "17

A little later Governor Cooke wrote the General again, suggesting that perhaps the Bermudians themselves might bring the powder to the mainland. Washington replied on 14 August that "The Voyage is short, our Necessity is great, the Expectation of being Supplied by the Inhabitants of the Island under such Hazards as they must run is slender so that the only Chance of Success is by a sudden stroke . . . . "18 On the thirtieth, Nicholas Cooke wrote again, reporting the creation of the Committee of Safety or Recess Committee to direct the operations of the vessels of war along with other military maneuvers when the Assembly was not sitting. He had hesitated to lay General Washington's proposal before the entire Legislature. "At present," he wrote, "the undertaking appears to me to be extremely difficult. The most suitable man we have for the purpose [Captain Whipple] is confined to his bed by sickness. We have accounts that a number of vessels have sailed lately from Boston, which we apprehend, are designed to plunder the stock along the coast . . . We have now about three hundred men employed in that business . . . . "19 The letter ended with the good news that the powder vessel the *Washington* was cruising for (it had been sent out by John Brown) had arrived safely at Norwich, Connecticut.

Three days later the Deputy Governor had still more cheering news for the General. The newly formed Recess Committee had given his project full consideration, and resolved to make the attempt. "Captain Abraham Whipple, the Commodore of the two armed vessels in the service of this Colony, who hath been very ill, but is now upon the recovery, hath been consulted and will undertake the enterprise as soon as his health will permit . . . . He requests your Excellency to give him a line under your hand assuring the people of Bermuda that, in case of their assistance, you will recommend it to the Continental Congress, to permit them to fetch provisions for the use of the Island. He does not propose to make any use of it, unless he shall find it utterly impracticable to obtain the powder without their assistance."20

The readiness with which they committed themselves to this daring scheme speaks for the temper of the patriots on the Recess Committee (Mr. Bowler excepted) which, sensible of the danger involved, promised an extra month's pay for all hands should the mission be successful. Abraham Whipple's prompt acceptance of the hazardous assignment showed the same spirit that had unhesitatingly burned the *Gaspee* and earned him special mention from a king.

General Washington, ever on the lookout for new action, had still another idea for this project, which he propounded to Governor Cooke on 6 September. Enclosing the requested message to Bermudians (see Appendix D) and expressing gratification at "the Concurrence of the Committee in the Bermuda Voyage," he went on to explain the importance of gaining intelligence of the enemy's plans and to suggest the interception of the next British mail packet, hourly expected from England. "If the Vessel proposed to go to Bermuda should cruize for a few Days off Sandy Hook," he wrote, "I have no Doubt she would fall in with her; In which Case she might with little or no Delay land the Mail, in order to be forwarded to me and proceed on her Voyage . . ."[21]

Captain Whipple, true to form, made no objection to this addition to his orders and on 12 September was handed his instructions. Embracing "the first suitable wind and weather," he was to cruise off Sandy Hook for fourteen days looking for the mail packet. If he were so fortunate as to meet her, he was to land the mail, taking along with it any warlike stores or light sails that might be useful on the *Katy*, and then dismiss the said packet to pursue her voyage. In case of resistance, he was to take her by force.

> After taking the packet, or the expiration of the said fourteen days, you are immediately to proceed to the Island of Bermuda to possess yourself of a quantity of powder in a magazine upon the said island and to take the same on board your said sloop and immediately return therewith. In conducting this enterprize every thing is submitted to your judgment and direction with respect to the most prudent measures to be taken to become Master of the powder. We only recommend to you to effect it, if possible, without desiring any other assistance from the inhabitants than being piloted in and having a guide to the magazine; and of course you will make no use of General Washington's Address to the Inhabitants unless it be absolutely necessary . . . .[22]

It is easy to imagine the excitement that fired the *Katy*'s crew as they loaded aboard the supplies for her first cruise as a fighting ship. Here at last was a chance to end the months of serving as guardian of the river and seagoing barnyard, a chance to get out of the Bay with the prospect of high adventure at sea and extra pay to boot. It was a cheerful bunch of sailors who raced to the halyards to set sail for the run down the Bay and, when the British fleet had been left safely astern, to trim the sheets for a course for New York Harbor and the British mail.

General Washington was gratified to hear from Governor Cooke that Captain Whipple had sailed with sixty-one men on board, "his Vessel being clear and in every Way in good Order." Since Captain Broughton in the schooner "Hannah" had sailed a week earlier, first of Washington's fleet to put to sea, the General could take pleasure in reflecting that he now had two ships out in the service of the Continental army.

It is axiomatic that many a sound enterprise, however carefully planned and brilliantly executed, has been defeated by faulty timing. In the eighteenth century the fastest express could carry messages scarcely a hundred miles in a day, while communication by sea at any distance was a matter of weeks. Many a Revolutionary enterprise failed to come off because the information regarding it was out-dated before the project was begun. The first hint that the *Katy*'s mail-gunpowder expedition might be one of these was voiced by Governor Cooke in a letter to General Washington. Just three days after the *Katy* had sailed, on 15 September, he wrote,

> I observe that in the Cambridge Paper of Yesterday—there is an Extract of a Letter from Bermuda to New York giving an Account that upwards of 100 Barrels of Powder had been taken out of the Magazine, supposed to have been done by a Vessel from Philadelphia and another from South-Carolina. This Intelligence appears to me to be true; and I beg to know your Excellency's Opinion of it as soon as possible, that if it be thought best to relinquish the Expedition I may recall Capt. Whipple as soon as his Cruize for the Packet is out.—His Station in this River is very necessary as Capt. Wallace hath equipped a Sloop with Six and a Schooner with Four Carriage Guns who may be very troublesome here.[23]

Washington's reply on the eighteenth was apologetic.

> I should immediately have sent you Notice of the Paragraph in the Philada Paper (which is all the Account I have of the taking the Powder at Bermudas) but I supposed it had come to your Hands, before it reached ours; I am inclined to think it sufficient to suspend Capn. Whipples Voyage . . . .[24]

Governor Cooke lost no time after receiving this letter in dispatching the *Washington* to intercept the *Katy* off Sandy Hook.

Lieutenant Grimes carried orders for both vessels to cruise an extra week for the packet and then return directly to Providence.

It was already too late. Shortly after arriving at the mouth of New York Harbor, Captain Whipple had picked up "authentic intelligence" that the mail packet had already landed. He had therefore at once set all sail for Bermuda. Unbeknownst to him, the powder from the magazine there had indeed been taken off long since—on 14 August, nearly a month before the *Katy* left Providence. Such being the fortunes of war in times when communication traveled by horse or by sailing ship, the *Washington* cruised in vain for a *Katy* which was on her way to Bermuda for powder that was no longer there.

In the meantime, *Katy* sped along under "light, flattering winds" until, nearing Bermuda, she ran into a violent gale. It was certainly a hurricane at that time of year, and its screaming winds and towering seas pounded the *Katy* harder than any broadside. Even with her guns dismounted and stored in the hold, the little sloop must have wallowed sickeningly under staysail, lifted by one giant wave after another to plunge over the crest in a mad slide before steadying herself for the next wild climb. Nothing and nobody aboard could have stayed dry. The slashing rain and seas sweeping her deck made a nightmare of the watches on the quarterdeck, while below the pumps were manned around the clock to keep her afloat. By the time the storm had blown itself out and it was possible to take a bearing again, the *Katy* was three degrees south of Bermuda, with a long 200-mile beat back northward ahead.

It was well into October when the lookout at the crosstrees gave the cry "Land ho!" and Bermuda was in sight. This glad news was shortly followed by the disagreeable word that ships had been sighted—a British man-of-war and a big transport lying in the harbor at St. George. Captain Whipple kept well out of their reach, dropping *Katy's* hook at the western end of the island. Here the inhabitants, taking her to be yet another of the King's ships, were thrown into confusion, and women and children fled. However, Captain Whipple soon established contact, and five members of the King's Council accepted an invitation to come aboard. Seated around the table in the great cabin whose stern windows looked out on the blue-green water, they enjoyed the hospitality of the ship. They also broke the bad news about the powder to Captain Whipple, and gave him a report on the plight of the islanders. Most of them were friends to the American cause and heartily disposed to serve it, they said. For their cooperation in the theft of the powder, they were being treated like rebels by the Loyalist governor. The British ships had come in response to his pleas for help and were taking provisions from the island in order to punish its citizens.

The *Katy* could not linger long to enjoy her welcome or the delights of Bermuda. Her stores of wood and water were renewed, and on 14 October she was ready to sail. From the shore her new-found island friends watched with regret as the creaking windlass brought the anchor up and the sails filled to take the *Katy* back to Rhode Island. In contrast to the stormy outward voyage, she made a quick passage home, coming smartly to her mooring at Providence on 20 October.

It had been a frustrating mission and a costly one, both for the Colony and for the career of the *Katy*. It had, however, at least one beneficial result. Captain Whipple's first-hand account of the plight of the Bermudians was relayed to General Washington, who urged the Congress to send them supplies. This action was in due course taken, and it is to be hoped that the islanders credited it to the visit of the *Katy*.

Governor Cooke's final letter to the General on the Bermuda venture ended on a somewhat rueful note. After reporting the results—or lack of them—of the cruise, he added, "We are fitting out Capt. Whipple for a cruise to the eastward with all possible expedition, which I hope will prove more fortunate than his last."[25]

CHAPTER III

The Continental Congress
Authorizes a Navy

SEPTEMBER—NOVEMBER 1775

DURING THE FIVE WEEKS that the *Katy* was away on her Bermuda misadventure, events that were to shape her future occurred both in and out of the Colony. British-American relations continued to worsen. Vice Admiral Graves, deploring what he considered the soft attitude of the British Ministry, gave his captains all the latitude he dared. On 17 September 1775, he sent new orders to Captain Wallace. Citing the many rebel-armed vessels "infesting the Coast of America particularly about Providence, Rhode Island," and other places, the Admiral enjoined his captain not only to take or destroy all such pirates but to lay waste every harbor, together with its shipping, in which they were sheltered or fitted out.[1] Along with these orders, Admiral Graves also sent Captain Wallace still further reinforcement, and the bomb brig *Bolton* joined the *Rose, Swan,* and *Glasgow* at Newport.

On the patriots' side, determination for resistance also stiffened. The struggle over livestock continued, centering now on the island of Rhode Island. The *Katy* was sorely missed when on 4 October the Colony's Committee of Safety ordered two captains of the minutemen to take the sloop *Washington* with as many men as they could enlist up to sixty and proceed to Rhode Island to prevent the British from taking off stock. This operation was carried out in conjunction with four hundred troops under Esek Hopkins, commander in chief of militia and minutemen. They succeeded in removing "60 or 70 Head of Cattle, 100 Sheep, besides Hogs, Turkies &c" that were being guarded by British marines.[2]

Captain Wallace responded to this action with characteristically violent threats to destroy Newport. Although he never did actually cannonade the town, turning his guns on Bristol instead, many terrified inhabitants moved out—the start of a general exodus that ultimately cost Newport its prominent position in the Colony.

It was not only at home that Rhode Islanders were attempting to stiffen resistance. In the Continental Congress at Philadelphia there lay on the table a resolution for the creation of a Continental navy, a resolution that had been submitted by Delegates Hopkins and Ward on instructions from the Rhode Island General Assembly on 26 August. It stated that,

> This Assembly is persuaded that the building and equipping an American fleet, as soon as possible, would greatly and essentially conduce to the preservation of the lives, liberty and property of the good people of these Colonies and therefore instruct their delegates to use their whole influence at the ensuing congress for building at the

Continental expenses a fleet of sufficient force, for the protection of
these colonies, and for employing them in such manner and places as
will most effectually annoy our enemies, and contribute to the common defence . . . .[3]

This motion met with both vigorous support and violent
opposition in the Congress, which repeatedly postponed debate on
it. Matters were brought to a head, however, on 5 October, when
the Congress was informed that two defenseless British ships
loaded with military supplies were on their way to North America.
The suggestion that they should be intercepted caused the erup-
tion of that long-overdue debate—to have, or not to have, a navy.

John Adams described the opposition to the proposal as "very
loud and vehement." The idea of a navy was represented as "the
most wild, visionary, mad project that ever had been imagined. It
was an infant, taking a mad bull by his horns . . . ; it would ruin
the character, and corrupt the morals of all our seamen . . . It
would make them selfish, piratical, mercenary, bent wholly upon
plunder, &c. &c. These formidable arguments and this terrible
rhetoric were answered by us by the best reasons we could allege,
and the great advantages of distressing the enemy, supplying
ourselves, and beginning a system of maritime and naval operations, were represented in colors as glowing and animating. The
vote was carried, the committee went out, returned very soon, and
brought in the report."[4]

This first Naval Committee was composed of three
members—Silas Deane of Connecticut, John Langdon of New
Hampshire, and Christopher Gadsden of South Carolina—all
ardent advocates of a naval force. Its report cited the sailing of the
two brigs from England on 11 August 1775, loaded with arms,
powder and other stores, for Quebec, without a convoy. In order
to intercept them, ships should be despatched at once. Accordingly
a letter was to be sent by express to General Washington, requesting the use of two Massachusetts vessels. Another was to go to
Governor Cooke, "desiring him to despatch one or both the armed
vessels of the colony of Rhode Island on the same service."[5]

The report made the first mention of the distribution of prize
money—a thorny matter that was to trouble the infant navy for
years to come. On this occasion, it said, the master, officers and
seamen should be entitled to half the value of the prizes taken, in
addition to their wages. The "sd ships and vessels of war to be on
the continental risque and pay, during their being so employed."

John Hancock lost no time in getting off the required letters, together with a similar request to Governor Trumbull of Connecticut, and so on 10 October 1775, Nicholas Cooke in Providence opened a despatch from the President of the Congress. It reported the "sailing of two north Country built Brigs of no force from England on the 11 of August last loaded with 6000 Stand of Arms and a large quantity of powder & other Stores for Quebec without a convoy: and it being of importance if possible to intercept them, I am directed by Congress to desire you with all possible expedition to dispatch the armed vessels of the Colony of Rhode Island on this Service that the vessels you dispatch be Supplied with a Sufficient number of men, stores &c and particularly with oars: That you give the commander or commanders Such instructions as are necessary as also proper encouragement to the Marines & Seamen that shall be sent on this enterprise, which instructions &c are to be delivered to the commander . . . . Sealed up with ordrs not to open the same until out of sight of land on account of Secrecy . . . . "6

The *Katy* was just working her way back to Bermuda after battling the hurricane when Governor Cooke had to break the bad news to the Congress. On the same day that he received John Hancock's letter, he wrote to delegates Hopkins and Ward, informing them that "Our large Vessel is upon a Voyage to Bermuda and the small One is unfit for the Service. I have given Information of this to Genl Washington and Gov. Trumbull that they may not make any Reliance upon our assisting in this important Expedition.—I have strongly recommended to the latter to employ their Colony Brig which is fitted and mounts 14 Carriage Guns in this Enterprise. I am not without Hopes however that the large Sloop will return in a Day or Two, in which Case I shall have her immediately cleaned and dispatch her . . . . "7

Meanwhile the Naval Committee went ahead with its work without having received Governor Cooke's disappointing report that the *Katy* was unavailable. On Friday, 13 October 1775, the Congress passed a historic act that is generally considered the first piece of American naval legislation.

> The Congress, taking into consideration the report of the Committee appointed to prepare a plan, for intercepting vessels coming out with stores and ammunition, and after some debate . . .
> *Resolved,* That a swift sailing vessel, to carry ten carriage guns, and a proportionable number of swivels, with eighty men, be fitted,

with all possible despatch, for a cruise of three months, and that the commander be instructed to cruize eastward, for intercepting such transports as may be laden with warlike stores and other supplies for our enemies, and for such other purposes as the Congress shall direct.

That a Committee of three be appointed to prepare an estimate of the expence, and lay the same before the Congress, and to contract with proper persons to fit out the vessel.

Resolved, That another vessel be fitted out for the same purposes, and that the said committee report their opinion of a proper vessel, and also an estimate of the expence.[8]

There is something about this piece of landmark legislation that is at once both curious and familiar. It is the specific detail used to describe the first vessel—contrasted with the vagueness about the second. It is as though this is a description of a particular vessel already selected—much like that June resolution of the Rhode Island General Assembly that in everything but name designated the *Katy* as the first Colonial flagship. Not only much like—almost exactly like. Here are the same ten carriage guns, the swivels, the eighty men. In fact, the Congress, unaware as yet that she was out at sea, had fixed on the *Katy* for the first vessel to be sent on its first naval mission.

Proof, if any is needed, that it was indeed the *Katy* that the Congress wanted, is furnished by a letter from Silas Deane to a Connecticut friend, in which he wrote, "A Naval Force, is a Favorite object of mine, & I have a prospect now, of carrying that point, having succeeded in getting Our Connecticut, & the Rhode Island Vessels into Continental pay."[9]

Thus it is clear that it was little *Katy* which had been chosen as the first ship of her country's first navy. Unaware that she would be unable to accept this signal honor, the Congress, once launched on the scheme to create a navy, was proceeding full speed ahead. Having on 13 October authorized the purchase of two ships, the *Katy* and Connecticut's *Minerva*, it soon went one step further. On 30 October 1775, it adopted the resolution that is generally considered the authorization for the creation of the Continental Navy.

Resolved, That the second vessel ordered to be fitted out on the 13th Inst, do carry 14 guns, with a proportionate number of swivels and men.

That a Committee be appointed to carry into execution with all possible expedition the resolution of Congress of the 13th Inst, the one of ten and the other of 14 guns, and

That two other armed vessels be fitted out with all expedition; the one to carry not exceeding 20 Guns, and the other not exceeding 36 Guns, with a proportionate number of swivels and men, to be employed in such manner, for the protection and defence of the united Colonies, as the Congress shall hereinafter direct.[10]

This resolution, confirming the earlier authorization for the purchase of the *Katy* and *Minerva*, provided for the acquisition of two larger vessels as well. Those actually purchased were the *Alfred* and the *Columbus*, and when both *Katy* and *Minerva* (whose crew refused to go) proved unavailable, their authorization served just as well for the procurement of the *Andrew Doria* and *Cabot*. Thus that hurricane that was responsible for *Katy*'s absence at a crucial moment cost her not only the chance to be the first ship to sail for the Congress, but a greater distinction as well—that of being the first ship taken into the Continental Navy.

The immediate problem that had prompted the naval resolutions, that of supplying vessels to intercept the two British brigs, was solved in the end by General Washington. His clear realization of the value of sea power had been responsible for his sending the *Katy* to Bermuda. It also had persuaded him to fit out a number of merchant vessels to intercept British supply boats coming into Boston. The first vessel of the "Army's Navy" had sailed only a week before the *Katy* left for Sandy Hook, thus giving to Captain Nicholas Broughton's schooner *Hannah* instead of the *Katy* the honor of being the first ship to sail on a mission for the United Colonies.

To carry out this new Congressional assignment, General Washington had only to issue orders for intercepting the British brigs to his little fleet already at sea. There was still time for the *Katy* to join that fleet when she arrived home from Bermuda on 20 October, and she immediately began fitting out for that "cruise to the eastward" which Governor Cooke had mentioned to the General.

The fitting out was completed by November 9 when the *Katy* and *Washington* enjoyed a bit of action with the British bomb brig *Bolton*, which had fired at some boys digging clams in Newport the day before. The *Rose*'s journal noted, "Saw 2 of the Rebel Sloops off Gould Isl'd Sent the Bolton Brigg and 4 Tenders in Chace of them."[11] The *Newport Mercury* gave a more vivid account.

Last Thursday about noon, the bomb brig, schooner, and 3 tenders, part of the ministerial navy in this harbour, weighed anchor and

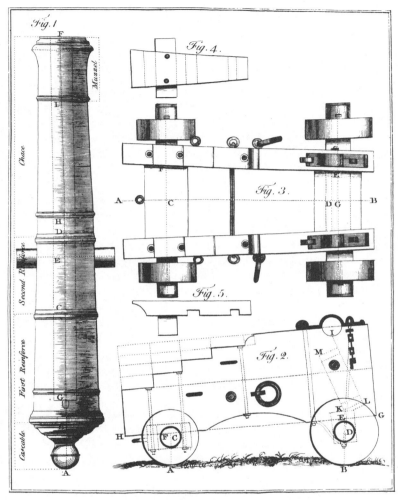

A ship's gun and carriage of the Revolutionary period. Line engraving originally published in A Treatise of Mathematical Instruments, *by John Robertson, London, 1775. Courtesy, The Naval Historical Center.*

went up the Bay, near Warwick Neck, where they met two Provincial sloops, who engaged them warmly for a short time, when night coming on, and the wind blowing excessively hard at S. E. they parted; and the next morning the brig, schooner, &c. came down again.

Tis said two of the tenders were hull'd, and received some considerable damage in their sails and rigging; the Provincial sloops, we hear, received scarcely any injury at all.[12]

As if in celebration of this action, on the following day the General Assembly finally got around to buying the *Katy*. They had chartered her from John Brown all summer for $90 a month, and now they paid him $1250 for her. Presumably this action would clarify responsibility for her future disposition. It would also avoid complications about division of prize money, should *Katy* fulfill Governor Cooke's hope that the forthcoming cruise for Congress would prove more fortunate than her last.

Captain Whipple's orders for the brig-intercepting cruise were handed to him on 12 November 1775. They specified as his quarry any ships carrying men or supplies for the Ministerial Army and Navy "now acting in America against the United Colonies." He was to cruise between Nantucket and Halifax for no longer than six weeks. Half of the prize money from any ships taken was to go to the *Katy*'s officers and crew. A postscript advised that "There are some Sloops & Schooners cruising upon the Same Service Should You meet any Vessels as the Means of knowing whether they are upon the same Service the Signal agreed upon is Your hoisting your Ensign upon the Topping Lift."[13]

As things turned out, however, the *Katy*'s topping lift remained bare. These orders were never carried out, and Washington's navy, which enjoyed some success including the notable capture of the ordnance brig *Nancy*, had to get along without the services of the *Katy*.

The reason behind the rescinding of these orders was undoubtedly the receipt of news coming up to Providence from Philadelphia. Not only was the Continental Navy about to become a reality, but the Colony's own Brigadier General Esek Hopkins, brother to Stephen and uncle of Mrs. Abraham Whipple, had been offered command of it. Rhode Islanders began volunteering to enlist, and when it was learned that on 10 November the Congress had voted to raise two battalions of marines, still more patriotic recruits signed up. Esek Hopkins, after enlisting a number of seamen and marines, took off for Philadelphia. Nicholas Cooke, now named by the General Assembly governor in title as well as in fact, wrote some new orders for Captain Whipple. Dated 21 November, they were addressed to Abraham Whipple, commander of the sloop *Katy* in the service of the Colony, by "the Honorable Nicholas Cooke, Esq., Governor, Captain General and Commander-in-Chief of and over the English Colony of Rhode Island and Providence Plantations in New England, in America." The orders read, "You are hereby directed to take on board the said sloop *Katy* the seamen engaged by Brigadier General Hopkins, in the Continental service, and with them and the officers and men to the sloop belonging, you are to proceed immediately to Philadelphia. If the Honorable Continental Congress are equipping a naval force to act against the enemy upon the coast of New England, that will sail soon, you are to remain there in order to sail with and assist such fleet in their operations upon the said coast; and in that case you are to obey the orders of the Commander-in-Chief of the said fleet during his expedition upon the said coast. But "—here came a proviso that was to cause some problems—" if the fleet of the United Colonies is destined for any other part of America, you are to apply yourself to the Honorable Stephen Hopkins and Samuel Ward, Esqs . . . whom you will find at Philadelphia, who will furnish you with a cargo of flour upon account of the Colony, which you are to lade on board the said sloop, and return therewith immediately to this place . . . . "[14]

Captain Whipple received these orders on Tuesday; by the weekend he was ready to sail. The *Katy* must have been pretty crowded below decks, with her own complement augmented by the new recruits. Among them were four whose names were to be closely associated with this sloop—Lieutenants Jonathan Pitcher, John Peck Rathbun, and Hoysteed Hacker, ex-skipper of the flour packet *Abigail,* and John Trevett, midshipman of marines. There was a crowd of families and well-wishers at the dock to see them off, both tearful and cheerful, waving handkerchiefs and shouting last-minute messages that soon became inaudible as the sloop gathered way to move downriver, her sails filled by the crisp November breeze.

For once Captain Whipple could enjoy having extra hands aboard—naval captains were constantly plagued by the difficulty of finding enough men to tend sail, work the guns, and man possible prizes. He found use for them almost immediately. Off Sakonnet Point, the lookout in the crosstrees hailed the deck with "Sail Ho!" and the *Katy* bore down on what proved to be a schooner in ballast heading into Newport. She carried a cable and anchor for the *Rose*, which had lost hers in August when the sloop carrying them had been chased by the *Katy* and *Washington*. After delivering her cargo, she was to load provisions for the British in Boston. Instead, her three crew members were transferred to the *Katy* for a free trip to Philadelphia as prisoners,[15] while a prize crew was sent aboard to sail the schooner up the bay to Providence. Apparently Captain Whipple appointed as prizemaster Lieutenant John Peck Rathbun who, having been married for only a few months, welcomed the chance to spend a little more time ashore with his young wife, Mary, in South Kingstown (now Kingston), Rhode Island.[16]

When the *Katy*'s boat had completed its ferry service and was safely lashed amidships again, Captain Whipple turned the bow of the sloop southwestward, reflecting with considerable satisfaction that he had twice deprived Captain Wallace of the *Rose*'s stream anchor and cable. With this jaunty farewell, the *Katy* left the shore of Rhode Island astern to head for Philadelphia and whatever new adventures awaited her.

CHAPTER IV

Sloop Providence *Sails with the Fleet*

JANUARY—MARCH 1776

WHILE THE *KATY* sailed the wintry Atlantic on her way to Philadelphia, the Congress weighed the question of how best to employ its infant navy—to send it southward into the Chesapeake, or northward into Narragansett Bay. There was need of it in both places. In the south, the Earl of Dunmore, royal governor of Virginia, had fled aboard a Tory vessel from which he directed a loyalist fleet. Reinforced by British warships and commandeered American vessels, Lord Dunmore's squadron controlled the Virginia capes, threatening the colonial hold on both Virginia and Maryland.

The need for the fleet in Rhode Island was also great, and Captain Whipple aboard the *Katy* carried an urgent statement of the case for sending it there first to the Rhode Island delegates in Congress. Providence merchant Nicholas Brown wrote to Hopkins and Ward, stressing the importance of communication through Rhode Island by water to supply the Continental army in Boston. "If the Isld of Rhode Isld should be taken possestion of by our Unnatural Enemys," he warned, "said Communication by water in & out, to this port would be Intirely Shut up, And the Colony Swallow'd up & ruined . . . This Colony of it self is Insignifecant Compaired with the whole, or some Single Colonys, but Its Communication & situation &c of the Utmost Importance–We are now Infested with a Fleet whose Commander is the most Inhuman of all Mankind."[1]

Mr. Brown went on to suggest that if a "United Force" could be sent to Rhode Island, the entire enemy fleet could be easily captured in a few days. The addition of the conquered British ships would make of the Continental fleet a sizeable maritime force that would then be available to proceed southward or wherever needed.

This persuasive argument came too late. Before the letter reached Philadelphia, pressure from the southern delegates had prompted Congress to decisive action. On 2 December 1775, it instructed its naval committee to acquire as many as four more vessels from Maryland, to "proceed immediately to cruize on, take or destroy as many of the armed vessels, cutters, and ships of war of the enemy as possible, that may be found in the bay of Chesapeake, or any of its dependencies, or coasts of Virginia and Maryland."[2]

Immediately following this resolution came the passage of another. It added the *Katy* to the Continental fleet. "Resolved, that the committee for fitting out armed vessels be directed to employ the armed sloop, commanded by Captain Whipple of Rhode Island, now on a voyage to this port, and despatch her forthwith to aid the marine business to the southward . . . "[3]

In view of Captain Whipple's instructions to sail the *Katy* back to Rhode Island unless the Continental Navy was to proceed there at once, this resolution posed a problem for the Rhode Island delegates. They promptly communicated it to Nicholas Cooke. Reporting that "Genl Hopkins has arrived very well, his accepting the Command of the Fleet gives universal Satisfaction," they went on to note that Captain Whipple had not yet arrived, and to confess to a bit of embarrassment about the *Katy*. They had been informed by the Rhode Island Committee of Accounts in Congress that "the Colony considers her as belonging to the Continent & in their Service & propose to be repaid for her & the Wages of the People if so will not refusing to let her cooperate with the Fleet wherever destined frustrat the Design of repayment for her & past Services. We wish your Honors farther Directions on this Head & Hope they may arrive before there is a Necessity of coming to any Resolution about it, but if not We shall advise Capt Whipple to follow his Instructions."[4]

On the next day, 3 December, the *Katy* landed safely at Philadelphia, volunteers, prisoners and all, and Samuel Ward wrote to his brother Henry in Providence, "This Day I shall enjoy Myself highly; next to the Pleasure of being at home is that of seeing our Friends when abroad; Govr Hop, his Bror and Son, the Comee for Accts and Capt Whipple all do Me the Favor to dine with Me; never did I expect the Pleasure of seeing so many of my Countrymen on this Side Rhodeisland . . . "[5]

The question of whether the *Katy* would return to Providence or sail southward with the Continental Navy was certainly the chief subject of discussion at Mr. Ward's little dinner party. The Colony's view of the matter was not forthcoming until receipt of a reply from Governor Cooke to the delegates' request for instructions. His letter, written on 12 December, included an account of a raid on Jamestown by Captain Wallace in which many of the houses had been burned—an attack that pointed up with alarming clarity how helpful the *Katy* had been in protecting the islands in Narragansett Bay. The General Assembly considered the sloop as belonging to the Colony, although they expected payment from the Continent for her voyages to Bermuda and Philadelphia.[6]

The letter closed with the suggestion that it would be best to follow Captain Whipple's instructions, but a few days later Governor Cooke wrote again. Reluctance to part with their flagship had not, apparently, blinded Rhode Islanders to the plight of their neighbors to the south. "The stopping of Lord Dunmore's Progress in Virginia is an Object of Importance," wrote the Governor. "Indeed I think he ought instantly to be crushed at all Expense and Hazard."[7]

With the objection to a southern expedition removed, there was no further obstacle to implementing the congressional resolution of 2 December. Sloop *Katy*, having missed her chance to be the first, was officially welcomed into the Continental Navy as vessel number five.

The four ships that had been purchased under the 30 October authorization were already lying at their piers being converted from merchant vessels to naval cruisers. The largest of these, a three-masted square-rigger, had been rechristened *Alfred* in honor, said John Adams, of the founder of "the greatest Navy that ever existed"—an ironic tribute to the enemy—and was being equipped with 20 nine-pounder and 10 six-pounder cannon. The second ship (a designation used for a three-masted vessel, square-rigged on all masts) was a little smaller. Renamed *Columbus*, she was to carry 18 nine-pounders and 10 six-pounders. The other two vessels were both brigs—two-masted square-riggers. The *Andrew Doria*, misnamed after the great Genoese admiral, was being fitted with 16 six-pounders, and the *Cabot*, named after the explorer, would carry 14 six-pounders.

Captains for the four vessels had already been chosen, the Naval Committee's appointments reflecting a certain degree of family influence. Commodore Esek Hopkins' son, John Burroughs Hopkins, who had been in on the burning of the *Gaspee*, drew command of the *Cabot*, and Abraham Whipple, related by marriage to the Hopkins brothers, was appointed to the ship *Columbus*. The *Andrew Doria* went to the young Philadelphian Nicholas Biddle. He was the only one of the captains to have served in the Royal Navy, and had, like young Horatio Nelson, given up his commission in order to sail on the expedition to the north pole. Command of the flagship, the *Alfred*, was given to Dudley Saltonstall of Connecticut, more because his wife was Silas Deane's sister than that he possessed outstanding abilities. Since Saltonstall had not yet arrived in Philadelphia, the *Alfred* was fitting out under the supervision of her first lieutenant, a young Scotsman named John Paul Jones. On 3

December, just when the *Katy* was sailing up the Delaware, perhaps in time to watch the ceremony, Lieutenant Jones under the direction of the Commodore raised the Colonial flag—its canton the British jack, with 13 stripes in the field—for the first time on an American naval vessel.

In the meantime the Congress, having provided for its first five vessels, including the *Katy,* had ordered two more to be fitted out at Baltimore. Sailing full speed ahead with its naval program, on 13 December it at last took official action on the Rhode Island proposal for the building, rather than buying, of a navy. Authorization was given for the construction of thirteen frigates, designed as warships from the start, to be built in various colonies—four in Pennsylvania; two each in Massachusetts, Rhode Island and New York; and one each in New Hampshire, Connecticut, and Maryland. At an anticipated cost of $67,000 per ship, this appropriation showed the determination of the Congress to provide a really effective fighting force at sea.

However, the frigates were not yet on the drawing boards at the time the conversion of the merchantmen was being carried on at Joshua Humphreys' shipyard in Philadelphia. The work proceeded with frustrating slowness, attended by delays and shortages, but it was finally nearing completion by the time the *Katy* joined the other vessels lying at their piers in the Delaware. Since she was already equipped as a warship, she needed very little alteration. The only real change was to add two more long four-pounder cannon to her armament so that she would mount eight carriage guns on her open gundeck and four on the quarterdeck.

The bill for work done on the sloop was reasonable enough. It came to £20, 12 shillings, of which labor at 8 shillings per man day, about $1.20, accounted for £15. Other items totaling £4 included "Heaving down Wharfage & Capston, 2 Stages 1 day & 1 ditto 3 days, 2 Potts & Ladle 1 day, 4 Poles" and some planking—12 feet of 1½ inch, 36 feet of 2 inch, and 56 feet of 2½ inch. These timbers may have been used for hull repairs or decking over part of the hold for more berth space, as well as in the construction of the two new gun carriages. A final charge of £1 went to "Joshua Humphreys for His Attendance."[8]

The bill for chandlery supplies for "Sloop *Kitty* for the Congress," as she was listed at first in the chandler's day book, was a bit steeper. It came to £37 charged for "1 Cask Tallow, 2 Tallow Brushes, 2¼ Gallons paint oyle, 2 lb Lamp black, 1 Gallon Lamp Oyle & Jugg, 2 Tarr Brushes, and 1 Gallon boild oyle."[9]

The work was apparently completed sometime shortly after the turn of the year. Meanwhile the Naval Committee had decided to change the *Katy*'s name to *Providence* in honor of the Hopkins brothers and the other Rhode Islanders in Philadelphia, as well as her home port. Probably a few days after Christmas, 1775, a little ceremony was held on board as the Congressional delegates and naval officers gathered in the great stern cabin. If there were no bottle broken across the sloop's bow, there was certainly one broken out below as the little party raised its glasses to bid farewell to flagship *Katy,* 10 guns, of the Rhode Island Navy and to wish success to sloop *Providence,* 12, latest addition to the Continental fleet.

Command of the newly christened *Providence* was first offered to *Alfred*'s first lieutenant, John Paul Jones. To his later regret, Jones turned it down, largely because he had never sailed a sloop before, his experience having been in English square-riggers. Her captaincy then went to John Hazard, of whose origin and background little is known. Captain Biddle characterized him as "A Stout Man Very Vain and Ignorant—as much low cunning as Capacity"—a description that later events proved remarkably apt. His commission was dated 9 January 1776 and, like those of the other captains, was signed by John Hancock. It appointed him commander of the armed sloop called the *Providence* "in the service of the Thirteen United Colonies of North-America, fitted out for the defence of American Liberty, and for repelling every hostile Invasion thereof" and enjoined him "carefully and diligently to discharge the Duty of Commander by doing and performing all Manner of Things thereunto belonging."[10] It was an injunction that he would soon and frequently find it expedient to overlook.

Captains were easier to come by than seamen, and when the recruiting that had been so successful in Providence proved far less productive in Philadelphia, the fleet faced for the first time the problem that was to be its constant plague—shortage of men. On 9 December Stephen Hopkins had written to his friends Nicholas and John Brown, suggesting that the small sloop *Fly,* belonging to Providence merchants Clarke and Nightingale and about to sail from Philadelphia back to Rhode Island, "shall return hither again directly and bring as many able seamen as she can carry—If her owners shall agree to this plan to Whom we have wrote for this purpose we shall be greatly obliged to you to use your utmost influence for the procuring of such seamen, it being slowly that we raise seamen here has put us upon this project and we hope that

Model of Sloop Providence. *Courtesy, Rhode Island Historical Society.*

the Rhode island seamen who come to Philadelphia for this purpose will very soon see their own homes again . . . "11

This time recruitment went slowly even in Rhode Island.
Nicholas Brown answered Hopkins' letter on Christmas Day,
acknowledging receipt of "yours In behalf of the Comte of Naval
Affairs" on the twenty-first. "I emediately laid the same before
Govr Cooke & Mr. Ward . . . whereupon Capt Nicho Power . . .
s[e]t of[f] the next Morng for Newport where we hope to get a
Number of Seamn But they being Mostly Inlisted into the
Artillery & other Compys in Deffence the Colony, & the Influence
of the Toreys prevented his getg Any . . . We Call'd together the
(Council) this day, who upon Consideration of the Importance of
Maning the Contenental fleet wch in Turn after a Short Time
hoped to receive Some *emediate* Benefiet by sd fleet Granted Liberty
for Capt Power to return to Newport & get all the Seamen from
Any . . . compy he Could tho' the Govermt at this Time is in the
Graitest Confution, All the Minute men being Ordrd on to the
Island The Alarm list Includg *all* persons in the Collony between
16 & 60 . . . "12

Captain Power's second attempt was more successful, despite
the desperate nature of affairs at Newport. Once volunteers in the
army had been released, the *Fly* was despatched again for Philadelphia, carrying 40 seamen for the fleet.

As the work of fitting out the five vessels proceeded, supplies
were gradually accumulated and sent aboard for a three-month
voyage. Cask after cask of provisions was loaded and stowed. The
Congress did not intend its seamen to starve, and had allotted for
each man a weekly allowance of food that, if not by modern stand-
ards a balanced diet, was both filling and sustaining. A pound of
bread every day and, except for Wednesdays, a pound of either
beef or pork—on Wednesdays a half-pint of rice with two ounces
of butter and four of cheese took the place of meat. A half-pint of
dried peas on Mondays, Thursdays, and Saturdays; four ounces of
cheese on Mondays and Saturdays, and a pound of turnips, potatoes and onions every week. Pudding was to be served twice a
week, and a half-pint of vinegar and a half-pint of rum per man per
day, with a discretionary allowance for "particular Occasions, such
as Action, extra Duty, and the like."13

Food was more plentiful than gunpowder, which was in desperately short supply. The Pennsylvania Committee of Safety
came to the rescue by selling almost its entire stock to the Naval
Committee for use aboard the fleet.

Finally preparations were complete, or nearly so, and the moment arrived for the issuing of the "Come Aboard" order on 4 January. It stated that

> The Naval Committee give possitive Orders, that every Officer in the Sea and Marine Service, and all the Common men belonging to each, who have enlisted into the Service of the United Colonies on board the Ships now fiting out, that they immediately repair on board their respective Ships as they would avoid being deemed deserters, and all those who have undertaken to be Security for any of them are hereby called upon to procure and deliver up the men they have engaged for, or they will be immediately called upon in a proper and effectual Way.
>
> Boats will constantly attend at Messrs. Willing and Morris's Wharf to carry all people on board the Ships.[14]

Among the officers as well as the men who stepped into the boats to be rowed out to their ships, huddled against the biting January wind, were many Rhode Islanders. In addition to Commodore Hopkins and Captains Whipple and Hopkins, several of the first and second lieutenants came from Rhode Island, as did many of the marine officers. Among the names that were then or later to be associated with the *Providence* were those of Jonathan Pitcher, Hoysteed Hacker, and John Trevett. Lieutenant Pitcher, assigned to the *Alfred,* actually went aboard the *Providence* as first lieutenant, responsible to Captain Hazard for the running of the ship. Lieutenant Hacker went to the *Cabot* as first lieutenant, and midshipman of marines Trevett boarded the *Columbus,* nearly all of whose officers were Rhode Islanders. Trevett was, besides a good officer, a faithful reporter, whose carefully kept journal provides one of the most vivid eye-witness accounts of the adventures of the Continental Navy. John Peck Rathbun, whose voyage to Philadelphia in the *Katy* had been interrupted by a hitch as prizemaster of the schooner captured in Narragansett Bay, was still ashore in Rhode Island. It would be several weeks before he would rejoin the fleet as second lieutenant of sloop *Providence.*

Those officers who left the safety of the Philadelphia wharves and their lives ashore for the slippery thwarts of pitching small boats heading out to the waiting ships faced a life of certain danger and hardship—low pay, hard duties, rude quarters—but one not without its compensations of power and authority. For the "common men" heading out to the Continental ships, the prospect was grim indeed. They would have to stand all the miseries of the officers and others of their own, including long hours, harsh working conditions, and often the brutality of their superiors. In their fight for freedom in general, they were sacrificing their own, to submit to the most rigorous discipline, with the lash, leg irons, or a rope from the yardarm waiting to punish infractions. Whatever devotion to God, country or principle impelled them, they were putting it to a terrible test.

Commodore Hopkins, piped aboard the *Alfred,* carried his orders from the Naval Committee. They clearly evinced the strong desire of Congress for Lord Dunmore and the British vessels to be cleared out of Chesapeake Bay. They instructed him to proceed with the utmost diligence with the fleet to sea and

> if the Winds and Weather will possibly admit of it to proceed directly for Chessepeak Bay in Virginia and when nearly arrived there you will send forward a small swift sailing Vessel to gain intelligence of the Enemies Situation and Strength—If by such intelligence you find they are not greatly superiour to your own you are immediately to Enter the said bay, search out and attack, take or destroy all the Naval force of our Enemies that you may find there—If you should be so fortunate as to execute this business successfully in Virginia you are then to proceed immediately to the Southward and make yourself Master of such forces as the Enemy may have both in North and South Carolina . . . ; either by dividing your Fleet or keeping it together–
>
> Having compleated your Business in the Carolina's you are without delay to proceed Northward directly to Rhode Island, and attack, take and destroy all the Enemies Naval force that you may find there . . .
>
> Notwithstanding these particular Orders, which 'tis hoped you will be able to execute, if bad Winds or Stormy Weather, or any other unforeseen accident or disaster disable you so to do, You are then to follow such Courses as your best Judgement shall Suggest to you as most useful to the American Cause and to distress the Enemy by all means in your power.[15]

The fleet was ready to embark on this bold program as soon as all the officers and men had reported aboard, and on 4 January 1776, the *Alfred, Columbus, Andrew Doria,* and *Cabot* cast off their Philadelphia moorings to drop down the Delaware River. Sloop *Providence* stayed behind to finish refitting and take on supplies. When Captain Hazard came aboard a few days later, he carried a message for Commodore Hopkins and a new yellow flag—the Revolutionary rattlesnake, bearing the legend "Dont Tread on Me." Casting off about 7 January, the *Providence* in her turn dropped down the river to join the rest of the fleet. She had not far to go. An unusually severe winter had choked the Delaware with ice, and the ships had gotten only as far as Reedy Island, less than sixty miles from Philadelphia, before being frozen in.

On 14 January the Providence sloop *Fly* arrived in Philadelphia with Captain Power's 40-odd recruits from Rhode Island, who gave, according to Delegate Ward, "new spirits to the whole fleet." It badly needed them. Patriotic fervor cooled rapidly on the icebound ships despite the half-pint of rum allowed each man daily, and desertion was a constant problem. Officers tried to keep the men busy—and warm—with drills and wood chopping and gun practice, but they still had to stand anchor-watch day and night to stop would-be deserters from leaving the ships.

The *Fly*, having landed her reinforcements, was taken into the Continental service, and command of her offered to Senior Lieutenant John Paul Jones. Thinking her nothing more than a despatch boat—she was small and extremely fast—he refused, and Lieutenant Hoysteed Hacker left the *Cabot* to become her captain.

The *Fly* had not lingered to take on supplies in Philadelphia, and on 27 January, Commodore Hopkins wrote to the Naval Committee from Reedy Island that "The River holds still froze so much that the Pilots will not undertake to carry us from here But perhaps we may Sail before the things can come for the small Sloop by Water think it will be best to Send some of the most Necessary things by Land such as some of the Swivel Guns Some Musquet Ball some old Canvas & six 20 feet Oars . . . "

In response to this suggestion, three wagonloads of supplies were despatched to Reedy Island on the thirtieth, containing, along with the swivel guns, ladles and worms, 5 "Quiles Riggin, 6 Tin Meashuers, Jacketts, Great Coats, and 2 barrels Cloaths."[16] There were also casks of cheese, bread, coffee and, doubtless most welcome of all, a barrel of rum.

February brought the long-awaited thaw to the Delaware. It also brought still more recruits, among them Lieutenant John Peck Rathbun, from Rhode Island and Connecticut. The *Fly* was sent to pick some of them up from the New Jersey coast, carrying a note from the Commodore, dated "febuy 10" and addressed "Gentlmen I Desier you will Come with Capt Hacker all the officers and men that are Designed for the Ameracin fleet as I understand you are arrived on the Jersey shore. Make What Dispatch you Can as the fleet will Saill the fir[s]t wind Esek Hopkins Cr in Cheff."[17]

On 10 February 1776, John Peck Rathbun reported on board sloop *Providence* to take up the duties of second lieutenant. First Lieutenant Jonathan Pitcher was delighted to welcome him aboard, to show him his quarters below the port side of the quarterdeck, and to fill him in on the condition of the sloop. It cannot have been a happy report. During those frozen weeks at Reedy Island, Lieutenant Pitcher had tried to keep his officers and crew occupied by working the guns, sail drill, clearing for action, teaching the landsmen the ropes, and getting them settled into daily shipboard routine. He had been hampered by the increasing restiveness of his men, stemming not only from the bitterness of the weather, but also from what seemed to them unnecessarily brutal discipline imposed by two of the officers—a midshipman and the captain himself. Lieutenant Pitcher must have had a growing awareness of Captain Hazard's imperfections. The "low cunning" and stupidity observed by Nicholas Biddle were already manifest, and dealing with them presented a problem to his executive officer. It was a relief to share it with Lieutenant Rathbun, whose advent raised morale both above and below decks on the *Providence*.

Another morale-builder was the prospect of getting under way at last. On 11 February, the wind freshened and, one by one, the six vessels hoisted sail and cast off. Like the others, the *Providence* came to joyful life again with the thrust of the wind against her great mainsail and the bow wave falling away under the bowsprit. Now the topmen could go aloft to handle sails and spars instead of chopping ice from frozen rigging, and the deck hands tending sheets and braces could feel the strain of motion on their lines once more.

It was not a long voyage down the river, and on 14 February the fleet came to anchor at Cape Henlopen on the western shore of Delaware Bay. Here it was joined by the 10-gun sloop *Hornet* and the 8-gun schooner *Wasp*, both of which had been fitted out at Baltimore.

Clear of the ice at last, his fleet reinforced with both ships and men, Commodore Hopkins could now carry out his orders to go into action in the Chesapeake. He chose instead to be guided by that paragraph in his orders that allowed him, in case of "unforeseen accident or disaster," to exercise his own judgment, which suggested that he avoid going into the Cheaspeake and head southeastward instead. He explained this decision in a later letter to Congress on the grounds that "We had many sick and four of the Vessels had a large number on board with the Small Pox . . . . I did not think we were in a Condition to keep on a Cold Coast." Although a vaccine against smallpox was available (the Commodore had been vaccinated in Philadelphia), its use was not general throughout the fleet, which was to be plagued with sickness for many months to come.

During the weeks of frozen immobility, Commodore Hopkins had frequently conferred with his captains, whose opinions must have carried some weight. Perhaps Captain Whipple's report of *Katy's* Bermuda voyage, and the warm welcome from the islanders, persuaded him to undertake an expedition to the island of New Providence to get gunpowder and other military stores from the poorly defended garrison there. On 14 February he issued orders to his captains, who were, if "Separated in a Gale of Wind or otherwise . . . to use all possible Means to join the Fleet as soon as possible—But if you cannot in four days after you leave the Fleet You are to make the best of your way to the Southern part of Abacco one of the Bahama Islands."[18]

Now in ironic contrast to the frozen weeks behind, the fleet lay at anchor at Cape Henlopen in summery weather. From the deck of the *Providence,* riding her reflection in a flat calm, it was an impressive sight. Most of the ships were glistening black with plain stems, but the *Alfred* sported gay yellow topsides and a figure-head of a knight holding a sword. The *Cabot* was also yellow with "white drifts" on her quarters, and the somewhat inappropriate figurehead of a woman. The *Fly* had scraped sides payed with tar. The *Providence* herself is described by a British observer as all black, long and low, with crane irons for oars over her quarters. Hanging limply from the flagstaffs of the fleet were their ensigns, the Grand Union flag, its canton the British Union Jack and its field thirteen stripes in various arrangements of white, red, and blue.[19]

At last the wind picked up, and in a brisk northeasterly on the eighteenth the *Providence* with the rest of the fleet weighed anchor and put to sea for the Abaco rendezvous. Monday the nineteenth brought hard gales and thick weather. Now old salts aboard had a chance to display their sea legs, and novices and ship's boys their lack of them, as the deck of the *Providence* pitched and rolled in heavy seas. Some of the hands were seasick—even the daily ration of rum failed of its usual cheer, and the cook's decision that it was too rough to light the galley fire left them unmoved.

Lookouts on deck had a hard time keeping the other ships in sight through the fog and driving rain, and when the weather finally cleared there was no sign of either *Hornet* or *Fly.* With the other five vessels, the *Providence* made a fast run to Abaco, coming

to anchor on Friday, 1 March.[20] Two local sloops were commandeered to get pilots for the tricky reefs of the Bahamas. On Satur-
day boats plied back and forth carrying marines from the bigger
vessels to the *Providence* and the two native sloops. Supplies of
wood and water were also renewed, and on Sunday the third, the
marines crowded below, the *Providence* with the rest of the fleet
sailed in the small hours before dawn for New Providence.

Nassau at that time was a small village sprawled along the
edge of the harbor behind Hog Island and guarded by two forts,
Montagu at the eastern, and Nassau at the western end of the
town, where a resort hotel now stands. All the gunpowder was
stored in Fort Nassau, but there were only civilians to protect or
use it as British military forces had been withdrawn, except for
one schooner, HMS *St. John,* which had put in for careening and
repair.

The fleet anchored in the morning but it was early afternoon
before the *Providence,* accompanied by the *Wasp* and the two small
sloops, made sail again to run into the eastern channel. There they
launched their boats to ferry the marines ashore, some two miles
east of Fort Montagu. Back and forth plied the boats until 250 men
under the command of Captain Samuel Nicholas had been landed.
They marched immediately for the fort, where they met with
almost no resistance. According to the journal kept by John Trevett, now a lieutenant of marines, "I took command of one of the
companies and marched to the first fort. They fired a few 18
pound shot, but did no damage. We saw an officer coming & I went
up to him to know what he wanted. He informed me that Gov.
Brown would wish to know who we were [and] what our business
was. we soon gave him his answer, and the first fort stped firing;
and that night we lodged in the fort."[21]

In the meantime, Governor Montfort Browne at sight of the
American fleet had summoned his council and, together with
Lieutenant Grant, commander of the *St. John,* and Captain William
Chambers of the sloop *Mississippi Packet,* the decision was made to
send the powder stored at Fort Nassau off to St. Augustine.
Accordingly, Captain Chambers' cargo of lumber was jettisoned
and, with the help of boats and men from the *St. John,* during the
night 162 barrels of gunpowder were carried from the fort aboard
the sloop. At 2:30 in the morning the two vessels weighed anchor.
Although expecting at any moment to be waylaid by the American
fleet, they went undetected as they crept across the bar. Thanks to
the efforts of Lieutenant Grant and Captain Chambers, the

powder was later successfully landed on the mainland, thus defeating a major purpose of the Hopkins expedition.[22]

On Monday the Commodore and the rest of the captains came ashore, only to learn the bad news that the powder had been evacuated before the marines got to Fort Nassau. Nonetheless a considerable quantity of military stores remained, including, according to the log of the *Andrew Doria*, "Large Quantitys of Sheel & Shott, Sixteen Morters of Different Sizes: 30 Cask of Powder & some Provisions fifty two Cannon Eighteens Twenty fore & Thirty two pounders loaded with Found Shott Double headed & Grape & several other Articles."[23]

Loading the loot aboard the fleet took the better part of two weeks, during which the *Providence*'s people were busy lowering ordnance into the hold. The sloop was experienced as a transport for heavy cannon, after having twice as flagship *Katy* removed the guns from Fort Island in Narragansett Bay. On 11 March, the *Fly* joined the fleet, Captain Hacker reporting that in the storm on 19 February she had collided with the *Hornet* which, her masthead carried away, had headed back to the mainland.

On 16 March the stores had all been loaded aboard the fleet, the marines returned to their ships, and three prisoners, Governor Browne and two officials, provided with seagoing quarters. At four in the afternoon the sails of the *Providence* swelled to a moderate tropical breeze as with the rest of the ships, including the two prizes and a borrowed sloop, she turned her bow seaward for the long voyage north.

CHAPTER V

In Home Waters—
Captain Jones Comes Aboard

MARCH—JUNE 1776

As THE FLEET left Nassau in mid-March, 1776, Commodore Hopkins had a second opportunity to follow his orders for action in the Chesapeake. With spring coming on, this was no longer the "cold coast" that had deterred him in February. However, the problem of sickness in the fleet was worse instead of better, and by this time his ships' bottoms were foul and in need of scraping. It seemed to the Commodore that he should turn his attention toward Rhode Island instead, and on 18 March he instructed his captains to sail northward and to rendezvous, if separated, "in 30 fathom Water South from Block Island."[1]

The fleet's voyage from New Providence to New England waters was generally uneventful, though not without incident. On 24 March the *Wasp* sprang a leak that her pumps could not contain. Making twenty inches of water an hour, it could not be stopped "no otherways than Stop in a pees of Beef"—and even this desperate remedy worked only temporarily. Two days later, leaking again, *Wasp* left the fleet to return safely to the Delaware.

On 25 March, a cloudy day with moderate wind, a strange sail was sighted to the north, and the *Alfred* hoisted the signal to give chase. It was the *Providence* who brought the chase to, and Captain Hazard sent a boarding party to look at her papers. To his disappointment, she turned out to be a schooner from Carolina bound for France, not prize material, and she was allowed to go on her way.

There was trouble aboard the *Providence*. Although she was not leaky, neither was she happy. The behavior of her captain, which made her officers uneasy, also caused unrest among her crew. Their complaints, voiced in a petition to the Commodore, were directed against two of their officers, a midshipman and Captain Hazard. They liked all the others, but these two, they said, beat them with heavy sticks and ropes ends, and kept them on deck from morning till night so that they hardly had time to eat. Lieutenants Pitcher and Rathbun, both extremely popular, had their hands full keeping the friction between quarterdeck and forecastle from interfering with the running of the sloop.

The ships ploughing northward toward Block Island had no word of developments that were taking place ashore. On 17 March 1776, the British troops had evacuated Boston to go aboard transports in the harbor, leaving the city to the Provincials. For another two weeks His Majesty's ships lay offshore, occasioning speculation as to where they might be going next. Rhode Island seemed a likely target, and there was considerable apprehension

that Newport might soon overlook a forest of British masts. However, the Ministry decided to send the troops southward and,
instead of reinforcing the squadron at Newport, to withdraw it.
Wallace was to send HMS *Glasgow* southward with despatches,
brought to Newport by HMS *Nautilus,* while the *Rose* herself was to
head for Halifax in company with the *Swan* and the bomb brig *Bolton.* Early in April the British ships sailed out of Newport Harbor.
The *Rose* and *Swan* returned to pick up stragglers. Captain Wallace
had ordered his tender *Hawke,* commanded by his nephew, and the
Bolton to cruise off Block Island until he joined them. Thus it was
that the *Glasgow* sailed alone with her tender while the *Hawke* and
Bolton cruised obediently off Block Island, appointed rendezvous of
the American fleet.

On 4 April that fleet sighted and brought to a small schooner
that turned out to be the *Hawke,* first British naval vessel captured by
the Americans. The next day the *Bolton* was forced to haul down her
colors—a particular satisfaction to those sailors who had fought her
in flagship *Katy* the summer before. A little later a brig and sloop
from New York for London were brought in, adding to the prize
list. At sunset on 5 April, "we were," wrote Marine Captain Nicholas, "twelve sail in all and had a very pleasant evening."[2]

Not only the weather was pleasant. There was also the antici-
pation of coming into friendly waters that were home to many of
the officers and crewmen. But the atmosphere of relaxation and
celebration with which the men turned in that night was about to
come to a rude and abrupt end.

Off to the southeastward of the fleet cruised the *Glasgow* and
her tender. At half past one in the morning of 6 April, she was
sighted by the lookout on the *Andrew Doria,* and the fleet changed
course to intercept. At the same moment, Captain Tyringham
Howe in the British frigate spotted "8 strange sail to windward . .
TKd, stood for them & prepar'd for action."

Commodore Hopkins had his ships deployed in two columns,
the *Cabot,* followed by *Alfred* to windward, *Columbus* behind *Andrew
Doria* to leeward, and sloop *Providence* bringing up the rear. All ships
were ordered to make ready for action, but Commodore Hopkins
left it to each of his captains to decide what action he would take.
The brig *Cabot,* captained by John Hopkins, was the first of the
American squadron to approach the *Glasgow.*

"At half past two," wrote Captain Howe, "a Brig much like the *Bolton*, but larger, came within hail, and seemed to hesitate about giving any answers, but still kept standing towards us, and on being asked what other Ships were in Company with her, they answered 'the *Columbus* and *Alfred*, a two and twenty Gun frigate.' And almost immediately, a hand Granadoe was thrown out of her top."[3]

The *Cabot*, having started the action without orders by tossing the grenade onto the deck of the *Glasgow*, promptly let go her weak broadside of 6-pounders and "instantly received a return of two-fold, which, owing to the weight of metal, damaged her so much in her hull and rigging, as obliged her to retire for a while to refit."[4] It also killed her sailing master and wounded several men, including Captain Hopkins.

The *Alfred* then came up, avoiding the drifting *Cabot*, and in her turn fired her broadside on the *Glasgow*. In an exchange of broadsides, lucky British shots cut away *Alfred*'s main brace and tiller rope, and while she broached helplessly, the *Glasgow*'s guns raked her fore and aft.

Captain Biddle managed to work the *Andrew Doria* into the action, pounding away at the *Glasgow*'s quarter, while Abraham Whipple in *Columbus* was blanketed by the other ships and slow getting into the fight. The *Providence* was even slower. What actually happened aboard the sloop remains a matter of conjecture, but from subsequent events we can make a fair guess at what really did go on. Captain Hazard, awakened by the mate, came up on deck, probably in his nightshirt, to find Lieutenants Pitcher and Rathbun already there. Through their telescopes they could make out the *Alfred*'s top light and the signal flying for action stations. Beyond her, the sails of *Cabot* gleamed in the pale moonlight, and still further off those of the *Glasgow*. Lieutenant Pitcher gave his captain the report of the officer of the watch, and prepared at his order to have the sloop cleared for action. No such order was forthcoming. Captain Hazard was content to leave the fighting to the other ships. Not so his two lieutenants. Seething with impatience and frustration, they watched the *Glasgow* exchange broadsides with first the *Cabot*, then the *Alfred*, disabling both. By the time the *Andrew Doria* had worked into position to engage, the *Providence*, keeping well to leeward of the embattled ships, had come up even with them. At this point the order was finally given to send the men to battle stations. The guns of the starboard battery were run out, and the *Providence* tacked to cross the stern of the *Glasgow*,

Wooden artifacts retrieved from a British frigate of the Revolutionary period, including a small plane, lignum vitae fid, buttons, and a trident. Courtesy, Underwater Bicentennial Expedition, University of Rhode Island.

raking her as she went. The shot went high. According to an American prisoner aboard the frigate, "the most of the shot went about 6 feet above the deck, whereas, if they had been properly levelled, must have soon cleared them of men."[5]

By this time the battle had lasted for an hour and a half, and the *Glasgow*, her despatch pouch already jettisoned, had had enough. Captain Howe cracked on all the sail he could and bore off for Newport, the American ships in hot pursuit. Several times they yawed to rake the *Glasgow*, but at too great a distance to do much damage. Having failed to cut her off, at daylight Commodore Hopkins, fearful that Captain Howe's gun signals would bring the rest of the British squadron out of Newport, hoisted orders to call off the chase. The fleet tacked to rejoin its prizes, one of which had taken the *Glasgow's* tender, and made sail for New London Harbor.

Abandoning chase was the wisest decision of the whole affair. The *Rose, Swan,* and *Nautilus,* already under orders to leave, had indeed prepared to come to the aid of the *Glasgow,* and cut their cables in their haste to get out of the harbor. Thus, in rather precipitate fashion, did Captain Wallace and his squadron take their final leave of Newport Harbor.

The *Glasgow* found scant sanctuary there. With holes through her hull and mainmast, her sails riddled with shot, her spars carried away and her rigging cut to pieces, it seems incredible that she could have outrun the Americans as long as she did, even considering the fact that she was at peak trim while they were heavy laden and foul bottomed. Scarcely had she anchored for desperately needed repairs, when a cannon rolled up within range by the militia opened fire, forcing her to move, first upriver, and with a later shift in the wind, out of the harbor for good. Captain Wallace sent her on to Halifax for temporary repairs, where she was patched up well enough to return to England for refitting, conveying a group of notable Tories heading for home.

The Americans had paid a high price for putting one British frigate out of commission. Against the *Glasgow*'s toll of one man killed and three wounded stood American casualties of 10 killed and 14 wounded. The rejoicing that should have attended the triumphant homecoming of the fleet, bearing quantities of military stores, seven prize vessels, and sundry prisoners, was shadowed by the escape of the *Glasgow*, and it was with mixed feelings that the officers and men rendezvoused at New London on 7 April.

The first reports of the *Glasgow* engagement began going out of New London even as the wounded and sick were being sent to hospital ashore, and repercussions of it set in train a series of problems that were to plague Commodore Hopkins and his captains throughout the spring of 1776, first in New London and later, with increased severity, in Providence. Even what should have been the fleet's chief accomplishment—the liberation of the New Providence ordnance, including 70-odd invaluable heavy cannon—was to earn Esek Hopkins more trouble than thanks, and his return to home waters was to bring him more difficulties than any he had encountered at sea.

Once arrangements had been made for caring for the 202 disabled men, most suffering from tropical fever, it was a matter of only a few hours to transfer them from the ships to billets on land. The officers of the *Providence* had a relatively easy task. Thanks to Captain Hazard's reluctance to engage the *Glasgow*, there were no battle casualties, and only sixteen of their men were sick enough to need hospitalization.

When this operation had been completed, the job of unloading the military stores could be begun. With it came the airing of opinions as to the merits and demerits of the *Glasgow* fiasco, and the taverns of New London were loud with charges and counter-charges. The fault lay, depending on opinion, with the Commodore, for his failure to give an order for fleet action; with Captain Hopkins of the *Cabot*, for having opened fire without orders; with Captain Whipple, for his slowness in getting *Columbus* into the fight; and with Captain Hazard for keeping the *Providence* so long out of it.

One conclusion that seems inescapable is that a lot of the trouble was due to inexperience. The Continental Navy had seen no action as a fleet before—of its captains, probably only Nicholas Biddle had ever sailed with one, let alone fought in concert. Gun crews, however hard they had practiced, had never been in action together, and the rest of the men, wrested from their hammocks to be plunged into the infernal din of a night battle, could hardly have been expected to perform at top efficiency. In any case, as an example of the Continental Navy's first action the engagement with the *Glasgow* surely stands as a vindication of Commodore Hopkins' decision to stay clear of the British forces in Chesapeake Bay.

Captain Whipple was stung by the rumors and reports flying around New London into writing an indignant letter to the Commodore, explaining that

> the Night that we fell in with the Glasgow Man of War, two of my Lieutenants was on Board of the two Prizes and fourteen of the best Seamen, when we was running down on the Ship getting in order to Engage and Quartering the Men in places of the others that was out, the Glasgow suddenly hauling to the Northward brought me to the Southward of her and brought her right into your and Capta Hopkins Wake, I hauled up for her and made all Sail with my three Top Gallant Sails, then Captain Hopkins beginning the Fire and the Glasgow returning the same and my being in her Wake and as far to Leeward as she it Instantly kill'd all the Wind which put it out of my Power to get up with her . . . at New London I found that the report was from the Alfred and the Cabot that I was a Coward and many other ill natured things which I say was a false report . . . Therefore I desire that there may be, by my own Request a Court Martial be called on me, and Tried by my Brother Officers of the Fleet and either acquitted with Honor or Broke . . .[6]

Still other problems occupied Commodore Hopkins. Getting men to take the places of those set ashore was the most immediate. The ships were so dangerously undermanned as to be unable

to sail, especially as it was not known just how many British vessels were cruising in Long Island Sound. On 15 April an express rider clattered into New London with an urgent message from General Washington in New York. It warned the Commodore that three British ships had left New York Harbor, "intended for New London in Order to block up your Squadron in that Harbour . . ."[7]

This bit of news served to keep the fleet closely in port, "under sailing orders," commented Captain Biddle with some annoyance, "but afraid to go out for fear of some Ships we heard was on the Coast." Actually this was a false alarm, as the General later conceded when the New York ships returned to their station. Captain Wallace had ceased to be a threat as well, having long since sailed for Halifax in company with the crippled *Glasgow*. However, the British had not entirely deserted these waters, and a small squadron that included the 28-gun frigate *Cerberus* and the 16-gun brig *Diligent* were standing off and on between Newport and Block Island, where loyalist inhabitants were supplying them with water and livestock.

While the shorthanded crews unloaded stores and speculated about British strength, the Commodore turned for help with his manpower problem to General Washington. Many army troops were passing through New London on their way from Cambridge to New York, and when Hopkins begged the loan of some men, the General graciously released two hundred, of whom 170 actually went aboard the fleet. Commodore Hopkins was able to write to his brother Stephen on 21 April that "We are much better Mann'd now than we ever have been."

The *Providence's* stay at New London, inactive though it was, was not without interest. With the acquisition of General Washington's troops, there was inevitably a shift of personnel within the fleet. Sloop *Providence*, which like the *Columbus*, had lent crewmen to the *Andrew Doria* for a brief cruise in Long Island Sound that netted one more prize, was in for some changes. Chief among them was the transfer of Lieutenant Jonathan Pitcher to the *Alfred*, and the arrival of Lieutenant William Grinnell to take his place as first lieutenant. John Peck Rathbun continued in his post of second lieutenant, a tower of strength to seamen and officers alike.

After nearly two weeks of idleness in port, the fleet was finally ready to sail on 19 April. It got as far as Fishers Island, where the *Alfred* ran aground on a ledge. It was five o'clock in the afternoon before she got off again, by dint of unloading all the cannon and starting her water. The *Providence* and the other vessels had been standing by all afternoon, and now accompanied their flagship back to New London.

Repairing the *Alfred* held the fleet in port again until the twenty-fourth when, leaving the *Andrew Doria* behind to careen, it again headed eastward. This time it had better luck. Without meeting either any rocks or any British vessels, it got safely to Rhode Island, and on 25 April the *Providence* sailed up the Providence River for the first time since she had left it as flagship *Katy* half a year before, and dropped her hook in her own home waters.

It is easy to picture the excitement in Providence as the town turned out to welcome the fleet. Although the new frigates were already under construction, only the *Providence* and *Fly* were familiar to Rhode Islanders, who crowded the wharves to inspect the other ships. There were joyful reunions and celebrations in the waterfront taverns that night as the officers and crewmen who had been away for six months were given a hearty welcome by their families and friends.

Return to her home port eased some of the tensions aboard the *Providence,* but it did not solve her problems. Her crew had already petitioned the Commodore:

> Cannot bear with it we like all our officers but Two Capt Hazzard and mr Spooner they carry stick with bullets and Ropes ends to beat us with and are kept from morning till night uppon deck and have scarce time to eat we hope that you will take it into consideration we mean to be true subjects to the country we mean to do all that lys in our power for the country but wee are used like dogs on Board the *Providence* we hope that you will find a new Captain or a new Vessel.[8]

After the engagement with the *Glasgow,* the officers of the *Providence* also lodged with Commodore Hopkins complaints about Captain Hazard's conduct. Since Captain Whipple had already requested that a court-martial be held to judge his behavior in the fight, the Commodore scheduled a hearing for him on 6 May, and arranged for the charges against Captain Hazard to be aired two days later.

Both courts-martial were held aboard the *Alfred* at her Providence mooring. With Captain Saltonstall presiding in the great cabin, both hearings were attended by Captain Biddle and Marine

Captains Samuel Nicholas and John Welch, together with four Marine and three naval lieutenants, among them John Paul Jones and Hoysteed Hacker. Captain Hazard sat on Abraham Whipple's trial, which was brief. After listening to his explanation of his failure to engage the *Glasgow* at close quarters, the court determined that "said Whipple's conduct . . . and his mode of attack on the *Glasgow* in our Oppinion has proceeded from Error in Judgment and not from Cowardice . . "9

Captain Whipple, exonerated, was free to sit on Captain Hazard's court-martial on 8 May 1776. The *Providence*'s captain, expecting similar gentle treatment, was in for a rude shock. The proceedings stated that,

> Captain Hazard aforesaid being brought before this Court a Prisoner on the complaint of a number of Officers belonging to the sloop *Providence* . . . setting forth a number of Crimes & Misdemeanors against him . . . The Charge being Read in the hearing of the Prisoner and the Question being put to him whether he was guilty or not guilty; he answered not Guilty; and desired he might be heard—Upon which this Court proceeded to hear him, and on trying the merits of the Case find him Guilty as follows—
> (Question 1st) Whether the prisoner was guilty of breach of Orders at Reedy Island, in not delivering a Certain parcel of Wood which the Commander in Chief had directed to be put onboard the sloop *Fly*-
>   Passed in the Affirmative Unanimous—
> (Question 2nd) Whether the Prisoner was Guilty of neglect of duty on the night the Fleet Engaged the *Glasgow*, in not preparing for Action before the Engagement began, he having timely Information
>   Pased in the affirmative Unanimous—
> (Question 3rd) Whether the Prisoner was Guilty of Embezling part of the Vessel's Stores
>   Passed in the affirmative Unanimous—
> (Question 4th) Whether the Prisoner was Guilty of breach of orders going up Providence River the 25th of April last-
>   Passed in the affirmative Unanimous-
>   In consequence of the foregoing Tryal, this Court are Unanimous in their Opinion, That the Prisoner John Hazard Esqr has rendered himself unworthy of holding his Commission in the Navy of the United Colonies of North America, and Adjudge him accordingly 10

When Captain Hazard received a copy of these proceedings, he promptly forwarded it to Commodore Hopkins with a request for a new trial. Calling his "Embeslement" a "Mear Triffle," and defending his conduct in the *Glasgow* affair, he accused Captain Saltonstall of having deprived him of many "Priviledges which I ought to have had at my Tryal."[11] Somewhat reluctantly the Commodore had on 9 May endorsed the guilty verdict with an order that Captain Hazard surrender his commission. In sending copies of both courts-martial to Congress, he remarked," . . . As for the rest of Captn Hazards Conduct I could have look'd it over, but as he was found Guilty in the affair of the *Glasgow* I could not pass it by."[12]

It was a lucky thing for the *Providence* that he could not. And lucky too for the *Alfred*'s first lieutenant, John Paul Jones, to whom Commodore Hopkins immediately, and for the second time, offered command of the sloop. This time Lieutenant Jones

Silhouette of John Paul Jones by Jean Millette, 1776. Courtesy, Franklin D. Roosevelt Library.

accepted with alacrity if not undue enthusiasm—he still had his reservations about fore-and-afters, and took this one on largely to get out of serving any longer under Captain Dudley Saltonstall.

On 10 May 1776, Captain Jones was rowed out to the *Providence* swinging gently at her mooring in the river. As the boat left the shore, the boatswain's pipe summoned all hands on deck where the men waited, heads bare, in respectful silence. On the quarterdeck stood Lieutenants Grinnell and Rathbun, the junior officers grouped behind them. Sideboys at the entry port stiffened to attention and pipes twittered as the boat came alongside and the new captain stepped aboard. With a brisk salute to the quarterdeck, he turned to face the men and to read them his commission as captain of sloop *Providence*.

It was always a solemn moment when a new captain took over a vessel. The fate of his men, over whom he had absolute authority, lay in his hands, and he had the power to break his officers as well. John Paul Jones cut á trim figure as he stood on the sloop's deck in the early May sunlight, addressing his men for the first time, reading in a slow firm voice, savoring the words. His hair was clubbed back neatly under his tricorne, his uniform spotless, and his boots newly polished—a pleasing contrast, thought the silent crewmen, to their late commander, fat Captain Hazard.

Commission-reading over, Captain Jones made a few remarks and, after dismissing the men, mounted the quarterdeck to shake hands with his officers. He already had his orders from Commodore Hopkins and was anxious to lose no time in putting them into effect. They reflected the fact that, while fate was smiling on Jones, it was frowning on his Commodore.

The persistent problem of manning the fleet, temporarily held at bay with the loan of General Washington's troops, came rudely to the fore again with the receipt of a letter from the General at the end of April. His forces in New York fell far short of what he had expected, said Washington, and he needed his men back at once. On 1 May the Commodore wrote to John Hancock, "I was making all dispatch possible to procure Provisions & Stores in Order for a three or four Months Cruise when I received . . . General Washington's Orders to Send his Men immediately to New York which I must Comply with . . . I am ready to follow any

Instructions that you give at all times but am very much in doubt whether it will be in my power to keep the Fleet together with any Credit to my Self or the Officers that belong to it . . . . "13

Hopkins was also having his problems with Congress. Initial gratification at the success of the New Providence expedition had turned to mounting annoyance over the *Glasgow*'s escape and the Commodore's distribution of the captured ordnance to northern colonies. Thirty-four heavy cannon had been left at New London and twenty-four at Newport. The Commodore had, he said, hoped by this means to get more men for his ships, but the southern delegates in the Congress, already irked at the failure of the fleet to go into the Chesapeake, saw it as partiality for New England. Congress ordered twenty of the big guns to be sent immediately to Philadelphia. These were to be taken from Newport—a prospect that evoked a howl of protest from the Rhode Island General Assembly, which sent an emissary to Congress with a plea that the cannon be taken from New London instead. Connecticut's Governor Trumbull objected vigorously to this idea, and in the end the Congress compromised by ordering six guns from Newport and fourteen from Connecticut.

General Washington needed his men more urgently than Philadelphia needed the cannon, and the first assignment for the new captain of the *Providence* was to collect the borrowed soldiers and deliver them to New York. Captain Jones' orders—his first—were dated 10 May 1776. They enjoined him to "take Command of the Sloop *Providence* and put her in the best Condition you can—and you are to take the Soldiers onboard that belong to General Washington's army and carry them to New York as soon as you can and then return here with the sloop for further Instructions—If you should be in want of any Supplys further than what Money you have will answer you may draw on me for as much as will be necessary to furnish the Sloop with any thing you cant do without and if you have an Opportunity to Ship any Seamen, you are to get what Number you can or Landsmen—When you come back you may call at New London and take Onboard what of the Men is fitt in the Hospital there belonging to the Fleet." Signed "Esek Hopkins Comr in Chief."14

The job of corralling General Washington's soldiers was complicated by the fact that many of them had succumbed to the same sickness that beset the fleet, and several had disappeared—either deserted or already on their way to rejoin their regiments. Captain

Jones spent a week gathering what men he could and getting supplies loaded aboard the *Providence* for the run to New York.

During that week he got acquainted with his officers and men. It was a mutually agreeable experience. His crew he later characterized as the best he ever sailed with, and he was equally fortunate in his officers. Although First Lieutenant William Grinnell was a relative newcomer to the sloop, in his second lieutenant, John Peck Rathbun, he found not only an officer who was thoroughly familiar with the *Providence,* but a kindred spirit. They were almost the same age—Jones just under, and Rathbun just over, thirty—and they shared a driving energy, quickness of mind, and cool courage that would be hallmarks of their respective careers.

Captain Jones was not inclined, however, to fraternize with his officers. He had reason enough for reticence. Born John Paul in Scotland, he had early joined the British merchant service, reaching master's rank by the time he was twenty-one. At the island of Tobago in 1773, he killed a mutineer aboard his ship. Although the circumstances appear to justify the act, Captain Paul found it expedient to repair to America, where he had already decided to make his home when he left the sea. There he added the *Jones* to his name, and two years later, John Paul Jones was granted the first lieutenant's commission written by the Continental Congress.

It was on the back of that commission that Commodore Hopkins wrote Jones' new orders as Commander of the *Providence.* The fact that he had no new captain's commission dated 10 May 1776 was to cost Jones later a loss in seniority that he resented for the rest of his life. His immediate concern, however, was to collect General Washington's troops. He managed to gather in more than a hundred in a week, added Henry Tillinghast as surgeon to his complement, and in the morning of 17 May got the *Providence* under way. Thirty-six hours later he dropped her hook in New York Harbor—a blessedly quick run for the crewmen and passengers crowded below decks.

The army men were ferried ashore, and Captain Jones turned his attention to recruiting more men. He found it hard going. On the evening of 19 May he took up his quill to write to his friend and patron in Congress, Joseph Hewes of North Carolina. The letter ranged over a number of subjects, and the oil in the lantern swinging gently over the table in the great cabin must have burned low before it was finished. Enclosing the minutes of the two courts-martial, he reported having been given command of the sloop, which he had accepted largely to get out of serving any longer under Captain Saltonstall, whose "Rude Unhappy Temper" made Jones glad that he had avoided quarreling with him, and that "I even Obtained his blessing at Parting . . . . "

> I left the A. *Doria* & *Cabot* at Rhode Island ready to Sail together on a four Weeks Cruise.—What will become of the *Alfred* & *Columbus* heaven only knows—the Seamen have been so very Sickly since the Fleet returned to the Continent, that it will be Impossible to man them without Others can be entered.—I have landed Genl Washington's Soldiers, and shall now Apply to Shipping men, if any can be Obtained but it appears that the Seamen almost to a man had entered into the Army before the Fleet was Set on Foot, and I am well informed that there are four or five thousand Seamen now in the Land Service.

It was in connection with his comment on the *Glasgow* affair that Captain Jones made some suggestions about running the Navy:

> I may be wrong, but in my Opinion a Captain of the Navy ought to be a man of Strong and well connected Sense with a tolerable Education. a Gentleman as well as a Seaman both in Theory and Practice—for, want of learning and rude Ungentle Manners, are by no means the Characteristick of an Officer.

Already worried about seniority, he was particularly concerned about Hoysteed Hacker's earlier appointment as a captain.

> Nor can I suppose that my own Conduct will in the Esteem of the Congress Subject me to be Superseded in favour of a Younger Officer, especially one who is said not to Understand Navigation—I mean the Lieutenant of the *Cabot* who was put in Commr of the *Fly* at Reedy Island after I had declined it—I was then told that no new Commission would be given and I consider her as a paltry Message Boat fit to be Commanded by a Midshipman.—but on my Appointment to the *Providence* I was indeed Astonished to find my Seniority Questioned . . . .
>
> When I get what men are to be had here—I am Ordered back to Providence for further Instructions.—the Sloop must be hove down— and considerably repaired and refitted before She can Proceed properly on any Cruise.—I should esteem myself happy in being Sent for to Philadelphia to act under the more immediate direction of Congress especially on one of the new Ships . . . .[15]

After he had recruited all the men he could, Captain Jones sailed on the first fair wind back to New London. There he took aboard the seamen who had recovered sufficiently to rejoin the fleet and carried them back to Providence, where he proceeded about the business of "heaving down" the sloop.

This rather ticklish process involved emptying the vessel of everything movable, including all the cannon, and stripping her of topmasts and rigging. She was then securely moored against a smooth portion of the Providence riverbank where she could be hauled over on her side to expose half her bottom at low tide. There she was scraped clean of barnacles, weed, and other impedimenta, and recaulked, tarred, and painted. Then she was turned around and the whole process repeated on the other side. It took some luck as well as skill to maintain the delicate balance. Captain Biddle had twice got the *Andrew Doria* full of water when he careened her in New London, though with no damage. Captain Jones was luckier and, with her bottom clean and newly painted, the *Providence* was refloated so that the work of rerigging and reloading could begin.

During this time, her officers were able to get some liberty ashore. Lieutenant Rathbun headed for South Kingstown (now Kingston) where his young wife Polly waited for him. Captain Jones sampled the delights of Providence in company with Abraham Whipple, whom he later chided for not giving him word "about our agreeable Widow, or my little affair of the Heart at Providence."[16] He managed to escape deep involvement of his affections, however, and by the time the *Providence* was ready for sea again, so was her captain.

CHAPTER VI

Providence *on the Prowl*

JUNE—OCTOBER 1776

By 13 June 1776, sloop *Providence* was clean, rigged and fitted out, and Commodore Hopkins had new orders for Captain Jones. He was to head for Newburyport (later changed to Boston) to pick up some cargo ships carrying coal, and convoy them to Philadelphia. First, however, he had other escort duties to perform. The Congress had ordered that cannon from Newport and New London be sent to General Washington in New York, and sloop *Fly*, commanded by Captain Hacker, was to deliver them. Because of British activity around Block Island where, in addition to the *Cerberus*, two other frigates and the brig *Diligent* were operating, she needed protection, and *Providence* was ordered to escort *Fly* to New London.

Getting the *Fly* past the British ships proved to be a frustrating assignment. Several times during the following week the two sloops left Newport Harbor, only to be driven back in by the *Cerberus* or one of her consorts. On one such sortie on 16 June, *Providence* and *Fly* encountered an American brig that was being hotly pursued by the *Cerberus*. Captain Jones fired his broadside, diverting the British frigate long enough for the brig to get safely into Newport Harbor. Meanwhile the sound of cannonfire had brought out the *Columbus* and *Andrew Doria* who, with the two sloops, went after the *Cerberus*. Finding herself under chase by a superior force, the frigate fled westward for the safety of Block Island. After a close chase that lasted all afternoon, she managed to get safely around Point Judith, and the four Continental vessels returned empty-handed to Newport.[1]

Captain Jones never did succeed in escorting *Fly* past Fishers Island, and after a week of fruitless attempts he wrote to the Continental agent in Boston that he had "determined to give it up and pursue my Orders for Boston." The *Fly* finally reached New London safely on 26 June in company with the *Andrew Doria*. Connecticut authorities refused to part with any cannon, however, and the next morning Captain Hacker sailed on a fair wind for New York with only the guns from Newport for General Washington.

The fleet had troubles other than British frigates. The shortage of men required that crews be shifted from one vessel to another or borrowed from the land forces. The Rhode Island General Assembly released 40 men to serve aboard the *Columbus* and the *Providence* so that the ships could sail. In May 1776, the launching of ships *Providence* and *Warren*, the two Continental frigates being built in Rhode Island, intensified the competition for seamen. A still greater deterrent to enlisting men was the

Brick hearth, as installed on board a small American armed vessel of the Revolutionary period. Courtesy, Smithsonian Institution, Washington, D.C.

attraction of serving aboard privateers, where a much more generous share of prize money went to the crew than was allowed in the Continental Navy. Bonuses offered for enlistment in the Continental service were snapped up by seamen who then deserted to serve, often at higher pay, in privateers.

The Congress in Philadelphia chose to ignore the very real manpower crisis, and to blame Commodore Hopkins for disregarding its orders to get the fleet to sea. On 20 June Hopkins received a peremptory summons to proceed immediately by land to Philadelphia to answer for his conduct; similar orders were issued to Captains Saltonstall and Whipple. Young Nicholas Biddle, senior captain remaining, was left in command of the fleet. Always eager for action, he might have managed to get it out, had he not received specific instructions not to do so from a peculiarly inconsistent Congress.

In the meantime, sloop *Providence* made an uneventful passage to Boston.[2] There she was delayed for fifteen days—because the agent was dragging his feet, complained her frustrated captain. She finally sailed on 12 July in convoy with some coal schooners bound for Philadelphia. Almost immediately one of the colliers, the *First Attempt*, began giving her escort trouble. Her master, instead of welcoming his protection, seemed to be trying to give the *Providence* the slip. As the ships approached Sandy Hook, where Admiral Howe had recently appeared with a sizeable British fleet, the behavior of the master of the *First Attempt* raised some grave doubts as to just where his loyalties lay.

Captain Jones summoned his officers as a committee to report on the matter. Gathered around the table in the great stern cabin were Lieutenants Grinnell and Rathbun, Surgeon Henry Tillinghast, Sailing Master William Hopkins, and Ensign Edmund Arrowsmith. They concluded that,

> Whereas Nicholas Johnson Master of the *First Attempt* hath paid no proper attention to the signals made by the *Providence* for his Government Since our departure from Boston Especially Yesterday while the *Providence* was in Chace before the Wind & had given him the Signal to make Sail—When, instead of obeying, he took in his Sails till he fell a Considerable way a Stern And then hawled Close by the Wind.—And Whereas he hath persisted in this Obstinate & Unjustifiable Conduct ever Since by not bearing down in the Night nor Since Day Light this morning, When he could plainly discover the Signals made from time to time on board here . . .
>
> Therefore the members of this Comittee being the principal Commission'd & Warrant Officers of the *Providence* who have hereunto Subscribed are Unanimous in their opinion & do Verily believe that the Said Nicholas Johnson hath Used & is using his utmost Endeavours to get away from the *Providence* & that without any Just reason and perhaps from bad Motives.[3]

In consequence of this meeting, Captain Jones sent an officer and some men aboard the *First Attempt* and, whatever the nefarious motives of her captain, she stayed thereafter close by the side of her escort. The *Providence* managed to guide her convoy safely past the British forces around Sandy Hook and to escape the perils of the New Jersey coast, including the predatory activities of the notorious Barnegat pirates. On 29 July she made a safe anchorage in Little Egg Harbor, where the next morning Captain Jones penned a brief report to the Congress, forwarding the verdict on the *First Attempt*'s captain, and adding, "I should not have put in here had not the wind been directly contrary with an appearance of Bad weather and none of us well acquainted on this dangerous coast."[4]

Making sail again that afternoon, the *Providence* made good time rounding Cape May and running up the Delaware to Philadelphia, where she arrived on the first of August. There Jones found Commodore Hopkins still waiting to answer for his conduct before the Marine Committee, which had already sent Captains Saltonstall and Whipple back to their ships early in July with a mild rebuke. The Commodore would not get his hearing until 12 August, or a verdict until the fifteenth, when his conduct was censured but, thanks to a vigorous defense by John Adams, he was not cashiered.

Captain Jones used his time in Philadelphia to renew his friendship with Joseph Hewes of the enlarged Naval, now renamed Marine, Committee, and to be introduced to the other members. He made such a good impression on them that he shortly received not only a regular captain's commission, but new orders that contained that desideratum of all enterprising naval captains—instructions to go out on an independent cruise. The Marine Committee suggested that he

> proceed immediately on a Cruize against our Enemies & we think in & about the Lattitude of Bermuda may prove the most favourable ground for your purpose.
>
> You must by all opportunitys transmit us an Account of your proceedings & of such Occurences as you meet with, You are to be particularly attentive to protect, Aid & assist all Vessells & property belonging to these States or the Subjects thereof. It is equally your duty to Seize, take Sink Burn or destroy that of our Enemys. Be carefull of the Sloop her Stores and Materials, use your People well thereby Recommending the American Naval service to all who engage in it, and we also Recommend Humane kind Treatment of your Prisoners . . . [5]

It was a jubilant Captain Jones who took the *Providence* down the Delaware on 21 August 1776. He was on his own in a vessel that he had come to appreciate for her speed and handling qualities. The Marine Committee had offered him command of the brig *Hampden,* which had been bought by the Congress after Jones rescued her from the *Cerberus,* but he chose to stick with the *Providence* instead. His crew, the best he ever sailed with, he said later, was headed by two able lieutenants, William Grinnell and John Peck Rathbun, who had already become Captain Jones' right hand man. The sloop's surgeon was Henry Tillinghast and her sailing master, William Hopkins. Ensign Edmund Arrowsmith headed a contingent of Marines, some twenty-five in all, including a fifer and a drummer, most of whom had come aboard at Rhode Island. Just before sailing, Jones had acquired twenty men from the *Hornet* to fill out his complement of 73 officers and men—enough to sail the sloop, man the guns, and furnish prize crews.[6]

The *Providence,* amply manned, rigged and provisioned, was in good sailing trim for a cruise of several months. Below decks were carefully stored casks of beef and pork, bread, butter, cheese, bushels of onions, turnips, dried peas, and potatoes, plenty of vinegar, molasses, brown sugar, coffee and, best of all, rum. The sloop's 16-foot boat, lashed between quarterdeck and mainmast, provided temporary quarters for crates of chickens to supply the captain's table and wardroom with fresh eggs, and tethered nearby were any livestock—a pig and a sheep or two—that had been brought aboard. Until their appearance as fresh meat on the table, they would be tended by the ship's boys.

The hold was comfortably filled with barrels of fresh water, stacks of wood for the galley fire, and oil and candles for light. Below Captain Jones' cabin the powder magazine held its precious store of gunpowder, some of it already tied in canvas bags as cartridges. When the sloop went into action, the boys would serve as powder monkeys, kept on the run carrying cartridges to the busy gun crews.

Sloop *Providence* and the people aboard were willing and able, but it was a little late in the season for the best prize pickings. The choicest were apt to be East Indiamen returning to England from the Caribbean, and in search of them, Captain Jones set the bow of the sloop toward Bermuda. On 26 August the whaling brigantine *Britannia* was sighted and brought to. Jones sent Lieutenant Grinnell aboard in charge of a prize crew, ordering her into Philadelphia. Neither now nor later did Jones care to part with John Peck Rathbun to a prize. His reliance on Rathbun's skill and judgment in his handling of the sloop's fore-and-aft rig was obvious on this cruise, and its wisdom was soon to be shown by the strategy, surely Rathbun's, that they employed when the sloop faced a real crisis. Rathbun now took over the duties of first lieutenant, in charge of a crew that included several additions from the *Britannia*. Captain Jones was good at persuading his prisoners to serve under him,, and in this group he got a midshipman, master's mate, third mate, six seamen, and three landsmen.

After this promising beginning, the *Providence*'s luck deserted her. The next four ships she brought to were all homeward bound for friendly European nations and, not prize material themselves, were unable even to provide useful information as to where prizes might be taken.

On the first of September, things seemed to be looking up when five sail were sighted, hull down over the leeward horizon. One of them looked to Jones and Rathbun like an old Indiaman or a homeward-bound Jamaican three-decker, in either case a fat prize. The *Providence* stood for the stranger. As the distance closed, the lookout through his glass could make out details of the "Indiaman's" hull, and the dismaying word was passed below—"She's a frigate, Sir!" She was, in fact, His Majesty's 26-gun ship *Solebay* which, a few months earlier, had brought a famous prisoner back to America—General Ethan Allen, who had been taken to England after being captured at Ticonderoga.

The *Providence*, her four-pounders no match for the frigate's cannon, took to her heels, and the *Solebay* left her convoy of merchantmen to sail in pursuit. All hands were piped on deck to tend the sloop's sails. She was a good fast sailer, but a strong cross sea gave the heavy frigate an advantage through the water, and slowly but surely the *Solebay* began to overhaul the straining *Providence*. For four tense hours the two vessels raced by the wind, the Englishman firing his bow guns and steadily narrowing the distance between them. Finally the frigate pulled up within musket shot on the sloop's lee quarter. Captain Jones ordered the colors run up and the leeward battery to fire. Even as the guns recoiled, plunging inboard in their tackles, American colors soared aloft on the frigate and her leeward cannon went off. This broadside, directed at the empty sea, was the signal for "I am friendly." It fooled neither Jones nor Rathbun, who, like everybody aboard, knew there was no such ship in the Continental Navy. *Providence* was in a desperate fix and they knew it. As soon as the *Solebay* drew alongside, her battery of heavy guns would blow the sloop out of the water unless she struck. But Jones and Rathbun had had plenty of time to foresee this moment and to prepare for it. Their strategy depended on the sloop's chief advantage over the square-rigger—agility in maneuver—and on split-second timing. During the chase, topmen had gone aloft to set spars and canvas for the running sails—topsail, top gallant, and stuns'ls—and had stayed at the yard to wait for orders from below. Agonizing minutes dragged by as the frigate came inexorably on. At last the moment came. Captain Jones ordered the tiller put hard over, and Lieutenant Rathbun signaled to the men aloft for the sails to be run out. The *Providence* turned sharply to lie helpless right across the looming bow of the onrushing *Solebay* until the running sails, suddenly blossoming from the yards, fluttered and filled to send her flying downwind to safety.

Reporting his narrow escape from the frigate, Jones wrote,

> Before her sails could be trimmed and steering sails set, I was almost out of reach of grape, and soon after out of reach of cannon shot. Our "hair-breadth 'scape" and the saucy manner of making it, must have mortified him not a little. Had he foreseen this motion, and been prepared to counteract it, he might have fired several broadsides of double-headed and grape shot which would have done us very material damage. But he was a very bad marksman, and though within pistol shot, did not touch the *Providence* with one of the many shot which he fired.[7]

There was an extra ration of rum that night and three cheers for the captain as wardroom and messes buzzed with the rehash of their near-miraculous escape. Even Captain Jones' reticence was broken down in the general rejoicing. The perfect teamwork between officers and crew, coupled with sheer audacity, that had bought their freedom forged a bond of mutual confidence that was to be a hallmark of this cruise. Small wonder that John Paul Jones would remember it as the happiest of his entire career.

The next excitement for the *Providence* came on the evening of 3 September when she brought to the Bermuda-built brigantine *Sea Nymph,* bound for London from Barbados with a delectable cargo of rum, sugar, ginger, oil and wine. "The brig is new and sails very fast," reported Captain Jones to the Marine Committee, sending her to Philadelphia under Sailing Master Hopkins, "so that she is a pretty good prize."[8]

The scarcity of prizes, however, was disappointing, and the fact that the *Solebay's* convoy had been unusually small for the services of a frigate indicated that the taking of storeships from England was not going to be easy. On 6 September another Britain-bound brigantine, the *Favourite,* laden with sugar from Antigua, fell prize to the *Providence,* but Jones was discouraged about his future prospects. His report to the Marine Committee was carried aboard the *Favourite* by Prize Master Joseph Vesey.

"The West Indies are very much thinned of shipping," wrote Jones on 7 September, "and I have already succeeded beyond my expectation; however I will not yet give up the pursuit."[9]

Another few days of fruitless cruising enlivened only by an encounter with a prize of the *Columbus,* persuaded Jones that the season was indeed over in these waters, and he decided to take the *Providence* northward for Nova Scotia or Cape Breton, where he could replenish her dwindling supplies of wood and water. "I had besides a prospect of destroying the English shipping in these parts," he explained modestly.[10]

On 16 September, lowering weather turned to a howling gale from the northwest—a violent equinoctial storm. As the sloop pitched wildly in the tossing seas and screaming wind, her crew battled to dismount the twelve heavy cannon, striking them into the hold, and battening down gunports and hatches. For two days the storm lashed the little sloop, her men jammed uncomfortably below while she rode it out. On the nineteenth the storm subsided, and the *Providence* made landfall on the west coast of the Isle of Sable.

The next morning the sloop rode quietly at anchor, and fishing lines were dropped over the side for the sailors to catch their dinner. This peaceful occupation was interrupted by the sighting to windward of a frigate escorting a merchantman. She was HMS *Milford* and, at sight of the anchored sloop, she bore down on the *Providence.* The fishing lines were reeled in and the anchor hauled aboard, but Captain Jones coolly let the frigate come within cannon shot before making sail "to try her speed quartering." Finding the *Providence* far faster going to windward, Jones ordered Lieutenant Rathbun to shorten sail "to give him a wild goose chase and tempt him to throw away powder and shot." So for eight hours, they played games with the *Milford,* letting her get close enough to fire, and then cracking on sail to take the *Providence* out of reach again. "He excited my contempt so much by his continual firing at more than twice the proper distance," reported Captain Jones to the Marine Committee, "that when he rounded to to give his broadside, I ordered my Marine officer to return the salute with only a single Musquit."[11] Night put an end to this game of hare and hounds, and when at dawn the frigate was seen standing to westward, it was likely, as Jones suggested, that he was heading

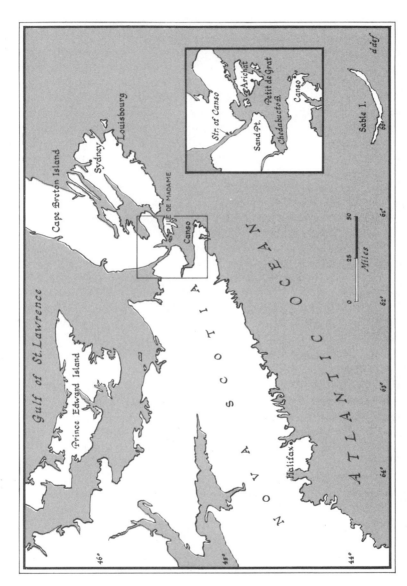

Area of operations at Nova Scotia and environs.

for Halifax where he would tell his friends "what a trimming he
gave to a 'Rebel privateer' that he found infesting the coast."

Although Halifax was the principal British port along the
Atlantic seaboard, all Nova Scotia was not entirely loyal to the
King, and there were many, if prudently silent, sympathizers to
the American cause. Lying off the harbor of Canso in the evening
of the twenty-first, Captain Jones sent his boat ashore to find out
how the land lay; the news was good and in the morning the *Providence* sailed in to drop anchor in the harbor. The day was spent taking on wood and water and recruiting some willing fishermen for
extra hands. There were three British schooners loaded with fish
lying at Canso; Jones had one of these burned, another sunk, and
made off with the third, the *Defiance,* after having filled it with fish
from the other two. The prize crew that Jones sent aboard the
Defiance was headed by Midshipman Bernard Gallagher, lately of
the *Britannia,* and included the bright young steward of the *Providence,* James Rogers. These two, together with the rest of the
crew—three seamen, a soldier, a drummer, and a landsman—were
slated for some interesting but not altogether pleasant adventures.

From a friendly informant at Canso (it is interesting to note
how much sympathy for the United States' cause was to be found
in other British colonies) Jones learned that at two small harbors
on the Ile de Madame on the east side of Canso Bay nine British
fishing vessels were lying at anchor—ships, brigs, and schooners—
which Jones decided would be fair game. "These I determined to
take or destroy, and to do it effectually," he said.

Suiting action to word, he sailed the Providence across the bay
to Ile de Madame. There he sent twenty-five armed men ashore at
the harbor of Arichat (he called it Narrowshook), and proceeded at
once to Petit de Grat [Peter the Great], where his boat carried a
similar landing party ashore. The *Providence* then stood off and on
between the two harbors, "to keep them in awe at both places."
The surprise was complete, and three hundred fisherman from the
Island of Jersey surrendered without opposition, together with all
the vessels in the harbors, which were being loaded for the homeward voyage and were unrigged. Lacking both men and time
enough to get them ready for sea, Jones made a deal with the Jer-
seymen whereby, in return for their help in rigging his prizes, he
would leave them three vessels to sail home in. Under this arrangement, the work of re-rigging was carried on with despatch, the Britishers assisting the *Providence's* men with "unremitting application." Jones left the fishermen two small schooners and a small

brig in which to make the Atlantic crossing, providing the master of each with sufficient supplies for the voyage and a safe-conduct strictly prohibiting "any subject of the Free States of America from offering any violence or interference at their utmost peril."[12]

The night of 25 September brought a violent gale with wind and rain—another hurricane perhaps—which the *Providence* rode out at the entrance to Arichat with both anchors and whole cables ahead. Two of her prizes were not so successful; one schooner loaded with oil was driven on the rocks and had to be burned, while another broke up on a reef, her prize crew lucky to escape on a raft with their lives.

By noon of the next day the winds began to die down, and Jones prepared to set sail for further adventure. He ordered a ship still unrigged and some storehouses to be burned and, accompanied by two prizes, the *Alexander* and the *Kingston Packet,* went to meet the rest of his men at Petit de Grat. There he learned that Midshipman Gallagher in charge of the landing party had sailed away in the *Defiance* at the beginning of the gale, taking with him the *Providence*'s boat and the entire shore party. The loss of so many men put an end to any possibility of further raids (Jones had contemplated destroying a British coal fleet at Louisburg), so shepherding his little flock of prizes, he reluctantly turned the bow of the *Providence* toward home.

At the time, Captain Jones rightly assumed that his *Defiance* prize master, Bernard Gallagher, had acted from good motives, but in a letter written on 3 November he would hear the particulars of his midshipman's misadventures. "After having missed you the day you sailed," wrote Gallagher from Boston to Jones in Newport, the *Defiance* had stood on and off Canso Harbor, waiting for the *Providence*. There she was brought to by another American vessel, the privateer *General Gates,* whose captain, finding she had no papers, "took us for imposters, carried us into Canso, took our arms from us and would not promise to let more than two have passage in her." But the next day at ten two British brigs hove in sight:

> We all being aboard the privateer was obliged to run into Peter the Great thinking to escape them there, however they pursued us through the woods with all the Exasperated inhabitants and took 30 of us out of 55 prisoners, nine of them belonging to us. Dividing us between both vessels I being put on board Captain Dawson where he paid me the compliment to put me in Irons for 14 days . . . We were all fetched to Halifax where we were obliged to live on 2/3 lb. bread and about 2 oz./pork, 100 of us being confined in a vessel's

hold about 40 tons, but then with a guard of soldiers to watch us. There we were obliged to stay for two weeks more when we had the pleasure to be put on board the cartels [vessels of truce for exchange of prisoners]. We arrived at Marble Head yesterday and got to this town last night, the only persons that is got so far belonging to us being James Rogers, George Nicholson and myself, we being obliged to leave sick on board the cartel Benjamin Allen, John Fears and Monroe.

Midshipman Gallagher ended his letter with a request that his effects left aboard the *Providence* be sent ashore at Boston. They included a chest, bundle, case, bed, 2 quills, 2 blankets, a sheet with some sea clothes, a quadrant, spyglass, ten-gallon case of spirit, barrel of sugar and a hat—quite a bit of gear for a captured midshipman![13]

Captain Jones, sailing the *Providence,* minus her boat, back to Rhode Island, was not actively looking for more prizes, but when on 27 September two sail were sighted, presumably Quebec transports, he found them too tempting to be passed up. Appointing a rendezvous with his other prizes in three days at Sable Island, Jones took after them. They had a long head start, however, and managed to get safely into port at Louisburg, and the *Providence* turned away to rejoin her prizes.

Once again at Sable Island on the thirtieth, Jones addressed another report to the Marine Committee. "I have had so much Stormy weather," he wrote, "and been obliged, on divers Occassions, to carry so Much Sail that the sloop is in no condition to continue long out of Port.—I am besides very Weak-handed and the Men I have are scarce Able to Stand the Deck for want of Cloathing, the weather here being Very Cold.—These reasons induce me to bend my thoughts towards the Continent.—I do not expect to meet with much, if any, Success on my return—But, if Fortune should insist on sending a transport or so in my Way—weak as I am, I will endeavour to Pilot him Safe.—It is but Justice to add that my Officers and Men behaved incomparably well . . . "[14]

Fortune provided no transport, but one more prize, a whaling sloop, and after an uneventful run down the coast, the *Providence* sailed into Narragansett Bay on 7 October. She had made a marvelously successful cruise. Of her sixteen prizes, six reached port safely—four brigantines, one ship, and a sloop—the others having been burned or lost. Captain Jones could take pride in having carried out his self-appointed mission to effectually wipe out the British fishery at Canso.

In doing so, he had established an international reputation for himself and sloop *Providence*. A London newspaper of 1 November 1776, carried an item from Ile de Madame. "On the 21st of September, a number of armed men belonging to the sloop *Providence*, Jones, Master, with fourteen guns, came in a shallop to Arichat from Petit-de-Grats, and took possession of the vessels and storehouses; . . . on the 24th they went off with the *Alexande*, and *Luce*, having twenty-two hundred quintals of fish on board. On the 25th they burnt the *Adventure*, and plundered the storehouses. This privateer took at Petit-de-Grats, the *Success*, Balliene, loaded with fish." The item closed with British wishful thinking. "The *Alexande*, *Luce*, and *Success*, Balliene, are supposed to be retaken by the *Millford*, man-of-war, and carried to Halifax, with the *Providence* privateer."[15]

However, the *Providence* privateer was otherwise engaged, having anchored safely in Newport for rest and repairs. Return to Rhode Island after an absence of four months meant homecoming to many of the sloop's crew and a stay in a new port for those who had signed on in Philadelphia. They were in need of money, and one of Captain Jones' and Lieutenant Rathbun's first acts ashore was to get cash from the local agent to pay off the men. Some $500 was handed over to them by John Manley, Deputy Continental Agent, who had also paid several bills incurred by the *Providence* for such items as a squaresail yard, 1 ½ cords of wood, sawed and split, mending some compasses, replacing binnacle glasses, furnishing paint, and butchering meat. There were also some transportation charges occasioned by the sloop's prize ship *Alexander* having put into Bedford.[16] It cost 9 shillings sixpence to move baggage "for sailors" from the *Alexander* to Newport, and an additional 8 shillings to send around some "Junk and Sails much wanted on board several of the Continental vessels," according to the Commodore, who assured the Massachusetts agent that prompt despatch of "them articles" would "forward the Service."[17]

Other ideas for forwarding the service had been coming to Commodore Hopkins from the Marine Committee, which was constantly urging him to take the fleet into southern waters. Hopkins chose instead to listen to John Paul Jones' opinion that there were still plenty of British fisheries on Nova Scotia that could be destroyed with a stronger force than one lone sloop. Further intelligence that a hundred American prisoners were being forced to work in the coal mines at Sydney persuaded Hopkins to send Jones eastward again—this time as Commodore of a squadron consisting of the *Alfred*, sloop *Providence*, and the *Hampden*, the brig that had been taken into the Navy after her narrow escape from HMS *Cerberus*.

CHAPTER VII

The Cruise with the Alfred

OCTOBER—DECEMBER 1776

CAPTAIN JONES WAS anxious to carry out his orders to take the *Alfred*, *Hampden*, and *Providence* on a second expedition to the eastward before ice threatened to block Nova Scotian ports and the British fishing fleet headed for home. In trying to fit out the three vessels, however, he was frustrated by the eternal problem of manpower.

Competition from privateers was particularly irksome. These were privately owned vessels authorized by the Congress in March 1776 to take prizes, proceeds from the sale of which went entirely to the captors, while prize money for Continental naval vessels had to be divided half-and-half with the Congress. Wages were lower, too, on naval ships, and when bonuses or cash advances were offered as inducements to sign on in the Navy, volunteers frequently pocketed the extra money and promptly deserted—usually to sail on a privateer.

To compound Jones' difficulty in getting men, the two Rhode Island-built naval frigates had been launched in May—ship *Providence* (whose identity would predictably often be confused with the sloop's) commanded by Abraham Whipple, and the *Warren*, now Commodore Hopkins' flagship under the command of his son, John Burroughs Hopkins. In the face of this increased competition, Jones found it impossible to man his three vessels. With only thirty men aboard the *Alfred*, whose normal complement was over two hundred, he decided to leave sloop *Providence* behind, transferring her entire crew to the *Alfred*, and taking only the *Hampden* in company.

Hampden was the brig that John Paul Jones in the *Providence* had rescued from the pursuing *Cerberus* some months before. Her command, refused by Jones, had been given to Hoysteed Hacker, formerly of the *Fly*. She had been fitted out in Connecticut and brought around to Newport to sail with the squadron.

When the fifty-odd men transferred from the *Providence* boarded the *Alfred*, some warm reunions took place. Among others, Lieutenant Jonathan Pitcher, *Alfred*'s first lieutenant, welcomed aboard his new captain and his old friend and shipmate, John Peck Rathbun. There were several men with whom Jones had served as first lieutenant, including midshipman Esek Hopkins, Jr., son of the Commodore, and Walter Spooner,[1] who had, with Captain Hazard, been accused of cruelty by the crew of the *Providence*.

The *Hampden*'s list of officers under Captain Hacker was headed by First Lieutenant Philip Brown and Second Lieutenant Adam W. Thaxter. Among her crewmen was one James Bryant, who had served as gunner aboard the *Providence*, but missed the cruise under Jones when he was left sick at Rhode Island. Now he was in trouble with Commodore Hopkins, who on 19 October sent a note to "Histate Hacker" that gives a glimpse of the kind of problems Hopkins had to deal with and the spelling he used when his clerk was not at hand.

> I have a Complant Enter a gainst Mr James Bryant your goner for Carring a way with out Leave out of the *alfred* a pare of pistoles and Sum other things belonging to the goner of the *alfred* and on Rescept of this you are to Lett Leut Saunders have the pistoles if to be found and Lett him Sarch to his Satisfaction for the other things mising.[2]

A second complaint against Bryant, more serious than pistol-stealing, was lodged by Lieutenant Philip Brown, whose accusation of having been abused by the gunner prompted Jones to convene a court-martial on him aboard the *Alfred*. Among those sitting on the court were Captains Jones and Hacker, and Lieutenants Jonathan Pitcher and John Peck Rathbun. The proceedings resulted not only in Bryant's dismissal from the service, with loss of prize money though not his wages, but also in the production of an historic document that contains the signatures of no fewer than four of sloop *Providence*'s commanders, all of her captains save John Hazard.[3]

Albeit with maddening slowness, the business of manning and provisioning went forward, and finally on 27 October 1776, *Alfred* and *Hampden* were ready to sail. They didn't get very far. Captain Hacker, perhaps unfamiliar with his square-rigger since, as a former packet boat captain, he should have known the rocks and shoals of Narragansett Bay, promptly ran the *Hampden* onto a ledge, putting her out of commission with a badly damaged keel.

Captain Jones, who already held a low opinion of Hacker's navigational ability, was thoroughly disgusted and showed it in a report to the Commodore. Hopkins on 28 October acknowledged receipt of Jones' "Disegrable Letter" and instructed him to shift the entire complement of the *Hampden* to the *Providence*. The Commodore also wrote a new set of orders for Captain Hoysteed Hacker, "now Commander of the Sloop *Providence*," to follow the instructions given him for the *Hampden* to cruise under the command of John Paul Jones.

The *Providence*'s new captain was about the same age as Jones, but darker in complexion and taller. John Paul Jones, about 5 feet, 7 inches tall, fit nicely under the heavy deck beams of the sloop, while Hacker, at 5 feet, 11 inches, had to guard against bumping his head when he went below.

Once again in a game of nautical musical chairs an entire crew was transferred. Lieutenants Brown and Thaxter were joined in the wardroom by Marine Lieutenant John Trevett, who had served on the *Columbus* and *Andrew Doria* and whose carefully kept journal during his *Providence* tour furnishes a detailed account of the sloop's activities. (See Appendix E.)

Stores and provisions as well as men were shifted from the *Hampden* to the *Providence,* and Captain Hacker incurred a last-minute butcher's bill that included a quarter of beef from John Manley's. This time the two vessels negotiated the perils of Narragansett Bay without incident, and headed eastward for Vineyard Sound. There in Tarpaulin Cove on Naushon, one of the Elizabeth Islands, lay the Rhode Island privateer *Eagle,* which Jones had been informed was harboring deserters from the Navy.

Captain Jones sent Lieutenant Rathbun in charge of a boat's crew to bring the schooner alongside the *Providence,* where she lay overnight under guard. Before sunrise the next morning, Lieutenants Rathbun and Brown and Marine officers Arrowsmith and Trevett took an armed boarding party onto the schooner to look for deserters. They found four hiding behind a false bulkhead and, according to a later deposition by one of the *Eagle's* officers, claiming they had further orders to take all the men on board, "by FORCE and VIOLENCE they took out of sd. Schooner 24 of their best Sea Men at different times in different Boats" and carried them aboard the ship and sloop. "In the last Boat which came on Board were a Number of Indians armed, who were ordered by sd. Rathbone . . . to go into Hold and prick about with their Cutlasses to discover any concealed Men, which they did—Rathbone abus'd the first Lieut. of sd. Schooner by heaving him on the Deck, and many other Acts of high insult were committed by Rathbone's Orders . . ."[4]

The *Eagle* episode epitomized the frustration of the Navy at the stealing of its men by privateers. It resulted in a £10,000 lawsuit by the owners of the schooner against Jones, Rathbun, and Brown; a countersuit for an equal amount ordered by Commodore Hopkins; and a permanent rift between the Commodore and John Paul Jones, who felt that he had acted in accordance with verbal orders which Hopkins refused to acknowledge. It was an altogether unpleasant affair that added fuel to the conflict between

At a Court-Martial held on board the Ship Alfred at Newport in the State of Rhode Island, on the 23ᵈ Day of October, 1776, by Order of the Honourable Esek Hopkins Esqᵉ Commander in Chief of the American Fleet for the Trial of James Bryant Gunner of the Brigantine Hamden for Mutiny

Present. Captains.

John Paul Jones   President
Hoysteed Hacker
Joseph Olney
Matthew Parke

Lieutenants
Edmund Arrowsmith
Jonathan Pitcher
John J. Rathbun   Members
Brosett Sanders
Peter Swille
Edward Burke
William Hamilton
Adam W. Thaxter

James Bryant aforesaid being brought before the Court as Prisoner on the Complaint of Philip Brown Esqᵉ for Mutiny on board the Brigantine Hamden bearing date the 20ᵗʰ of October 1776. The Charge being Read in the hearing of the Prisoner, he plead Not Guilty. Whereupon the Court proceeded to examine the Evidences who Deposed as follows, Viz.

Adam W. Thaxter appeared before the Court and gave Evidence. That on the 20ᵗʰ of October, James Bryant applied to the Commanding Officer Philip Brown Esqᵉ for leave to go on shore, and upon being denied that Liberty, behaved in a Mutinous manner by giving him abusive language; and upon being again denied going on shore repeated his abusive language Collared and otherwise abused the Commanding Officer. Afterwards questioning him concerning his Behaviour to Mʳ Brown he replied that Were it the Captain or Admiral he would behave in the same Manner; and challenged Mʳ Brown to single Combat

William Earle, Joseph Allen, and William Wardwell all confirm the above Evidence.

Benoni Taylor confirmed the above with respect to the first part of the Evidence but was absent at the latter part of the Disturbance and further saith not

John Davis confirmed the above Evidence, and added that Mʳ
... ... Headed Shot

The court-martial of James Bryant, crewman aboard **Hampden**, *October 1776. The document contains signatures of four of sloop* **Providence's** *commanders. Courtesy, Rhode Island Historical Society.*

naval and civilian service, although it did have the virtue of contributing to the success of the forthcoming cruise.

Leaving the *Eagle* with her fuming captain on Naushon, the *Alfred* and *Providence* sailed for the open sea. Off Cape Breton they took their first prize, the brig *Active*, bound for Halifax with an assorted cargo from England. Jones put Walter Spooner aboard as prize master with orders to sail her to North Carolina, a friendly gesture to Jones' patron in Congress, Joseph Hewes. Spooner, for whatever reasons and to his captain's great annoyance, took her into Dartmouth, Massachusetts, instead.

Almost at once off Nova Scotia the two vessels took their next prize, a juicy one. She was the ship *Mellish*, bringing 10,000 winter uniforms to General Bourgoyne's army in Canada. Additional cargo included a set of lighthorse accoutrement, with carbines, a valuable invoice of medicine chests and trunks of silk gowns and dry goods. The *Mellish*, mounting 12 carriage guns, hauled down her colors to the sloop *Providence*. "In this ship was every article complete for a soldier, from the hat to the shoes," wrote Lieutenant Trevett. "At that time I can say with pleasure, I had rather have taken her than a Spanish Gallion loaded with hard money."[5]

The *Mellish* also had aboard a number of passengers, including the families of British army men. Captain Jones, unwilling to risk sending such a valuable prize and her prisoners alone into port, put Lieutenant Philip Brown of the *Providence* aboard as prize master with 25 men, 10 guns, and orders to stick close to the *Alfred*.[6] In choosing his prize master, Captain Jones adhered to the policy that he had adopted on his first cruise in the *Providence*. He showed extreme reluctance to part with Lieutenant John Peck Rathbun, despite his first lieutenant's undoubted eagerness for a command of his own. Officers above and below Rathbun in rank were sent off in prizes, but Jones found it hard to spare his second in command.

The orders that the *Providence*'s first lieutenant carried on board the *Mellish* were typical of those issued by Jones on this cruise. Addressed to Philip Brown "By John Paul Jones, Captain of the American ship of War the Alfred, Senior officer of the original fleet and Commander of the present off the coast of Newfoundland 15 November 1776," the orders read,

Sloop Providence *capturing the ship* Mellish, *November 1776. The unknown artist has reversed the flags. Courtesy, Franklin D. Roosevelt Library.*

You are hereby appointed Commander of our prize the Ship Melish and as she is now manned and equipped and armed for war you are to endeavor to keep company with me and observe and obey all signals made on board here. You receive herewith a copy of signals for your government. Should we fall in with any of the Enemy's ships of war you are directed to give us all possible assistance and you are to follow our future directions which you may receive from me.

Should you unfortunately be separated from the squadron you are to proceed with all possible dispatch to the most convenient port within the United States of America. I would advise you to proceed through Nantucket Shoals to Rhode Island. Your careful attention to these things will secure my regard and promote your own interest.

The *Mellish* was to take station astern of the *Alfred* and the enclosed signal directions described the "day and night signals to be made with or without a gun: Meeting after separation—those to windward should clew up their main topsail and spread an ensign on the main topmast backstay from the crosstrees downwards and those to leeward shall answer by clewing up their fore topsail and spreading an ensign on the fore topmast backstay."[7]

The departure of her first lieutenant intensified growing apprehension aboard the *Providence* as to the condition of the sloop. On 14 November, Captain Hacker was handed a message signed by Lieutenant Thaxter, Sailing Master William Earl and his two mates, and four midshipmen.

> We take this method to acquaint you of the present situation of our vessel and crew since the afternoon of our chasing the Brig which we made prize of We have Leak'd in such a manner as to oblige us to keep our pumps constantly going, owing to our being obliged to carry Sail hard and the wind blowing very fresh, which strained her very much. The last night being obliged to lay too by Reason we cd not carry Sail as she kept both Pumps constantly going. Should we meet with a severe gale, it is our opinions both Pumps will not keep her free unless we scudded. We have a quarter part of our hands sick and the prizes we have taken will still reduce our number, as they are of great value. Should you think proper to continue further to the northward, we are ready and willing to do everything in our power for the good of the expedition, but we are of opinion it will too much endanger the vessel.[8]

While the two vessels lay off Louisburg, Captain Hacker's "round robin" was rowed across the choppy seas to the *Alfred* for John Paul Jones' perusal. It failed to weaken his determination to carry out the objectives of the cruise, though it did prompt him to make an eloquent appeal to *Providence*'s crew to rescue their captive countrymen laboring in the Sydney coal mines.

Nonetheless, apprehension aboard the sloop continued to mount. When, a few days later, a vicious snowstorm lashed the north Atlantic—the "severe gale" feared by the "subscribers"—Jones had both vessels hove to in order to prevent separation, but Captain Hacker, perhaps taking advantage of a sudden squall's blotting out the *Alfred*'s masthead light, weighed anchor in the night and set a course southwestward for home. At the end of November, her pumps clanking away day and night to keep her afloat, the *Providence* sailed safely into Narragansett Bay.

Captain Jones was infuriated at finding the *Alfred* abandoned, without, as he saw it, any "just foundation," and considered that Captain Hacker's having given him the slip entirely "overset the expedition." However, he had himself described the *Providence* on his return from Canso as being in no condition to stay long out of port, and as she had been pressed too hastily into service on this cruise to have had time for extensive repairs, it would appear that there was considerable justification for Captain Hacker's action—a supposition borne out by the fact that he was never officially reprimanded.

On board the *Alfred* there were also complaints about the severity of the weather. Lieutenant Rathbun transmitted the men's grievances to his captain, but Jones insisted on finishing the cruise alone.

Shortly after (according to *Alfred*'s log) or before (according to Trevett) the *Providence*'s unceremonious departure, three colliers, the *Surprise, Betty,* and *Molly,* were captured, manned, and ordered to stick close to the *Alfred*. From their crews, Jones learned that his "brethern" in the coal mines had enlisted in the Royal Navy, and the Sydney mission was scrapped.

Turning southward, on 25 November the *Alfred* captured the 10-gun letter-of-marque (a cargo vessel entitled to take prizes) ship *John*. For the first time Captain Jones saw fit to relinquish his first lieutenant to a prize—and with good reason. After the surrender, the rebellious crew of the *John* had tried to retake their ship, and Jones wanted Rathbun's firm hand in control. After sending Lieutenant Rathbun aboard as prize master, he ordered the rebels and the *John*'s captain to be confined aboard the flagship, an order to which Rathbun replied with a note that shows he could be compassionate as well as decisive. "As your order . . . works such an afect upon the Capt.," he wrote, "and I can't find that he any way Encouraged the People to behave as they did but on the Contrary took a Cutlass from one of them, I would beg it as a favour if your Honr would please to let him tarry on board as he is unwell . . ."[9]

Alfred, trailed by her prizes, cruised southwestward in squally weather until 8 December when, near nightfall, her lookout sighted a sail that proved to be a British frigate, none other than Jones' old adversary HMS *Milford*. Captain Jones signaled the *John* to close with the *Alfred*, and having no desire to take on a frigate without his first lieutenant at hand, summoned Lieutenant Rathbun on board the flagship. Lieutenant Robert Sanders was sent to command the *John* with orders to stay with the *Alfred*. The other prizes, *Mellish* and the colliers, were ordered to take a divergent course under cover of darkness, and to pay no attention to any further deceptive signals from the *Alfred*.

To divert the Britisher's attention from his fleeing prizes, Jones hoisted a conspicuous masthead light, which enticed the frigate to follow him. The ruse worked, and at daybreak the prizes were safely out of sight. The *Alfred* fired her broadside at the enemy, but, outmatched by the strength of the frigate, took to her heels and escaped. The *John*, however, was recaptured by the *Milford*, as were ultimately two of the colliers.[10]

The other two prizes reached port safely, and when the *Alfred* sailed into Boston Harbor on 15 December, Jones learned that Lieutenant Brown had brought the *Mellish* safely into Bedford, where her cargo was already being loaded onto wagons headed for New Jersey. Some of the clothing reached the American troops before they embarked on their Christmas crossing of the Delaware, in time to warm the spirit that won the Battle of Trenton. For Burgoyne's soldiers, waiting in vain for their scarlet uniforms, the loss was devastating. Instead of pressing on toward a rendezvous with General Howe's forces in New York, they were forced to go into winter quarters, a delay that contributed largely to Burgoyne's ultimate defeat at Saratoga the following year.

John Paul Jones had good reason for taking the *Alfred* into Boston instead of into Rhode Island. Sloop *Providence* had made safe anchorage in Narragansett Bay at the end of November 1776. There she lay in company with frigates *Warren* and *Providence*, and ship *Columbus*. Early in December Commodore Hopkins had received on board flagship *Warren* urgent messages from Governor Nicholas Cooke and the Rhode Island General Assembly warning him that a British invasion of Newport appeared imminent and urging him to take his ships around to Boston at once to avoid being blockaded. For reasons of his own, the Commodore chose to remain deaf to warnings of approaching danger, and left the four vessels right where they were.

It was a fatal decision. The ships were lying peacefully off Gould Island when on 7 December catastrophe struck Rhode Island. It came in the form of a huge British squadron under the command of Sir Peter Parker, and occasioned a late-night note on the eighth from Governor Cooke to General Washington:

It is with great concern, I give you the disagreeable intelligence that the enemy, with a fleet consisting of seventy-eight ships-of-war and transports, entered the harbor of Newport yesterday. We had about six hundred men upon Rhode Island, who were obliged to evacuate it, with the loss of about fifteen or twenty heavy cannon; having taken off the ammunition and stores, and the greatest part of the stock. The enemy have full possession of the island.

I am informed . . . that they landed this morning, about eight o'clock, with eight thousand men, who marched in three divisions; one towards Newport, the second toward Howland's Ferry, and the third to Bristol Ferry; where they arrived time enough to fire upon the boats that brought over our last men, but without doing damage . . .[11]

The American vessels, surprised by the sudden appearance of the enemy, were forced to move up the bay and into the Providence River, where they were to lie in frustrating idleness for months to come. Lieutenant Trevett reported that

While the British fleet was running into Narragansett Bay, the sloop *Providence* had some men on shore on Gould Island cutting wood. I perceived a large quantity of hay stacked up there, and I ordered one of the men to give me a brand of fire, with which I stepped into the barge, and our sloop hove to until I set fire to all the hay on the island, as I well knew it would fall into the hands of the British. All I received for this was the loss of a silver knee-buckle and a waistcoat, but had great contentment of mind, which money cannot purchase.

While the flames leaped and crackled on Gould, the journal continues,

We then hauled our wind for the north end of Jamestown Island, the wind being S.W. As soon as we opened Narragansett Bay there was nothing to be seen but ships. We were under easy sail and wishing some of them would give chase, we lay in the way until we gave them three shots, when immediately three of their ships, with all the sail they could pack, gave chase, which we wanted. We, under easy sail, stood up for Warwick Neck. Finding we intended to get them aground, signal was given from the Commodore of the British fleet, and they gave up the chase and we went up to Providence.

CHAPTER VIII

Behind the Blockade— and Out to Fight

DECEMBER 1776–JUNE 1777

THUS BEGAN LONG dreary months for the fleet, bottled up in the Providence River. It was an old story to sloop *Providence*, whose days as flagship *Katy* of Rhode Island's navy in the summer of 1775 had been spent dodging the British in these waters, but Sir Peter Parker's fleet was a very different force than Captain James Wallace's little squadron, and running this blockade would be in no way the quasi-sporting event that *Katy* and the *Washington* had made of evading the *Rose* and her consorts when they needed to get out. Furthermore, this time Newport was lost to the Americans, entirely in the hands of the redcoats billeted there, while the town of Providence was in hardly less dire straits, cut off from its commercial lifeline to the sea.

Naval affairs, like Providence's maritime trade, were at a low ebb. As though the blockade weren't bad enough, the situation was further complicated by action taken by the Marine Committee in October 1776, in issuing a captain's seniority list that was a marvel of sectionalism and influence-peddling. Twenty-four captains were named, including many who had never sailed for the Continent, but were nevertheless given the sought-after commands of the new frigates, still building in the several colonies. Nicholas Biddle ranked fifth, assigned to frigate *Randolph*, just below Dudley Saltonstall, who drew frigate *Trumbull*. Abraham Whipple, No. 12, would command one of the Rhode Island frigates, ship *Providence*, and the Commodore's son, John B. Hopkins, No. 13, got the other, the more heavily armed *Warren*.

Among other peculiar assignments, Hoysteed Hacker turned up with command of the brig *Hampden*, senior to John Paul Jones, who was outraged to find himself assigned to sloop *Providence* once more. In view of the fact that, at the time he learned of the list, he was in command of the *Alfred*, which he had taken into Boston for repairs after finishing the Cape Breton cruise alone, his lack of enthusiasm for taking up his post on the blockaded sloop is entirely understandable. She fell instead under the care of her former first lieutenant, Jonathan Pitcher, who had come into Boston on *Alfred* in mid-December and returned home to Providence. Adam W. Thaxter was still aboard as second lieutenant, and it appears that Esek Hopkins, Jr., also home from Boston, was assigned to the sloop as well.

As a matter of fact, it made very little difference who was assigned to what, as none of the vessels in the river was going anywhere for a while. The fleet was, as always, woefully short of men, with scant prospect in their present predicament of getting any. Sir

Peter Parker's having landed some seven thousand troops at Newport had raised the spectre of their making a land assault on Providence; this had prompted the legislature to issue an urgent call for
troops to defend the state. The supply of volunteers, already
reduced by competition from privateers as well as the filling of
Rhode Island's quota of two battalions for General Washington's
army, was thus still further curtailed. Recruiting for a navy that
could hold out some promise of prize money was hard enough; persuading men to sign on for the dubious honor of running an enemy
blockade was next to impossible.

If convincing men to enlist aboard idle ships was a problem, getting them to stay there was no less a one. Attempts at desertion
were a constant plague, and those who got caught at it had a sorry
time of it; doubtless they were made an example to their fellows by
that time-honored custom inherited from the British—flogging
around the fleet. Typical was the punishment of one unfortunate
who was sentenced to receive his "red-checked shirt" by 64 lashes of
the cat-of-nine tails. While he was rowed from one vessel to
another, all ships' crews at the rail to watch, 19 lashes were delivered alongside the *Warren*, and 15 each alongside ship *Providence*,
Columbus, and sloop *Providence*.[1]

There was an occasional opportunity for some excitement
other than watching a flogging, especially for sloop *Providence*,
whose shallow draft gave her an advantage in the river over the
larger ships. On the second of January 1777, the monotony of life
behind the blockade was broken by news that the British ship *Diamond* had gone aground on Warwick Neck. Flagship *Warren* was
lying off Fields Point at the time, and sloop *Providence* a few miles
south at Pawtuxet. Commodore Hopkins took 22 men in his pin-
nace and headed downriver for the sloop, where he found Captain
Whipple already aboard with some men from his frigate *Providence*.
Also on board was Joseph Vesey, who was on his way to report to
Captain Jones in Boston after sailing to Philadelphia as prize master of the brig *Favourite*.

The grounding of the *Diamond* looked like a shining opportunity to get back at the British—perhaps to recapture the glory of
the destruction of the *Gaspee* three and one-half years before, and
to wipe out the memory of the *Glasgow* disgrace.

According to the Commodore's own account of the incident,[2] the wind was blowing hard from the west as sloop *Providence* dropped down the river to Warwick where, on a shoal off Patience Island, lay the enemy frigate. Although stuck fast, with the tide falling, she was on a soft bottom and had not careened, so that her guns were still operable. Also, unlike the *Gaspee,* she was not alone; a mile and a half to the southwest lay a 50-gun British ship ready to sail to the aid of her stranded sister.

Commodore Hopkins went ashore at Warwick, where he learned that two 18-pounder cannon had been sent for; returning to the sloop, he had Whipple take her down just outside of musket shot of the *Diamond's* stern. *Providence* let go with her 4-pounders, getting return fire from the Britisher's stern guns. The shore battery on Warwick Neck opened up, but soon stopped shooting, out of ammunition. Wadding was sent ashore from the sloop, but her 4-pound shot was much too small for the big cannon, so nothing further was accomplished before darkness fell. Hopkins went ashore again in response to a hail; this time it was a request for bread from the *Providence.* The Commodore obligingly sent his boat out to the sloop to fetch it, and when the boat, improperly secured, drifted away, was stranded ashore overnight. At 2:00 a.m. the water had risen enough for the *Diamond* to be lightened and floated off the shoal without further interference from the Americans. Although far from being destroyed, she was badly enough damaged so that several days later she was still undergoing repairs at Newport to "stop up the bruises" given her by sloop *Providence.*

Joseph Vesey, reporting to Captain Jones in Boston, gave a very different account of the *Diamond* affair. Jones, no friend to the Commodore since the *Eagle* impressment, lost no time in forwarding it to Philadelphia. According to Vesey, the *Diamond* "was suffered to depart" though the wind was directly down the river so that none of the English ships could come to her assistance.[3]

Jones' letter reached a Congress already thoroughly disenchanted with Commodore Hopkins. So did a petition signed by several officers of the *Warren,* accusing him of profanity, disrespect to the Congress, and refusal to get the fleet out of Narragansett Bay before the blockade. Although it was later proved that the petition was the result of a plot against Hopkins, instigated by Providence merchants who had neither forgiven nor forgotten his efforts to ban privateering, the Congress made no attempt to investigate the charges. Neither did it inform the Commodore that

The Continental Fleet at anchor in the Providence River, 1777. From a powderhorn engraving, 1777. Courtesy, Henry Finn and John F. Millar, Newport, Rhode Island.

they had been made against him. When he learned of them, he ordered a court-martial held on 3 April on the ringleader of the plot, one Lieutenant Marvin. The court, which included among others Abraham Whipple, Hoysteed Hacker, Jonathan Pitcher, William Grinnell, Philip Brown, and Adam Thaxter, found Marvin guilty, and cashiered him.[4]

It was already too late. The Congress gave the Commodore no chance to defend himself, and his own explanation of the *Diamond* incident arrived after the decision had been made. On 26 March, Hopkins was suspended from his command, and on 2 January 1778, the anniversary of the *Diamond* affair, the suspension became dismissal. Henceforth maritime affairs of the eastern colonies would be conducted by a Navy Board of the Eastern Department, which would direct, among other matters, the future career of sloop *Providence*.

The *Providence*'s performance as temporary flagship of the United States fleet had done her Commodore no great service, and the testimony of her Acting Master Vesey played a sizeable role in the downfall of Esek Hopkins. Although his removal may have been in the best interest of the service, the manner in which it was carried out was inexcusable. In assessing the merits of Mr. Vesey's criticism of the *Diamond* affair, it should be remembered that Abraham Whipple was in command of sloop *Providence*, and he was not a man to let an opportunity for close action slip by. Furthermore, both he and Commodore Hopkins knew the Providence River better than their own back yards, while Joseph Vesey, who had first come aboard the *Providence* from the *Hornet* in Philadelphia and left her off Bermuda, was a total stranger to Rhode Island waters. All things considered, Hopkins' dismissal was, as Admiral Morison remarks, "a nasty way to turn out a loyal officer whose ability was unequal to his task."[5]

Back in the Providence River, soon after the *Diamond* incident, sloop *Providence* served in another abortive attempt against the British. This time it was an expedition to burn a ship stationed at Warwick Neck. One calm, dark night the *Providence* slid quietly down the river accompanied by two fire ships—a brig and a sloop—which were to be chained to the ship under cover of darkness. "The time shortly came," wrote Trevett, "when we undertook to chain them, but a sudden breeze of wind sprang up before we could chain them, and the sloop-fire-vessel got so near the ship she was obliged to run ashore, near East Greenwich, and we set her on fire rather than she should fall into the hands of the enemy. The brig and sloop *Providence* returned to Providence."[6]

Another break in the monotony of life behind the blockade came for Lieutenant Trevett, who late in January was ordered to take two midshipmen from the *Providence* to work a cartel—a flag of truce boat carrying prisoners for exchange—bound for Newport with British prisoners sent down from Boston. His account of his adventures on this mission (see Appendix E), which included an unauthorized and risky trip ashore, in disguise, visiting old friends under the very noses of the British soldiers billeted in their houses, must have hugely entertained his shipmates upon his return. Governor Cooke on 9 February wrote to General Washington, "Agreeably to Your Excellency's recommendation, I have sent to Newport all the prisoners in the land service, that were in the care of this state, and enclose you one of Lord Percy's receipts for them."[7]

Sloop *Providence* cast off her mooring again on the afternoon of 14 February, when word came that a big armed schooner from the enemy's fleet had gone ashore on the north part of Prudence Island. Captain John B. Hopkins, now recovered from his *Glasgow* injury, was in command as the *Providence*, her crew reinforced by men from the *Warren*, stood for Narragansett Bay. She reached the schooner just as the sun was setting; at her approach, the British crewmen scrambled ashore, having first set fire to the vessel. Just as a boarding party was being readied on the *Providence* to put out the flames, the schooner blew up—a powder train having been set, Commodore Esek Hopkins surmised, "to go off about the time they expected our people to board her."[8] So it was that the *Providence* could return to port with her crew intact and satisfied that the British squadron at Newport, then consisting of one 50- and one 40-gun ship, with eight smaller vessels and their tenders, had been deprived of the services of one large schooner.

While sloop *Providence* served as maid-of-all-work for the blockaded fleet, her official commander, John Paul Jones, busied himself in Boston. Ever full of helpful suggestions about the running of the Navy, he had an idea about the prize ship *Mellish*, whose cargo of uniforms was warming George Washington's soldiers, that he communicated to Robert Morris on 16 January 1777. Morris, who had remained in Philadelphia when the Congress, the Marine

Committee included, had fled, was conducting naval affairs almost single-handed.

"The *Mellish*," Jones wrote, "would make a much better ship of war than the *Alfred* . . . . lately a Bomb in the British service and from the Bins downward she is one solid bed of timber. She sails as well as the *Alfred* and is not near so Crank so that her lee guns could be serviceable when the *Alfred*'s will not . . . . Could mount 18 or 20 9-pounders on one deck . . . . "9 The idea of replacing *Alfred* with *Mellish* was never carried out, but her price at auction, with the value of her precious cargo, must have made her a wonderfully profitable prize.

All during the months of the blockade, sloop *Providence* had been officially under the command of Jones, according to the October seniority list. However, news of the success of Jones' two cruises to the eastward had boosted his stock with the Marine Committee, which on the first of February had written him some exciting new orders. Captain Jones was to take command of the *Alfred, Columbus, Cabot, Hampden,* and sloop *Providence* on a cruise to capture first the island of St. Kitts, then some British sloops-of-war and valuable merchant vessels in the Gulf of Mexico. This accomplished, the fleet was to "show the flag" in Florida, Georgia and the Carolinas, and then choose between sailing for the West African coast or to windward of Barbados to capture British slavers bound for the West Indies.10

Captain Jones received these orders on 19 February in Boston, where the *Alfred* was undergoing extensive repairs. Understandably delighted, he would have liked nothing better than to carry them out, but he soon realized the utter impossibility of doing so. As Commodore Hopkins reported to the Marine Committee, the *Hampden* was out, and the *Cabot* under sailing orders, but the *Alfred* was laid up in Boston, while "it is not likely that the *Columbus* and Sloop *Providence* can be mann'd here while the Harbour is block'd up." Even when the ships were no longer frozen in, the Commodore could "see no prospect of getting them out while the Enemy's ships keep at the mouth of this River."11

Captain Jones remained in Boston for several weeks, hoping that somehow the way might open for him to carry out his orders from the Marine Committee, and ignoring a directive from Commodore Hopkins, who had not yet learned of these orders, to come to Rhode Island and take command of the sloop *Providence.*

Although Lieutenant Pitcher had gone to Providence to take charge of the sloop, it is likely that Lieutenant Rathbun spent much of the winter of 1777 in Boston. Both he and Jones were being sued by the owners of the *Eagle* and in danger of being served a summons if caught in Rhode Island. Furthermore, Rathbun had warm Boston connections. He had spent much of his young life there in the household of his uncle, Thomas H. Peck, and had in May 1775 married the 16-year-old daughter of Benjamin Leigh, another prominent Bostonian. Despite his daughter's marriage, Leigh's sympathies lay entirely with the Loyalists, and it is not likely that John Peck Rathbun spent much time with his father in-law, although both he and Captain Jones must have frequently enjoyed the hospitality of the Pecks during the early months of 1777.

In the first week of March 1777, Lieutenant Rathbun made a trip from Providence to Boston, where he delivered to Jones a request for back pay from Henry Tillinghast, surgeon of the transferred *Providence-Alfred* crew. While Rathbun was in Boston, Jones, who now realized he could not carry out his glamorous orders from the Marine Committee to sail as Commodore of a sizeable fleet, urged his first lieutenant to join him in journeying to Philadelphia. Captain Jones had decided to see what new orders a personal appearance might produce and, since he had no intention of returning to sloop *Providence,* he suggested that Lieutenant Rathbun go with him to the Congress to make a bid for a captain's commission and command of the sloop.[12] Rathbun's objection that command of the *Providence* should properly go to his senior, Lieutenant Jonathan Pitcher, would have been met by Jones' assurance that, in view of the way the Marine Committee functioned, Pitcher was less apt to get the command than someone in Philadelphia better known to the Committee.

Lieutenant Rathbun yielded without undue reluctance to the persuasions of his friend and captain. By 13 March, he was back in Providence where, having delivered Surgeon Tillinghast's money, he was rowed out to Flagship *Warren.* After a smart salute to the quarterdeck, he was welcomed aboard to visit and exchange news with his old shipmates and the Commodore before picking up some letters that Esek Hopkins had written to Philadelphia. One of them contained the Commodore's explanation of his failure to capture or destroy the *Diamond,* but it would be delivered too late to change the Congressional decision for Hopkins' suspension.

In another letter, this one to William Ellery, who upon the death of Samuel Ward had become a Rhode Island delegate to the Congress, the Commodore gave a warm and, in view of Rathbun's prospective traveling companion, somewhat ironic recommendation of Lieutenant Rathbun. "The bearer Lieutt. Rathbun waits on you with this," wrote Hopkins. "He has Served since the Fleet went from Philadelphia there being no Vacancy whereby I could promote him agreeable to his Merits—if there Should be any Vacancy with you I can Recommend him as a man of Courage and I believe Conduct, and a man that is a Friend to his Country—and I believe the most of the Success Capt Jones has had is owing to his Valour and good Conduct . . . ."[13]

With the mail for Philadelphia safely in hand, Rathbun could return to his home in South Kingstown to be joined by Captain Jones for the journey southward. It is easy to picture the two officers setting off on horseback on a brisk March morning, Polly Rathbun waving them goodby at the gate. A dashing sight they must have made in the uniform that Congress had prescribed for naval officers the previous September. Their blue coats had stand-up collars, red lapels, yellow metal buttons stamped with anchors and, for Captain Jones, gold edging on the coat. Their waistcoats were red, breeches blue, and each sported a black cockade in his three-cornered hat.

Captain Jones surely also carried mail for Philadelphia, including some recommended changes in this uniform that he, with several other captains, had approved a few days earlier in Boston. The red lapels and waistcoat would be eliminated in favor of white, with white breeches and stockings. The new uniform, minus the tell-tale red, would be enough like the British officers' to permit deceptive tactics at close quarters. Rathbun, among others, would later use the stratagem of impersonating a British captain to good effect. Now, however, Jones and Rathbun were more concerned with avoiding British outposts between New York and Philadelphia as, with a final salute to young Polly, they turned their horses' heads westward on the Post Road for Westerly, New London, and points south.

In the meantime, back in the Providence River, it looked as though sloop *Providence* might see some real action at last. At the end of the letter of recommendation that Lieutenant Rathbun carried to Delegate Ellery, Esek Hopkins made reference to an event that has attracted singularly little attention from historians. It was an attempt, suggested by the Congress, for the Colony of Rhode Island, with help from Massachusetts and Connecticut, to drive the British forces out of Newport. Back in December 1776, when General Washington had heard from Governor Cooke news of the British occupation of Rhode Island, he had sent one of his generals, Joseph Spencer, to Providence "to pursue such measures as circumstances should seem to require" and "render you many essential services."[14] At that time, General Washington himself, having been forced to retreat southward from New York through New Jersey and across the Delaware into Pennsylvania, was in no position to offer any further help to the beleaguered colony to the eastward.

In March 1777, General Spencer, contemplating an assault on the British garrison at Newport, enlisted the help of Commodore Hopkins in keeping his plans as secret as possible. When he asked that the Navy stop any intelligence from getting to Newport by water, sloop *Providence* was pressed into service. On 9 March Hopkins wrote to Captain Whipple, directing that the *Providence* with forty men drop down to anchor "in some convenient place this side of Conimicutt point and Stop all Boats or other Craft from passing without General Spencer's Order for it . . . You may go in her yourself or send Mr. Pitcher to execute the above Orders. The Sloop will be ready there as ever, to Act in Concert with the Fire ship."[15]

No attempt to land troops on Rhode Island was made in the spring of seventy-seven because, according to the Commodore, of the same problem that plagued the Navy—shortage of men. However, the so-called "secret expedition" (a title remarkably apt in view of its historical obscurity) was actually launched in October when, because of high winds and an insufficient number of boats, it was promptly abandoned.[16] Shortly thereafter the assembled militia was sent home, and further challenge to the British position awaited the better known, though equally abortive, Battle of Rhode Island in 1778.

Meanwhile, the winter of 1777 was bleak behind the blockade, and the problem of manning the ships as severe as the weather. On 18 March there were aboard the four vessels in the Providence River fewer than three hundred men, most of them assigned to the two frigates. The *Columbus* had twenty and sloop *Providence* "but a few." With the coming of Spring, however, the complement of sloop *Providence* swelled, and Hopkins was able to write the Marine Committee on 8 April that "sloop *Providence* is nearly mann'd under the care of Lt. Pitcher and shall try to get her out soon."[17]

"Getting her out" meant running the gauntlet of all those British guns in Narragansett Bay—a risky business at best, but after the tiresome weeks bottled up in the river, officers and crewmen alike welcomed the prospect of action. Now with a skimpy but adequate crew on board, including Lieutenants Adam W. Thaxter and Esek Hopkins, Jr. and Marine Lieutenant Trevett, Acting Captain Pitcher waited only for a favorable wind and a good dark night to take the *Providence* down the river on her bid for freedom.

The opportunity was not long in coming. One evening in mid-April 1777, the wind veered into the northeast, promising overcast skies and a black night, and the decision was made—Go! At sunset, Captain Pitcher ordered Lieutenant Thaxter to weigh anchor and make sail. Followed by the fervent good wishes, not untinged with envy, of the rest of the fleet, the *Providence* gathered speed as she slipped quietly down the river.

Safe enough until Warwick Neck lay astern, and for the first time in five months she was well out in the familiar, now hostile, bay. Sloop *Providence* became a kind of ghost ship; showing no lights, her men padding silently to tend sail, she slid quietly through the black water in enveloping darkness. Past a ship anchored off Prudence Island and, the light wind holding from the northeast, on down the western channel. Another ship suddenly loomed above, so close that her cannon could be counted—she was the big British 50-gunner—and her crew could be heard talking aboard. No one breathed as the *Providence* slipped noiselessly by.

She had made it almost to what is now Beavertail light when her luck turned. As the sky began to lighten to the eastward, the wind died, and two miles from the lighthouse she lay with sails slatting uselessly, becalmed. Her men watched the sun rise over the masts of the British ships riding at anchor in Newport Harbor, and were watched in return for several tense hours. Finally at ten in the morning their prayers were answered. A whisper of air stirred the tell-tale—then a puff that settled into a light breeze from the southwest. Just enough to fill the *Providence*'s sails and bring her to life again, but of little use to the British squadron at Newport. It was a jubilant crew that sprang to the sheets and heard the lisp of water against her prow as once again she answered her helm, heading out of Narragansett Bay—free at last.

She ran for New Bedford, where she dropped anchor late that

night, first vessel of the Continental fleet to run the British blockade. There was surprise mingled with rejoicing at having escaped
the net. Lieutenant Trevett reported, "We had but few men on
board, as it was not expected that we should get out of Providence
river." The old problem of recruiting was still with them, but they
managed, by one means or another, to enlist an adequate crew in
New Bedford and, after taking on provisions and supplies, cast off
for a cruise to the eastward.

These waters were by now familiar to both Captain Pitcher
and sloop *Providence* but, unlike their earlier cruises, this one in the
spring provided no excitement until they came within a few miles
of Cape Breton. There several sail were spotted and in the distance
heavy cannon fire could be heard. When a brig bore down and
opened fire from long range, the *Providence,* not yet ready to engage
the enemy, took to her heels to clear for action.

As the roll of the drum sent the sloop to quarters, her decks
were suddenly alive with hurrying men. Under Lieutenant Thaxter's supervision, all movable equipment was sent down into the
hold, including furniture and bulkheads from the officers' quarters.
The galley fire was thrown into the sea, and tubs half-filled with
sand and water were placed between the guns, smoldering slow-
matches (cotton wicks soaked in lye) draped over their sides.
Marines guarded the hatches to prevent any unauthorized trips
below as the gun crews ran to unlash their cannon. Cannonballs,
and wadding to stuff the empty spaces around them, were near at
hand, and ship's boys ran to the magazine to bring up cartridges,
cloth bags filled with gunpowder. Besides cannonballs for pounding
away at hull and masts, langrage (bolts, nuts, miscellaneous iron
pieces) and grape (small shot) packed into bags could be used to tear
into sails, rigging, and men.

When the decks had been cleared and sprinkled with sand and
the men were all at their stations, Captain Pitcher ordered the
Providence's sail shortened so that the brig could come up close
alongside. If she counted on making an easy capture, she was in for
a rude surprise. "The sea being smooth," wrote Trevett, "we cut
away all her colors in forty minutes, and they began to be slack,
but in a few minutes they began to fire as brisk as ever, and cut
our sails and rigging badly." For another forty minutes the two
vessels exchanged broadsides at point-blank range. The *Providence*'s
gun crews went through their motions deafened by explosions and
half-blinded by smoke. With the gun inboard, load and ram home
cartridge, wadding, and ball; run the gun out for aiming and for
the match to be touched to the priming hole and blown into life;

and jump back when the gun goes off, lurching inboard again in its tackles.

During the action Captain Pitcher was badly wounded, but refused to leave the quarterdeck. Finally good shooting from the *Providence* brought down the brig's main topmast. A hail from the sloop—without need of a speaking trumpet, so close were the two boats—asking if the Britishers gave up was answered with a "yes." "Capt. Pitcher sent me in the barge first on board," reported Trevett. "I found them with a very bloody deck, and her spars, sails and rigging very much injured. I staid on board until I sent the Captain on board our sloop. The cabin floor was covered with the wounded, so that you could scarcely find room for your foot, and I found some of them were Irish, as they cried out for 'Jesus sake' to spare their lives; they were very badly wounded."

It had been the first real fight for sloop *Providence*, and in it her officers and men had proved that they could function as a team in battle. The gunners had gone through their routine of load, run out, aim, fire, with speed and accuracy, urged on by their officers, and the three cheers that went up from the deck of the sloop were an expression of trust and congratulation between quarterdeck and forecastle. Lieutenants Thaxter and Hopkins had carried out the orders of their wounded captain coolly and competently, while the conduct of valiant Captain Jonathan Pitcher evoked from Trevett the comment that a better officer there could not be. Fore and aft, the men aboard the *Providence* had earned a heartfelt "Well done!"

The brig *Lucy* carried, in addition to 25 soldiers and 2 officers, a cargo of King's stores destined for Quebec. Captain Pitcher ordered the men transferred to the *Providence*, and sent a prize crew under Lieutenants Thaxter and Hopkins aboard the brig, with orders to take her into New Bedford. Sloop *Providence* had herself sustained so much damage that it was necessary to send down her topmast and topsail yard. That night under shortened sail she was lashed by high winds with sudden squalls of driving rain, and Captain Pitcher, forced to abandon his cruise, set a course for Nantucket shoals.

During the storm the two vessels had become separated, and in the morning there was no sign of the brig. The *Providence* made an uneventful passage alone and limped into Bedford early in June. There her injured captain and the British prisoners were sent to hospital ashore, while the sloop was laid up for badly needed repairs.

The brig *Lucy* and her prize crew fared less well. On 5 June 1777, while trying to round Cape Cod on her way into Bedford, she was chased by three British frigates—the *Orpheus*, *Amazon*, and *Juno*.

Artifacts recovered from HMS Orpheus, including a swivel gun, cannon balls, brass belt and shoe buckles, brass, bone, and pewter buttons, and bottles. At bottom center is the brass trigger assembly and buttplate from a musket, dated 1746. Courtesy, Underwater Bicentennial Expedition, University of Rhode Island.

Unable to escape and faced with such formidable odds, Adam Thaxter had no choice but to surrender. He and his crew were carried to
Halifax where they were confined in gaol until arrangements could
be made for their exchange.[18] News of their capture was slow in
reaching Providence, and it was not until December that, on order
of the General Assembly, two British officers from the *Syren* were
released at Newport on parole to be exchanged for Adam W. Thaxter and Esek Hopkins, Jr., "acting lieutenants of sloop *Providence,* now
prisoners at Halifax." Sir Peter Parker was requested to bring the
two Americans to Boston or Newport for discharge to avoid the
dangers of the journey from Halifax,[19] and early in 1778 Adam W.
Thaxter and Esek Hopkins, Jr. were joyfully reunited with their
families.[20]

CHAPTER IX

Captain Rathbun Takes Command

APRIL 1777–JANUARY 1778

WHILE SLOOP *Providence* was preparing to embark on her adventures in the spring of 1777, Captain John Paul Jones and Lieutenant John Peck Rathbun were on their way to Philadelphia, where they arrived early in April. Lieutenant Rathbun at once sought out William Ellery to deliver the letters from Commodore Hopkins, and to be introduced to the members of the Marine Committee. He made the same fine impression that Captain Jones had made in August 1776, and both men were treated with great cordiality. More important, they both received new orders. Captain Jones was assigned first to the *Amphritite*, later changed to command of the *Ranger*, a three-masted sloop-of-war fitting out at Portsmouth, New Hampshire. On 19 April, Lieutenant Rathbun received a commission as captain in the United States Navy, with instructions to assume command of his own old vessel, the *Providence*.

So it was that, the high hopes of their mission fulfilled, Captains Jones and Rathbun could set out once more, following the spring northward. A warm welcome awaited them in South Kingstown, where Polly Rathbun was overjoyed at seeing them and hearing the news of her husband's promotion. Captain Jones was impatient to get to Portsmouth, and undoubtedly Rathbun rode with him as far as Providence where the two friends parted for the last time. It is unlikely that they met again. In November 1777 Captain Jones took the *Ranger* to France and on to glory in the waters around the British Isles. He would not set foot on American soil again until 1781, while Rathbun was never to go to France. The two men must, however, have followed each other's careers with consuming interest, and John Paul Jones, whose relationships with his officers were almost uniformly strained, remembered with affection his happy cruises with John Peck Rathbun.

Captain Rathbun's orders from the Marine Committee "after we have appointed you to the command of sloop *Providence*," were dated 23 April 1777, and probably reached him some time early in May after he and John Paul Jones had returned to New England from Philadelphia. The orders instructed him to

> loose no time in proceeding to join your vessel at Rhode Island where you must exert yourself to have her fitted and manned immediately . . . When ready for sea you are to proceed on a Cruize in a latitude as will be most likely to fall in with and intercept the enemy's trans-

port vessels coming to reinforce or supply their army at New York and you are to use your best endeavors to take, burn, sink or destroy as many of them as possible . . . .

You are to continue this cruise for 3 months . . . .

The orders closed with the usual injunctions about replenishing provisions and supplies, urging Rathbun to use his officers and people well, still preserving discipline and decorum, and treating prisoners with humanity.[1]

It cannot have taken Captain Rathbun long to discover that his vessel had broken out of Narragansett Bay and was no longer at Rhode Island. With no way of knowing when, or if, the *Providence* would return to Bedford, he could only wait with what patience he could muster to claim his new command. It was June by the time the sloop *Providence*, battered by her action with the *Lucy* as well as rough weather, limped into Bedford. Jonathan Pitcher went ashore to recover from his wounds while his old shipmate took over the sloop. Pitcher's command had been brief but glorious, evoking a fitting tribute from Lieutenant Trevett, who wrote, "A better officer than Capt. Pitcher there cannot be." It was not the triumphant coming-aboard that it might have been for the *Providence*'s new captain. His vessel was not only badly in need of repair, but she was also woefully short of men. Marine Captain Trevett (recently promoted) sent his drummer marching through the town to gather in recruits and notices were posted advertising the forthcoming cruise, but getting the sloop manned remained a slow and painful process.

The *Providence*'s muster roll was kept by James Rogers,[2] who had earlier served as Captain Jones' steward and member of the *Britannia*'s prize crew. Now taking over the duties of both clerk and purser, he was one of the few carry-overs from Jonathan Pitcher's crew. The roll shows the "time of entry" for each man, listing only a couple before 19 June, when Captain Rathbun seems to have officially taken over, and indicating that recruiting in Bedford went on until the first of August. According to Trevett, four men were pressed there, and a few more picked up at Martha's Vineyard.

Gradually the roll filled up, officers as usual being easier to come by than men. The wages of neither provided much inducement for entering the service, especially as the inflation that would plague the United States throughout the war was beginning to make itself felt. The prospect of prize money was a stronger attraction since, even split fifty-fifty with Congress, it could and usually did exceed navy wages several times over.

Rathbun's first lieutenant was Joseph Vesey, he whose account of the *Diamond* incident had helped to scuttle his Commodore. Vesey had first come on board from the *Hornet* as acting sailing master in August 1776, and sailed on the Nova Scotia cruise, prizemaster of the *Favourite*. Daniel Bears, an early volunteer from Rhode Island, was second lieutenant, and George Sinkins of Newport, sailing master, in charge of two mates. Marine Captain John Trevett headed a contingent of marines that included a master at arms, two quartermasters, and a sergeant, as well as the usual fifer and drummer. Rathbun had known Trevett since the Continental Navy's first cruise, and had worked with him on the joint *Alfred-Providence* cruise in 1776, impressing seamen from the *Eagle*.

As commander of the *Providence*, John P. Rathbun would earn $48 a month; Marine Captain Trevett, $30; and Lieutenants Vesey and Bears and Sailing Master Sinkins, $24. Surgeon Ebenezer Richmond would get $21.67; the three master's mates, $15; and two midshipmen, $12.

The sloop's muster roll lists as gunner Lillibridge Worth, who had served as gunner's mate on the *Providence* and *Alfred* under John Paul Jones; Boatswain John Webster, whose inexorable pipe would punctuate the crew's activities; and Carpenter Thomas Brewer, one of the busiest men aboard. Each of these men, like the surgeon's mate, were paid $13, and their respective mates, $9. Wages for the rest of the hands went from $10 for steward and sailmaker, $9 for coxswain, cooper, gunner's yeoman and master at arms, to $8.50 for cook and quartermaster, $8 apiece for 13 seamen, and $6.67 for marines.

Besides prize money, the offer of cash in advance was the chief incentive to enlisting. Forty men, whose pay averaged less than $8 a month, shared nearly $3,000, almost $75 apiece, in cash advances. In addition, many of them were supplied from the slops chest with clothing which was charged to their accounts. The contents of the slops chest were valued more for warmth than style, especially in cold months when many sailors were kept ashore simply from a lack of heavy clothing. Although there was no official uniform for sailors in the Revolution, most wore loose pants and shirts of brown homespun. Headgear consisted of a knitted cap or a scarf tied around the head to protect the ears when the cannon were fired, while footwear was usually either heavy shoes or bare feet. From the slops chest of the *Providence* for this cruise, 23 crewmen drew in all more than $700 worth of clothing.

One great drawback to this system of advances was the temptation for a man to draw what he could and then desert, usually to a privateer. One seaman, Toby Jacobs, signed on on 19 June, pocketed $108, and "ran" in mid-July. He was apparently persuaded back on board, however, as his name appears on a subsequent prize list. Only one other man, a marine, deserted the sloop; he was listed as "run" on 25 July, without having received any cash advance.

While the business of recruiting went on, carpenters and caulkers were busy repairing the sloop's damaged topmast and doing extensive work on her hull. It was apparently at this time that her bottom was sheathed with copper—a relatively new technique that, by protecting her timbers from barnacles, weed, and the ravages of teredo worm, would add to her speed and cut down on the need for cleaning. Very likely at the same time the black paint was scraped off her sides, which were then given an oiled finish.

When some 66 men had signed on, Captain Rathbun was convinced that he had taken on board all the men he could get at Bedford. Hopeful for a few more, he sailed the newly renovated *Providence,* the Grand Union ensign with its white, red, and blue stripes snapping smartly astern,* across Vineyard Sound, past Naushon Island's Tarpaulin Cove of unhappy *Eagle* memory, and into Old Town (now Edgartown) on Martha's Vineyard. There she lay at anchor for several days, acquiring four more seamen, a marine, and a boy.

August was nearly half over before Captain Rathbun could carry out his April orders to search out prizes in the waters around New York. In compliance with them, he set his course for Sandy Hook, New Jersey, where he hoped to waylay British merchantmen, en route to the West Indies, sheltering there under the protection of Lord Howe's fleet.

Sloop *Providence,* having steered clear of the enemy ships at Newport and New York, made safe landfall off Sandy Hook, and stood offshore looking for prizes. "We saw some large ships lying there," wrote Trevett, "and at the same time saw a ship, brig, schooner and sloop get under way and come out, standing to the S.E." Since Captain Rathbun had no intention of inviting action so

*Although the Stars and Stripes had been officially adopted by Congress on 14 June 1777, word of the change did not reach the fleet for many weeks.

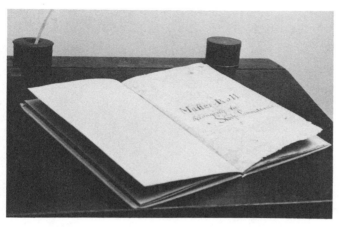

Muster Roll of Sloop Providence. *Courtesy, Rhode Island Historical Society.*

close to the British fleet, he bided his time. "We dogged them until the next day," reports Trevett, "when we had them a good distance from the Hook, and then stood for them." The ship was the primary target, for if she could be taken, the other vessels would have small chance to escape. Boatswain Webster's pipe shrilled, and the *Providence* cleared for action. The engagement that followed is described in Trevett's succinct prose:

> About 3 p.m. we came up with the ship, the other vessels being near to her weather bow, and hailed her. She had her pennant and ensign flying, but gave us no answer, and we gave her a bow gun intending to break her cabin windows. We drew very near her, but the wind being scant found we could not get to windward, so we bore away and went under her lee as near as we could and gave her a good broadside. She immediately gave us as good a one, and run us aboard on our starboard quarter, and hung there about five minutes, until she broke all our sweeps that were lashed there. At the same time the brig of 10 guns and schooner of 8 lost no time—all three of them firing on us at once. As the ship fell off she gave us her starboard broadside, and we shot ahead of them with our sails and rigging much cut to pieces. We then bore away, all hands employed in fixing our rigging.

The engagement should have ended there, as this was obviously no fat innocent merchant ship, and the *Providence*'s twelve 4-pounders were no match for the combined British can-

A Muster Roll of all the Offic[ers]
the Continental armed Sloop Prov[idence]
Rathbun Esqr. from June 19. 1777

Number	Names	Stations	Time of En[listment]	
			Year	Mon[th]
1	John Peck Rathbun	Captain	1777	
2	Joseph Vesey	1 Lieutnant		
3	Daniel Bears	2 ditto		
4	George Sinkins	Master	"	Jun
5	John Trevett	Cap. Marines	"	
6	William P Thurston	1 Mastr Mate		July
7	William Gregory	2 ditto do	"	"
8		3 do	"	
9	Richmond	Surgeon	"	A[ug]
10	James Rogers	Purser		Ap[ril]
11	Sam Bailey	Clerk		Jun
12	Oliver Whitwell	1 Midshipm		July
13	Joseph Deveber	2 ditto		"
14	Thomas Pain	Steward		July
15	Ellbridge Worth	Gunner		"
16	John Webster	Boatswain		Jun
17	Thomas Brewer	Carpenter		
18	Amos Potter	Gunn[er]		
19		Boatsn do		
20	Andrew Brewer	Carpr do		Jun
21		Surgs do		
22	Andrew Burnet	Cook		Jun
23	Richd Grennell	Ar[mourer]		
24	Peleg Slive	Carpenter		

Seamen & Marines belonging to ... Commanded by John Peck —

Wages per month	Run, Dead, Sick or Discharged	Promotions	
48			
24			36
24			
24			
30			
15		to 10	
		3-8	
21⅔		/	
		from Clerk to Purser	
12			
12			72
12			78
10			60 / 36
13			9
13			18
13			
9			60
9			
9			
135			
8½			

Muster Roll of Sloop Providence, *June 19, 1777 to August 11, 1777. Courtesy, Rhode Island Historical Society.*

non firing three against one. Furthermore the *Providence*'s sailing master, George Sinkins, responsible for the actual work of sailing the sloop, had been killed by a British ball, and two or three others wounded. The *Providence* and her people, however, were not so easily put out of action. The body of the sailing master was hove overboard, the rigging repaired with all possible speed, and back to the attack came stubborn little *Providence*.

"We came up with her just after sunset," wrote Trevett, "with a determination to board her, for we well knew if we carried the ship that the rest of the vessels would fall into our hands . . . We ran within half pistol shot and gave her a full broadside." This one shot away the Englishman's colors, and three cheers went up from the deck of the *Providence* in the belief that the ship had surrendered.[3] However, the Union Jack was soon hoisted again, and the enemy vessels "played their part so well," as Trevett put it, "we gave it up."

During the action with the ship, the schooner had got ahead of the other vessels, and, as darkness approached, the *Providence* was able to run alongside and take her. She was the *Loyalty*, mounting 8 guns and carrying a cargo of horses and carriages—a nice prize that Captain Rathbun manned and sent in to Bedford. From her master, Rathbun learned that all three vessels were bound for Jamaica in ballast and that the ship *Mary*, despite her appearance as an innocent merchantman, mounted 16 guns, and her captain held a commission in the Royal Navy. Undismayed by the news of her superior force, Captain Rathbun set his helm at nightfall on the course he calculated the ship to be on, hoping for another go at her by daylight, but in the morning she was nowhere to be seen.

The escape of the *Mary* was a bitter disappointment for the crew of the *Providence*, particularly for her new captain, whose reputation would instantly have been made by her capture. The significance of the engagement was recognized by the British as well. When a description of the action later reached England, the eminent marine artist, Francis Holman, immortalized the battle in the painting that appears as the frontispiece of this book.

The *Providence* cruised toward the southeast for several days, seeing some Dutch and Danish vessels, but finding no likely prizes until in the Gulf Stream a distant sail was sighted, hull down, and the sloop stood for her. At sunset she could be made out to be a ship, and the chase was continued until 1:00 a.m. when the *Providence* overhauled her. By starlight it could be seen that she was under full sail but, in Trevett's words,

> Her crew appeared to act strangely, she decoyed us before the wind, and sometimes shaking in the wind, top-gallants and all sail out . . . We came within pistol shot and hailed her, but received no answer. We gave her three shots at once, which made a cracking on board of her, but still no answer and no lights were seen. Captain Rathbun ordered the boat out, armed her, and told me to take command of her, and said for my consolation, if they killed me! he would not spare one of them. I set out and ordered the cockswain to steer under her stern; I held a lanthern and saw her rudder was gone, and hailed, but received no answer. I ordered the cockswain to steer round her larboard quarter, and go alongside, and I sent one man up with the lanthern, and followed him.
>
> I found no boats on deck, but saw on the quarter deck a deep sea-lead and line. I went into the cabin and found all the beds and all the trunks full of rich clothing, and chests with their keys in them. One of our men cried out, a man! a man! I asked where, and it proved to be a small dog, that opened all the eyes he had, but could not speak our yankee tongue. I then went into the hold and found her in ballast; no cargo or provisions, except bread, and 40 casks nails, and a few cases of French cordials.

Here was a real prize for the *Providence,* a fine ship that even without cargo would bring thousands of dollars sold at auction, if only she could be got into port. But how, as she had lost her huge rudder, could that be accomplished? Carpenter Brewer was sent to inspect the ship's stern, only to return with bad news—he had neither material nor facilities for rigging any sort of a makeshift rudder that might make the ship maneuverable.

Accepting this disappointment with his customary philosophy, Captain Rathbun ordered the trunks and chests full of French clothing to be transferred to the sloop. All day the barge plied between the two vessels, stacked high with boxes of women's silk shoes and gowns and, as Trevett put it, "apparel of finery, men's shirts all ruffled, small shirts and French pocket handkerchiefs, &c. Last of all we took out the dog and for fear she should fall into the hands of the English (she was a tight ship) we set her on fire and burnt her down to the water's edge."

It was quite a show that the crew of the *Providence,* now augmented by one small dog, lined the rail to watch. Flames licked up the towering spars, smoldered along the rigging and swallowed the yards until, as one by one the masts let go, a flaming mass of wood and cordage hurled itself into the sea with a hissing cloud of steam. A lingering cloud on the horizon as the *Providence* sailed away marked the last sight of the mystery ship.

Rathbun and his officers surmised that on her way from France the ship had been driven ashore, probably on Cape Hatteras shoals, and hastily abandoned by her passengers and crew. Refloated by the next high tide, she had been driven by westerly winds into the Gulf Stream. On the *Providence's* return home, however, careful scanning of Southern papers failed to produce news of any such ship, which remains the sloop's own mystery ship, her personal "Flying Frenchman."

The encounter with the ghost ship was the last excitement for the *Providence* on this cruise and, heading northward again, she arrived early in the fall back at Bedford to be laid up for badly needed repairs. The prize schooner *Loyalty* had also made port safely and, in spite of having lost two ships, the crew of the *Providence* could look forward to a sizeable windfall from her condemnation and sale, as well as the proceeds from the French ship's finery. Prize shares listed for the schooner and "wreck" amounted to more than $3,000. The Captain's share at £110 was worth $363, better than seven times his monthly pay. First officers received half that amount, and petty officers and crewmen proportionately smaller shares.[4]

While the Bedford shipyard workers were busy repairing the damage inflicted on the *Providence* by the *Mary*, Captain Rathbun and his crew enjoyed several weeks ashore. It was mid-November before Rathbun received instructions, this time issued by the Eastern Navy Board, to proceed "on his present cruise." The Board, set up in April, but plagued by slow communication and lack of funds, had finally gotten into action in September. Even after requesting a £3000 loan from the Rhode Island Council in order to do business,[5] it was still financially strapped, as it would remain throughout its service in spite of constant contributions from the pockets of its own three members, William Vernon of Providence, James Warren of Boston, and Connecticut's John Deshon.

With the Board's instructions for Captain Rathbun came word that it was unable to furnish him with "any slops, &c." Rathbun must have wished for some way to trade a few fancy French shirts for some warm clothing for his men, as at this cold season, lack of slops was a real deterrent to recruiting. However, it was gradually completed, albeit slowly, furthered by the decision to head immediately for warmer waters—Rathbun wanted no frostbitten sailors despite the clothing shortage. As usual, officers were in more abundant supply than men. First Lieutenant Joseph Vesey and Second Lieutenant Daniel Bears were still aboard, joined now by Lieutenant George House, and Marine Captain Trevett acquired a lieutenant, Michael Moulton.

Thanksgiving was approaching before the *Providence* was ready for sea. By this time the change in the American flag authorized by Congress in June had become official, and in place of her old Grand Union ensign the sloop now proudly flew the Stars and Stripes of the United States. Because of the lateness of the season Captain Rathbun planned on a rather short cruise, but such are the fortunes of war that it would be some months before the sloop saw the shores of New England again.

Trouble came almost at once. Rathbun set sail in a light northeast wind, heading for Block Island, but by nightfall the wind had freshened and it began to snow. All night the sloop pitched and wallowed in rising seas and winds that reached gale force by morning, when with a horrid cracking, her long bowsprit split. She rode out the storm hove to, while the hands cut away the broken rigging and, with the bowsprit temporarily "fished," bore away southwestward, heading for South Carolina.[6]

After an uneventful voyage, the *Providence* arrived off Charleston Bar just at nightfall in five fathoms of water. Captain Rathbun decided to wait for daylight and a pilot before going in, so kept the sloop standing on and off the bar, her guns in and ports closed, until at 2 a.m. in bright moonlight the lookout spotted a sail close inshore, heading for the *Providence*. The lieutenant of the watch roused his captain, and Rathbun and Trevett came up on the quarterdeck.

> She hailed us [wrote Trevett] and ordered the damned yankee beggars to haul down the colors. We had a foul weather jack at the mast head. In a few minutes she run under our lee-quarter and gave us a broadside without any courtesy, and run ahead of us. Capt Rathbone ordered the boatswain to call all hands to quarters, as still as he could, and not use his call. The Privateer (as she proved to be) bore away, and coming up again, was soon alongside; we were all ready for them and as soon as they made the first flash we gave them a yankee

welcome, with a handsome broadside. They up helm and ran to the eastward, and not having a man hurt, of any consequence, we made sail after them.

The enemy's broadside had cut the *Providence*'s rigging and torn her sails so badly that she was slow getting under full sail, but with hasty repairs soon began to overhaul the chase. When the privateer hoisted a lantern at her masthead, despite the moonlit brightness of the morning, it was surmised that she was signaling to another enemy ship, so Rathbun ordered that no more cannon be fired and that the chase be continued in silence. This proved to be a prudent precaution when, as dawn was just beginning to break, a large ship was sighted under the land to windward.

"About sunrise we neared the Privateer so much that the Lieut. from the round house fired several times at us, and the balls went a distance beyond us. I told Capt. Rathbone that we had beyond doubt as good muskets as they had." With two marines, Trevett went forward to take a shot at the lieutenant, "as he made a fine mark to be shot at standing on the round house. We had not fired more than three shot before we saw him fall, and instantly the Privateer got in the wind, and we were alongside of her in a few minutes; when we boarded her and found it was her Lieutenant we had shot, and he fell on the man steering at the wheel. This Lieut. belonged to the State of Virginia, and he expected to be punished if taken by the Americans, so he was determined to fight as long as he could. He had a handsome brace of pistols at his side when he laid dead on deck."

The Providence had inflicted considerable damage to the privateer's hull and badly wounded five of the crew. The captured officers provided information that the ship they had signaled to in the night, and that the *Providence* had sighted in the morning, was a British frigate that they had been on board the day before and were to meet off Charleston Bar—a rendezvous that never took place. Six negro pilots aboard the privateer had been captured the day before while they were fishing; arrangements were made to return them to their owners. The presence of the British frigate dampened enthusiasm for crossing Charleston Bar, and the *Providence* sailed up Winyah Bay to put into Georgetown, South Carolina, instead. There the prisoners were sent to the local jail, except the privateer's captain, who was to be delivered to the Commissary of Prisoners at Charleston.

On Christmas Day, the capture made the local newspaper.

Two of the enemy's ships have been frequently seen from the town since our last. Last Thursday two canoes with 8 negroes, were taken off the bar by a sloop, who was in company with the two men of war. The same sloop was taken on the morning following by the Continental Sloop Providence, Capt. Rathburne, after a short engagement, in which the enemy had three men killed and one wounded. She is the Governor Tonyn, carried 10 guns, is commanded by Capt. Demas, and fitted out as a privateer from St. Augustine. Both the Providence and her prize are in port. Six of the negroes abovementioned were on board the sloop when taken.[7]

Leaving their sloop repairing at Georgetown, Captain Rathbun and Trevett escorted Captain Demas overland to Charleston. There they had a chance to enjoy some real civilization for a change—to patronize the taverns and coffee houses frequented by merchant captains, and to meet old friends such as Captain Nicholas Biddle, who was preparing to take to sea a flotilla of four vessels under his new command, the frigate *Randolph*. From one of their coffee-house acquaintances, a merchant captain lately arrived from the island of New Providence, Captain Rathbun heard a startling piece of news. The ship *Mary*, the 16-gun privateer that had roughed up the *Providence* off the New Jersey coast in June, killing her sailing master, was lying in Nassau Harbor, where she had put in in distress after running onto a reef on her way from Jamaica. While she was undergoing extensive repairs, her captain had gone ashore sick, and for safety's sake, her ammunition had been stored in one of the forts. Here was provocative news indeed—an old adversary lying helpless in a none-too-well defended port—and Rathbun pressed for further information. It appeared that there was little British military strength on New Providence, and that the two forts were no better defended than they had been in March of 1776 when they had fallen without resistance to the Continental fleet. Moreover, the island was by no means entirely loyal to the King; some trade had been kept up with the Colonies, and there was a good deal of sympathy for their cause.

Both Rathbun and Trevett had taken part in that first New Providence cruise of the Continental navy, and were familiar with the lay of the land. The tempting thought of capturing the *Mary*, one of the *Providence*'s few escapees, gave rise to some fascinating speculation. If control of the two forts flanking the town could somehow be gained—in a surprise raid led by Marine Captain Trevett, for instance—under cover of their big guns, the *Providence* could sail in and at her leisure capture all the shipping in the harbor, including, of course, the prime target, the *Mary*. In addition to prize ships and cargoes, there would surely be useful military stores to be liberated and, if the safety of private property could be guaranteed, sympathetic townsmen might be counted on for necessary support. The scheme, risky as it was, was tempting, and Captain Rathbun kept turning it over in his mind.

He pictured the town of Nassau stretching along its waterfront on the north side of the Island of New Providence. A mile off shore lay Hog Island,* which protected the harbor and gave it two entrances. The western, and deeper, channel was guarded by Fort Nassau, while four miles along the coast Fort Montagu commanded the eastern channel. Fort Nassau at the west end of the town lay almost at the water's edge,** sheltered by hills rising behind it to the southward. The fort itself consisted of masonry walls 22 feet high, forming a square 100 feet long on each side. The walls, pierced with embrasures where 18-pounder cannon were mounted, were surrounded on the outside by a high stockade fence. Inside were living quarters for troops, storage rooms, casemates, and powder magazines.

When Commodore Hopkins had raided New Providence in 1776, the main goal of his mission had been frustrated by the removal of gunpowder from Fort Nassau before the Americans could get to it. Two mistakes, Rathbun reflected, accounted for the American loss of the powder—first, failure to keep the attack a surprise, and, second, delay in taking Fort Nassau. Captain Rathbun saw a way to avoid them both. To effect complete surprise, he would not only disguise the *Providence* to look like an island trading sloop as she approached Nassau, but he would also launch the attack under cover of darkness. In order to give the British no chance to remove the gunpowder from Fort Nassau, he would send his marines to assault Fort Nassau itself, instead of attacking the weaker Fort Montagu.

It was an incredibly daring scheme, whose infinite possibilities for failure might meet with extremely disagreeable consequences. Marine Captain Trevett, who would play a leading role, was not entirely sold on the idea, his confidence further shaken when Nicholas Biddle, to whom Rathbun outlined the plan, snorted that it was "downright presumption." Captain Biddle promptly offered Trevett a berth aboard the *Randolph*, which Trevett would have

---

* Now well-known as the site of Paradise Beach.
** On grounds now occupied by the Sheraton British Hotel.

accepted had not Captain Rathbun flatly refused to let him go. Captain Biddle, with a farewell handshake for both officers, said, "I am very sorry for I shall never see you more."*

The more Captain Rathbun pondered his plan, risks and all, the more feasible it began to seem. Although even the closest questioning of his informant could not give him exact information about the strength of the island's defenses, the report was encouraging. Newly appointed Lieutenant Governor John Gambier had no regular British troops to call on, and kept only a few local militia manning the two forts. No Royal Navy vessels were stationed in the harbor—in fact, the chief warlike activity in Bahamian waters appeared to be the depredations of a British privateer operating between Jamaica and New Providence. She was the 16-gun *Gayton*, commanded by the same Captain William Chambers who had carried off the gunpowder in 1776. With luck, the *Providence*'s arrival at Nassau would not coincide with one of Chambers' frequent visits to the harbor.

Having said their final goodby to Nicholas Biddle, Captains Rathbun and Trevett traveled back to Georgetown where the scheme was outlined to the other officers of the *Providence*. Lieutenants Vesey, Bears, House and Moulton, seated around the table in the great stern cabin, must have listened at first with thinly disguised incredulity as their captain unfolded his wild plan. The *Providence* would anchor off Hog Island at night, sending two boatloads of marines under Captain Trevett ashore to land near Fort Nassau. Carrying a scaling ladder, the shore party would climb through or over the fence, up and over the west wall, to overpower the few defenders and take command of the fort. Some of the big guns would be trained on the town, while others would cover nearby shipping in the harbor. At first light, the Stars and Stripes would be hoisted to the masthead, and the *Providence* would sail into the harbor to take her pick of the shipping there. Contact would be made with sympathetic local Whigs who, with assurances that no private property, but only military stores, would be touched, might be counted on for help. Captain Rathbun pointed out that, if the raid succeeded, it would be productive not only of glory and valuable supplies for the Continent, but probably a considerable amount

---

*This remark turned out to be prophetic, although perhaps not in the way Biddle intended. A few months later he and all but four of his crew were killed when the frigate *Randolph* unaccountably blew up in a gallant action with a 64-gun British ship of the line. Trevett could thank Captain Rathbun's refusal to let him leave the *Providence* for saving his life.

of prize money as well. Whatever his persuasions, his officers were convinced that the plan just might work, and they agreed to try it.

Preparations were begun at once. A good long scaling ladder had to be built, and a local seamstress was set to work stitching up a new flag, while wood, water, and provisions were loaded aboard. Finally, in the third week of January 1778 the work was finished. Sloop *Providence* cast off her lines and, as her officers waved goodby from the quarterdeck to friends ashore, she left Georgetown astern to sail out of Winyah Bay, bound for the open sea and high adventure.

CHAPTER X

Lone Raid on Nassau

JANUARY 1778

THE ADVENTURE CAME sooner than expected. On the *Providence's* second day out of Georgetown, bound for New Providence, a sail was sighted on the eastern horizon, then two more. They turned out to be British—a ship, brig, and sloop—but, no innocent merchantmen, they straightway made all sail for the *Providence*. She could handily outsail the smaller vessels, but was no match for the ship, which gained on her so fast that by two o'clock in the afternoon the grinning tier of British guns was discernible. Captain Rathbun had shown John Paul Jones how to make good use of the nimbleness of the sloop's fore-and-aft rig to escape from HMS *Solebay*, and he could see a way that he might again turn these qualities to advantage—and the dark hull as well—if only he could hold his lead until night.

With the enemy gaining steadily on the sloop, Captain Rathbun gave orders to lighten ship. Over the side went the casks of water so recently filled, the entire supply of wood for the galley fires, and all other expendables, including the newly made scaling ladder. Freed of this much weight, the *Providence* picked up just enough speed to hold the narrow stretch of water between her and those eager British guns. It seemed like an eternity before the light began to fade, but when the sun finally slid down below the horizon, welcome darkness fell fast on the sea. Rathbun turned the *Providence* abruptly off course, ordered all sails dropped fast and quietly, and all lights doused. The sloop lay, a silent, bare-sparred black hull, rocking on an inky ocean, waiting. Her deck hands lay at their posts, quiet as dead men, but ready to make all sail at once, should she be discovered.

It was not long before straining eyes could make out a gray blur looming against the blackness: the sails of the British ship, pulling hard as she raced safely past. The collective sigh of relief aboard the *Providence* must have been enough to fill her sails, which were, still quietly, reset for a new course to the southward. This course was held until daylight, when the lookout shouted down to the deck the welcome word—"No sail in sight!"

Lack of wood and water now prompted a change in itinerary, and like the earlier Continental fleet, the *Providence* turned eastward for Abaco. There, after an uneventful run, she spent a couple of days reprovisioning. A new scaling ladder was built, her topmast and topsail yard were sent down, and her guns neatly housed to hide her military appearance. Thus, with her crew ordered to disappear below decks if a sail were sighted, it was an innocent island trading sloop that weighed anchor at Abaco, bound for New Providence. Two days later, at midnight of 27 January, a light offshore breeze brought her abreast of Nassau Harbor, ready to lower the barge for the shore party.

Captain Trevett waited on deck, having, as he put it, "picked out my lambs!—better I could not wish—all smart and active, except one lame; he said to me, 'I cannot run.' I said you are the man I should choose." Captain Rathbun dropped the *Providence's* hook at the western end of Hog Island and ordered the boat lowered with as little noise and as few lights as possible. Marine Lieutenant Michael Moulton and 14 men climbed down into the barge, which was shortly swallowed up in the darkness as the faint splashing of muffled oars died away. After an agonizing half hour, the sound of oars again drifted across the water. The boat was back with welcome word from the coxswain that the party had been landed a mile from the fort and that everything seemed quiet ashore. This time Captain Trevett embarked with 12 men, taking "nothing with us to eat or drink, but filled our pockets with ball cartridges," and once more the barge headed for shore. When it reappeared out of the blackness, the word was good. The second landing had been effected as quietly as the first and, scaling ladder and all, the marines were ready to tackle Fort Nassau.

Now the action passed to John Trevett and his marines, while Captain Rathbun and the *Providence* had only to find safe anchorage outside the harbor until morning when, if the Stars and Stripes were flying over the fort, she would sail into the harbor in support of her landing party. However, the wind, which had generously held off while the barge was plying back and forth between sloop and shore, now suddenly freshened to gale force, threatening to drive the *Providence* ashore. Captain Rathbun had no choice but to put to sea.

At this point, not only was the whole enterprise in jeopardy, but the sloop herself was in danger. Her crew, the twenty-odd men left after Captain Trevett had taken his pick, had been expected only to maintain anchor watch overnight, not to tend sail while riding out a storm. There was no sleep aboard the *Providence* that night—least of all for her captain. John Peck Rathbun paced the quarterdeck where the binnacle light glowed like an evil eye, and cursed himself for nine kinds of a fool. The scheme that had, although risky, looked feasible in Charleston, now seemed sheer idiocy. He thought of Trevett and his little force assaulting the fort, and the thousand things that could have happened to prevent their taking it. He remembered Captain Biddle's derision of the plan, and his invitation for Trevett to transfer to the *Randolph*. Why had he not let him go, instead of sending him on this hare-brained mission on a hostile island?

The night seemed endless, but at length the wind died down, and Rathbun began working the *Providence* back toward Nassau. It was a long haul, and the sun was high in the sky before the look-out's cry "Land Ho!" brought the captain to the rail with his tele-scope. The leadsman was busy in the chains as the *Providence* picked her way through the reefs and shoals that guard the approach to the harbor. Captain Rathbun steadied his glass as details of the shore began to show—the hill dotted with houses behind the har-bor, Fort Montagu barely discernible down the coast to the east-ward, and to the west, the emerging shape of Fort Nassau. With a flag snapping briskly from the masthead—but which flag? Unbe-lievably after the nightmare of the night, it was the Stars and Stripes of the United States, swelling and rippling for the first time over foreign soil. All dignity and rank aboard the sloop was forgotten as the men jumped up and down, slapping each other on the back, and giving a cheer that would have done credit to a hundred men.

Captain Rathbun would soon learn how Trevett and his marines had carried out their assignment. Trevett's journal reports that

> . . . we landed about a mile from the Fort, and got our scaling ladder and all things ready. I recollected that when I was at the taking of New Providence with Com. Hopkins, I left out one of the pickets of the fort, and I thought this might prove fortunate if it had not been replaced. So I left my men and went myself to see, and found it as I left it, still out. I went through, and near the embrazures I heard talking in the fort, and instantly one of the sentinels came to the corner of the fort and cried "all is well!" and was answered from the other end of the fort, "all is well!" The ship that lay near the fort—[this was the *Mary*]—her sen-tinel also cried "all is well!" I lay still a few moments, as I supposed the sentinels were going their rounds. I then went back and we came on with the scaling ladder, and lay down near the fort until the sentry should come round again, for I expected they gave the cry every half hour, and so it was. We had been but a short time there before they came round and cried "all is well!" I waited a few minutes and then placed the scaling ladder near one of the embrazures and went over, every man following me.

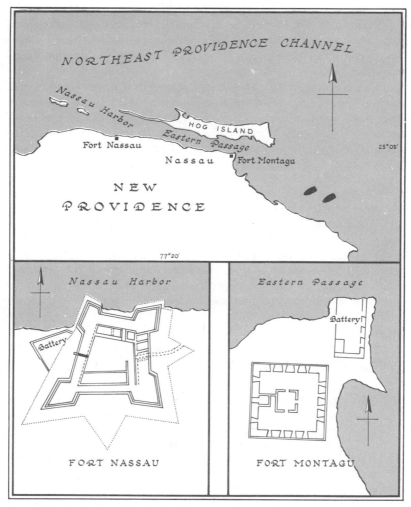

Scene of the landings on the island of New Providence, Bahamas, 1776 and 1779.

Having given stern orders for absolute quiet, Trevett felt his way cautiously along the wall of the fort, his men close on his heels. Arrived at a corner, he went around it—and ran smack into the British sentry. "I seized him by the collar, and ordered him in the first barrack door; he was much frightened, and exclaimed, 'for God's sake, what have I done!' " At this juncture an overzealous follower, forgetting his orders, fired his pistol at the sentinel, but fortunately the sound was muffled by the thick walls of the fort and failed to rouse anyone. "I spoke a soft word," continues Trevett, "and went into the barracks and examined the prisoner, and found there was only one more sentinel and he at the other end of the Fort." Trevett made short work of corralling him and installing him in a different barrack-room. Questioning each man separately, he heard the same story from both: "Gov. Gambier had sent into the fort every article necessary, about three weeks before we made them this friendly visit. I asked them the reason of having only two sentinels in the fort in time of war; they said if they had only time to fire one or two guns, that in less than ten minutes they would have more than five hundred fighting men in the fort."

The Americans were not disposed to put this assertion to the test, contenting themselves with a complement of twenty-eight, and two prisoners. Trevett kept them all busy.

> When I first got into the fort I found a number of 18 pounders loaded, and matches burning by them. I immediately ordered one of the prisoners to see what cartridges were filled, and took a lantern and went to the magazine of powder, where I found about three tons, but not so many cartridges as I thought necessary, so set two men filling cartridges. It was then two o'clock in the morning, and I continued their custom, every half-hour crying out "all is well," and the Jamaica ship and another, answered us as regular as they did the British sentries. We employed the remainder of the night in placing some of the heavy pieces of cannon to point on the different streets of the town, and on the ships. When daylight appeared we set our thirteen stripes flying at the fort.

The whole operation so far had gone with incredible smoothness, and it was thrilling to see the Stars and Stripes fluttering for the first time over foreign territory. Nonetheless Captain Trevett had his problems. He worried that the high wind that had sprung up during the small hours might have forced the *Providence* to leave her station at the mouth of the harbor and stand out to sea. When the sky began to lighten and he could scan the horizon, it seemed that his apprehension was all too well founded—there was no sign of the *Providence*. Perhaps she was just behind the island and would appear when the American colors were run up—but anxious scrutiny still produced no sign of a sail.

Providence or no *Providence*, however, stage two of Rathbun's operation had to be put into effect, and immediate contact made with the town. Accordingly, Trevett sent a small detachment to search out an old acquaintance from Newport, merchant James Gould. Gould hurried at once to the fort.

> I had the scaling ladder launched out of an embrazure, and went out to him. He knew me immediately, and asked me what our fleet consisted of. I made use of Com. Biddle's fleet, and informed him it was off the Island of Abaco, and I was sent in to see some of my old friends in a tender; and that we were bound to the north side of Jamaica, but hearing that Capt. Henry Johnson [of the *Mary*] was in your harbor, I came to wait on him and was determined to take his ship, and that my orders from the commodore were not to molest or disturb any private property, unless warlike stores.

This invention went over so well that Trevett, who was beginning to notice the lack of breakfast, improved on it with the information that there were 230 Americans holding Fort Nassau. He had plenty of provisions for his men, he said, but he needed a good breakfast for his thirty officers.

The accommodating Mr. Gould hurried off to round up suitable supplies. "He called on all the bakers and stopped a very large allowance of bread; and down came butter, coffee, and everything we wanted, and a very good breakfast we made and double allowance we had."

Three of the 28 Americans missed this repast.

> Before breakfast I sent Lieut. Michael Molton through the town to take the other fort, four miles off, with only two men to accompany him. I gave him particular orders, as I knew there were but two sentries, for him to give them no time to parley, but to inform them that we had possession of Fort Nassau, with two hundred men and thirty officers; and to keep possession until he heard from me. He succeeded without any difficulty.

Meanwhile, back at Fort Nassau Captain Trevett had been provided with some unexpected reinforcements. Four merchant captains from North Carolina, whose ships had been captured by the British privateer *Gayton,* Captain William Chambers, and sent into Jamaica, had made their way to New Providence, hoping to find passage back to the States. At sight of the Stars and Stripes flying over the fort, they hurried up there with several of their crewmen, offering to join forces.[1] Trevett was delighted with their help, especially welcome in the absence of the *Providence,* and immediately made use of it. Although Captain Rathbun's plan had counted on the sloop's guns to prevent any resistance from vessels lying in the harbor, Trevett decided to go ahead on his own with the next stage of the operation—capturing the ship *Mary.*

Captain Johnson had gone ashore ill, but the *Mary's* lieutenant was on board, in charge of her 45-man crew. Captain Trevett, himself remaining in the fort to command the authority of its cannon, sent a midshipman with the four captains down to the waterfront where they commandeered a barge moored at the wharf, and rowed out to the ship, lying only a pistol-shot from shore. Their instructions were to bring back to the fort all the *Mary's* men, together with their military gear—muskets, pistols, boarding pikes, and the like. At first the British lieutenant refused to let the Americans on board, but Trevett "was ready to settle this affair with him, and hailed him from the fort in hard language and some hard names, and he admitted them aboard." There the midshipman remained, while the Carolina captains escorted the prisoners and the ordnance back to Fort Nassau. The *Mary* had taken on cargo in Jamaica after her fight with the *Providence* the summer before, and her hold contained valuable supplies of rum, molasses, sugar, indigo, coffee, and cotton. Thus quietly and bloodlessly, half a year after having escaped from her, did the ship *Mary* fall prize to sloop *Providence.*

Besides the Jamaica ship, four smaller vessels were lying in the harbor. Captain Trevett sent out boarding parties, who added two sloops, the *Washington* and *Tryal,* and two schooners to the American prize list.

Still anxious watch to the northward brought no sign of the sloop *Providence.* Captain Trevett had kept his little group of marines constantly on the move to keep up that appearance of a sizeable force of Americans in the fort. "When we relieved guard, we took them from one part of the fort, and marched them with music and placed them on another part, doing duty all the time, day and night, to deceive the inhabitants, and to carry the appearance that our force in the fort was very numerous." Without sleep, food was of first importance, and when Mr. Gould reappeared to find out if breakfast had been satisfactory, Lieutenant Trevett reaffirmed the culinary needs of his 30 fictional officers. "I said yes, and enquired of him if there was any turtle in the crowls; he said there was. I told him we should like to have a good turtle, well cooked; he said it should be done. Accordingly the first ladies ordered their servants to work dressing a famous turtle, and we had a grand dinner with china dishes, &c., sent in for us to eat off."

Hardly had the hungry marines finished this sumptuous meal when at two o'clock came the long-awaited word that a sail had been sighted—the *Providence* was on her way into the harbor.

The joy of the men ashore at this news was akin to that of those afloat at the sight of the American flag flying over Fort Nassau. The pleasure of both was shortly tempered by the sighting of another sail running outside Hog Island, making for the western channel into Nassau Harbor. Trevett was told by the Carolina captains that she was the privateer *Gayton,* which had been expected. When Captain Rathbun learned that this was Captain Chambers' privateer, he housed the *Providence*'s guns and ordered the American colours on the fort to be replaced by the British Jack, hoping that the unsuspecting *Gayton* would soon come under the big guns of Fort Nassau. The ruse almost worked, in spite of vigorous efforts of loyal islanders to warn Chambers off. "The devil was in the men, women and children," wrote Trevett. "They turned out, covering the hills, men waving their hats, and women their aprons, and the Privateer running in for the bar."

From the quarterdeck of the *Providence* Captain Rathbun watched the colorful spectacle—the Union Jack flying once again at Fort Nassau's flagstaff as the *Gayton* worked her way into the harbor, while loyal natives on the hillside flapped anything available to warn her off.

Captain Chambers, taking all this activity for a demonstration of welcome, came steadily on. "At last some men got outside the harbor with a boat," wrote Trevett, "rowing hard for her and waving their hats, and the Privateer bore away. I run our Yankee-flag up, and gave her three eighteen pound shot, one of which went into her main beam, but never hurt a man; she went around the Island and came in another way, and came to anchor in sight of us."

The *Gayton* had run back of Hog Island to enter the eastern passage, in sight but just out of reach of the guns of Fort Montagu. Captain Trevett thought of the men he had sent over there.

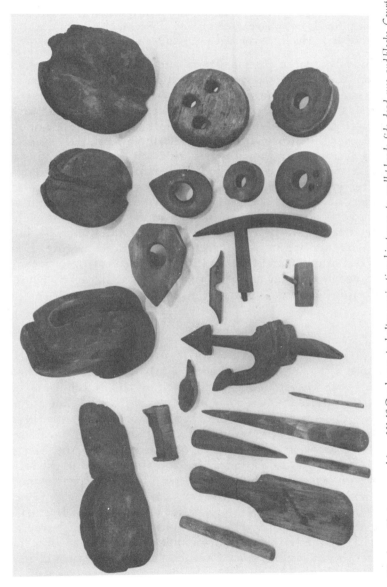

Wooden artifacts recovered from HMS Orpheus, including navigational instruments, mallet heads, fids, dead-eyes, and blocks. Courtesy, Underwater Bicentennial Expedition, University of Rhode Island.

I foresaw that I could not give Lieut. Molton any assistance at the other fort, being four miles from us; I therefore sent orders to him to spike all the guns and break all the rammers and sponges and completely dismantle the fort; to throw all powder into the sea, and discommode the enemy all he could, and return instantly to our fort, which, he did completely, and arrived safe with all his force, a little before dark. His force consisted of two men and himself.

This rather large order had been accomplished before Captain Rathbun, unwilling to leave his ship with the *Gayton* anchored so close, sent some of the *Providence's* crew ashore. "A good turtle dinner was reserved for them; and our vessel's crew at that time were quality, for they dined at seven o'clock, on a first-rate dinner. After dinner (I may say supper) Capt. Rathbone had the *Providence* moored abreast of the town with springs on her cables, and also our Prize-ship, so we were in good order for sailing."

After observing the dismantling of Fort Montagu, Captain Chambers had moved the *Gayton* westward, to anchor just out of reach of Fort Nassau's cannon. "It is now nine o'clock in the evening," reported Trevett, "and as for us we are tranquil and easy, but the inhabitants are in very great consternation, moving their effects out of town; and the people of color are very riotous. I say colored people for they are of all colors, from coal black to white. So ends this 24 hours."

Quite a 24 hours that twenty-eighth of January 1778 had been, for both Trevett and his weary marines and Rathbun and his tired sailors. Since the barge had first cast off from the side of the *Providence*, the Americans had captured two forts, dismantled one, taken the sentinels prisoner, acquired reinforcements, including some released American prisoners, obtained food for the "thirty officers" while the "two hundred men" marched around the fort, and taken five prizes, including the *Mary*. Much had been accomplished without the support of the *Providence*, now rocking gently at anchor below the fort. The sight of her was somewhat less reassuring than it would have been without the *Gayton* anchored to eastward, for the *Providence's* four-pounders were no match for the privateer's sixteen guns, even if Rathbun had had plenty of men to man them. By this time, with men aboard the prizes as well as enjoying their turtle in the fort, she was more short-handed than ever. "Tranquil and easy" as Captain Trevett may have felt, the

American hold on the hostile island, depending entirely on a few tired men holding the fort, was precarious at best.

The night passed without incident, however, despite unrest in the town, and the morning of the twenty-ninth dawned fair and mild. The crew of the *Providence* was occupied in getting the *Mary* ready for sea, together with the prize sloop *Washington* loaded with indigo. The third prize, sloop *Tryal,* was turned over to the Carolina captains and their men, "in consideration of their singular Courage and assistance during our stay on the island of Providence," wrote Captain Rathbun, "on behalf of Myself and the Sloop's crew."[2] Lacking enough men to man the two schooners, Rathbun ordered them to be unloaded and burned.

Captain Trevett, who remained in the fort, reported in his journal,

> The town continued in great confusion, many of the inhabitants moving their valuable goods, and numbers of all colors under arms, around the Governor's house, and all the hills around alive with them, their guns glistening in the sun. They gave me but very little uneasiness, as I had then in the fort twenty-five men beside myself, and all in good spirits, and many of them anxious for me to order them to fire on what they called black-beards; but I thought I knew what ground I stood on, and if I could do without it, I was desirous in my own mind not to shed blood. This morning came within half a pistol shot of the fort some of those colored troops, one of them hallooing to the others, seeing me on the wall of the fort, and pointing to me "See there is that d ____ d long nose Buckerer come again, that carried away Gov. Brown." I paid no attention to such small stuff.

A little later Trevett had visitors of higher rank; Governor Gambier sent his tax collector with two gentlemen to find out what the Americans' intentions were. Over the wall went the scaling ladder (no one could be let into the fort lest the true size of the force there be discovered) and down it climbed Captain Trevett. He informed the Governor's delegation that

> Com. Biddle had given orders to Capt. Rathbone to take Fort Nassau, and all armed vessels, and all American property we could find in the harbor of New Providence, and likewise to hold sacred all private property; with which orders I meant to comply; and that the Governor might rest assured, and he might take to himself and give to his friends, on the honor of an American officer, that his person and those of the inhabitants, should be protected.

While he was at it, Trevett also announced that he wanted some sails and rigging, in store for Captain Chambers, sent down below the fort for use on the prizes. The deputation left to convey this news to the Governor, while Trevett retired into the fort to await developments. Nothing happened, and when an hour had gone by, he decided to take some action himself.

> I then told Lt. Molton that I would have the scaling ladder launched and go in person among the rabble of colors, then in sight of the fort, and if he saw any confusion among them when I reached them, not to pay any attention to my being there, but to give them two or three eighteen pounders, which were all loaded with grape and langrage. I gave myself one hour to go and come in, and took my sword in my hand as a walking stick, and set out.

Captain Trevett had gone only a few steps before he ran into the tax collector, in whose company he proceeded to the cordage-agent's house, where arrangements were made for the sails and rigging to be sent down to the wharves. He returned to the fort without interference and was able to report in his journal that "these 24 hours ended peaceably."

Early in the morning of 30 January Captain Rathbun came on shore to consult with Trevett about procuring pilots to take the prizes over the bar. They would, he said, be ready to sail early the following day after the ammunition and ordnance from the fort had been loaded aboard the *Providence*. When his captain had left to return to his sloop, Trevett walked over to have dinner at Mr. Gould's house. His meal was shortly interrupted by one of his men running to bring the news that Captain Chambers was landing men and guns from the *Gayton*. With reinforcements from the town and cannon brought up on a hill near the Governor's house, he planned to attack the fort that night.

Trevett hurried back to the fort, taking the opportunity as he went to announce loudly that any attackers would have a hard time of it if they made the attempt as they would be met with four times their force. In case this information failed to prove a deterrent, when Trevett had gone back over the wall again, in accordance with his captain's instructions, he sent a messenger out with "a polite billet-doux" for the Governor. There were too many hostile-looking men on the hills, he said, and if they did not disperse in short order, Trevett would cannonade the town, neither giving nor expecting any quarter. To emphasize this point, he sent an agile young Rhode Islander shinnying up the flagstaff with a hammer to nail the Stars and Stripes in place, so that they could not be lowered. This gesture of determination to fight to the last man was made "all in sight and in hearing of the Governor," and in a very short time there was scarcely a man to be seen on the hills. "All had peaceably dispersed at sunset," wrote Trevett, "and during the evening the whole town was as still as the grave."

That grave-like quiet was, unbeknownst to either Rathbun or Trevett, threatened by a British plan to launch a joint land-sea attack against the Americans. Although the natives had been removed from the hills, they were to return that night to march on the fort, while Captain Chambers was to bring the *Gayton* down to engage the *Providence*. Only a piece of luck, in the form of a clumsy native pilot, prevented the attack. As the *Gayton* started to make her approach at 11:00 p.m., she ran aground and, with sea support gone, the plan was abandoned.[3]

Even without an attack, there was little sleep for the Americans again that night, for all hands were busy carrying the military stores from the fort down to the wharves and loading them aboard the *Providence*. This accomplished, in the morning the chief task remaining was the dismantling of the fort which, however, could not be carried out until native pilots had been obtained for the three prize vessels. The day before, Captain Rathbun and Lieutenant Trevett had worked out an elaborate scheme for selecting and, in effect, kidnaping the most skilled men; it was now up to Trevett to put the plan into action. First he was to assemble a crowd, large and friendly enough to attract the natives; a cooperative Whig would point out three good candidates to Trevett, who would then give a signal, a vigorous head-scratching, to the *Providence*'s barge, concealed behind a sloop, to come inshore and gather in the victims.

The first part of the program was the most difficult—it took some ingenuity for an occupying force to gather together a friendly crowd of hostile natives. To achieve it, Trevett made use of several casks of rice that he had found in the fort. Soon after sunrise he marched with his drummer to the marketplace in Nassau where, introduced by military drumbeats, he announced that at eight o'clock a rice sale would be held at the fort. The price would be cheap, and any rice not sold would be thrown into the sea.

Not long after Trevett's return to the fort, "large numbers of men and boys collected around the fort, and I had three casks headed up, one head of each knocked in. I then addressed the children and told them to run home and fetch some bags and baskets, and I would give them what rice they wanted. I told them to tell their mothers it was banyan day, and they must have rice pudding and butter. I kept laughing and talking with them as familiarly as though we had been well acquainted, and they filled their bags &c., and very soon carried home the three casks of rice."

All the time that Trevett was bantering with the children, his friend was quietly pointing out the best pilots in the crowd.

> I soon got the marks and numbers of them. I went up to one of them who was moving off, I said what price will it be best to fix? I intend it shall go soon and very cheap. I lifted my hat and began to scratch my head as though I had some enemies there. I looked on one side and saw the barge coming ashore, and as soon as she struck the shore, I picked out my three Pilots and informed them for what purpose I wanted them, and pledged my word and honor, that as soon as they carried the vessels over the Bar, I would have them landed. One and all declared they were not Pilots.

Unimpressed by this unanimous denial, Trevett "opened a book of hard names upon them," and ordered them at once into the barge. They finally went aboard and were rowed out to the prizes, which they piloted safely over the reef.

Once his mission had been accomplished, Trevett quickly finished up his sale and turned his attention to dismantling the fort. The big guns were spiked, rammers and sponges broken, and all other ordnance destroyed, while across the bar the three prizes waited and below in the harbor sloop *Providence* lay with "anchor short apeak" and sails up until the shore party could get aboard. By ten o'clock the job was done, and presumably with few regrets at leaving what had been home for the past three days, the men marched out of the fort and down to the waiting barge.

Just before Trevett stepped aboard, he was accosted by a gentleman with a message from Captain Chambers of the *Gayton*, a "very polite invitation to come up and drink a bowl of punch with him" at Mrs. Bunch's nearby tavern, "swearing at the same time that no one should hurt me, and proffering a great deal of friendship. Not old enough for a yankee yet! I sent back to Capt. Chambers, by the politeness of the gentlemen-like man, an invitation to come over the bar and take the sloop *Providence*, and then I would take some punch with him."

It was a warm welcome that awaited Trevett aboard the sloop, along with congratulations from Captain Rathbun for a job well done. Certainly the crew of the *Providence*, watching the Stars and Stripes, firmly nailed, still fluttering over Fort Nassau, could take credit for a considerable accomplishment. Not only was their prime target, the *Mary*, safely in hand, together with two other prizes, one of which had been turned over to the Carolina captains, but two schooners had, for lack of men to man them, been burned in the harbor. Some thirty American prisoners on the island had been released and both forts put out of commission for some time to come. The hold of the *Providence* was crammed with military stores, including a generous supply of gunpowder, while the cargoes of the two prize vessels promised a rich reward in prize money. All of this had been accomplished in just three days, without bloodshed, and, except for some powder that Trevett had commandeered from a local agent, without the taking of any property of private citizens. Quite a feat for one small sloop with half a hundred men, who had conquered an island to capture a ship!

CHAPTER XI

Captain Rathbun's Last Cruises in the Lucky Sloop

JANUARY 1778–FEBRUARY 1779

THERE WAS A party mood aboard the *Providence* that afternoon of 31 January 1778, as Captain Rathbun ordered an extra ration of rum for all hands to celebrate the astonishing success of the Nassau raid. Marine Captain Trevett had distinguished himself by his conduct of the operation ashore, and Rathbun decided to reward him with command of the prize ship *Mary* for the voyage home. Accordingly he signaled Lieutenant House, who had taken the *Mary* out of Nassau Harbor, to bear down on the *Providence* and come aboard. Captain Trevett, who from his berth had overheard Rathbun and his first lieutenant discussing the matter in the great stern cabin, got up to protest the decision. Lieutenant House, however, "sided with Capt. Rathbone and Lieut. Vezea," wrote Trevett, "so I finally went on board the ship, and had with me one half of our sloop's crew, amounting to 30 men."

The prize sloop *Tryal* had been turned over to the captains from Carolina on 29 January, when John Peck Rathbun and the *Providence* crew gave up all rights and shares in the prize, in exchange for the captains' services. On 7 February, the *Tryal* arrived safely in New Bern, North Carolina, where an account of the New Providence raid appeared in the *North Carolina Gazette* of Friday, 13 February:

> About 11 o'clock at night, on the 27th of January, the Continental sloop of war Providence, mounting twelve 4 pounders, carrying 50 men, commanded by John Peck Raithburne, landed 25 of her crew under the command of his captain of marines on the island of New Providence. They were joined by 18 or 20 Americans who had been prisoners on board different ships of war, and made their escape from Jamaica and were there waiting for opportunities to return to their respective homes.
>
> They took possession of fort Nassau with the cannons, ammunition and 300 stand of small arms. A ship mounting 16 guns, 45 men, Johnson commander, with rum, sugar and coffee, from Jamaica to New York, lay there in the road, as also five vessels captured by the privateer sloop Gayton, Capt. Chalmers, of Jamaica, and sent in there for condemnation.
>
> At day break 4 men were sent on board the 16 gun ship to take possession and send the officers and crew into the fort, the commanding officer being shewn the 13 stripes hoisted in the fort, and informed that it was then in the hands of the Americans, who would sink the ship if the order was not instantly complied with, thought proper to submit, they were carried to the fort and put in irons. Other parties were sent to take possession of the five prizes, which they soon effected, and secured their prize-masters in the same manner.

This being done, a party marched to the Governor's and demanded the keys of the eastern fort, which after being informed what had happened (it being then only sunrise) he delivered. They took possession of this fort also, removed some powder and small arms, spiked up the cannon, and returned to fort Nassau.

All this was effected by ten o'clock, by which time the inhabitants were in the utmost surprise and confusion, and were removing their effects out of town, but were informed by the Americans that they did not intend to molest the person or property of any inhabitant of the island unless reduced to the necessity in their own defence.

About 12 o'clock a motley crew of negroes, molattoes, and whites, the number of 150 or 200, appeared armed, and threatened to attack the fort, but on being told if they presumed to fire a gun, the town would be laid in ashes; and seeing preparations made for that purpose, they dispersed.

The Providence now came into the road, and anchored near the ship, and very soon after the Gayton also appeared. Continental colours were immediately struck, and the guns on board the Providence housed in hopes the Gayton would come to an anchor, but signals being given by a number of persons from the beach and hills adjacent, she tacked and stood off, on which the fort began to play on her with 18 pounders, from which she received considerable damage, but under cover of night made her escape.

No attack was made this night on the fort, but next day at 3 o'clock, two bodies of men, consisting of about 500 with several pieces of cannon marched within sight of the fort, and summoned it to surrender or that they should storm it and give no quarter, The garrison nailed their colours to the flag staff, in the presence of the messengers, cut away the halliards, and returned for answer, that they would not surrender while a man remained.

Until twelve at night the garrison expected to be attacked, but their enemy being more disposed to sleep than fight, retired to rest.

Next morning early the prizes were manned, the guns of the fort spiked, the ammunition and small arms carried on board the privateer, and the whole garrison with their prisoners embarked, and put to sea. Two of the prizes being of little value were set on fire, the rest stood for New England, except a sloop called the Tryall, which on the 7th instant safely arrived here with Captains Cockran, Morr, Annibal, Mr. Stanley, and some others belonging to this place.

A second prize of the *Providence*, sloop *Washington*, fared less well than the *Tryal*. Second Lieutenant Daniel Bears, sent aboard as prize master, soon found his vessel so unseaworthy as to be incapable of beating to the northward. Even after most of the cargo was jettisoned, the sloop nearly foundered, and Bears was forced to put into the West Indies. There he sold the sloop to buy passage to Charleston for himself and his crew. On the voyage to the mainland their vessel was chased and captured by a British frigate, and the unlucky Bears and his men spent the next couple of years in an English prison.[1]

No such fate awaited the *Providence* or the *Mary*, though they faced a perilous voyage into northern waters, well provisioned, but dangerously short of men. They had not long to wait for trouble. Soon after Trevett and his men boarded the *Mary*, a ship was sighted, bearing down fast. Captain Rathbun signaled Trevett to alter course and run, while he enticed the enemy into chasing the *Providence*. When the *Mary* was safely out of sight, Rathbun made his own escape with one of those quick maneuvers that had saved the sloop before, and set his course northward once again.

There was no sign of the *Mary*, nor would there be for three long, bitter weeks. Instead of sailing in company as planned, the two vessels had to make their separate ways back to New England waters, while the gay mood of the island raid was soon chilled by the hardships of the voyage. Trevett's journal describes the ordeal of the *Mary*; Captain Rathbun and the *Providence* can have fared no better.

> The first land we made was the Vineyard, and then we run down for Nantucket. This was on the 18th day after we parted with the sloop *Providence*, and we had experienced exceeding cold weather, and hard and heavy gales; out of 30 men there was only ten but what had got their feet or hands badly frozen, and one of our men . . . was frozen to death . . . The same day we anchored under Nantucket, the wind still blowing very hard, so much so that we could not land, and we fired signal guns of distress.

When the wind finally died down enough for boats to be put out from shore, Trevett replenished his supplies with five Nantucket sheep. Scarcely were they loaded aboard when a sail was sighted, running down the south side of the island and standing for the *Mary*. Supposing this to be a British privateer out of New York, Trevett got the *Mary* under way.

> We stood for the stranger, and she for us, but before we got up to her we discovered her to be our sloop *Providence*, that we parted with off Abaco. As they passed us we were so rejoiced to see them, that we had not time to draw our shot, so we gave them a salute, shot and all, and they returned it in the same way. We hove about and followed the sloop in under Nantucket, and came to anchor, as the wind would not admit of our going over the shoals.

The joyful reunion of the two vessels did not spell the end of their troubles. Trevett reported,

> On the 20th of February, 1778 we got under way, with a light air of wind from the N.E., which soon increased to a gale, accompanied by a violent snow storm. We were running for Cape Poge, when about twelve o'clock the ship struck very hard on a shoal near the Horse-shoe, and we lost our rudder, stove our boats on deck, and experienced a very hard time. We kept all sail on her until we beat over the shoal and deepened water, and then we let go our anchor.

Captain Rathbun met with similar difficulty taking the *Providence* into Old Town (Edgartown) Harbor in the blizzard. She ran aground on the way in, but Rathbun got her off again almost at once with no great damage. The next morning the *Mary*, assisted by boats, was brought into Old Town, and the work of unloading her valuable cargo was begun. A small part of it was to be sent to Hyannis and Boston, but the bulk of the supplies from Jamaica were destined for New Bedford. This, as time would prove, was an unlucky choice.

Leaving the *Mary* at Old Town for repair, Captain Rathbun took her crew back aboard the *Providence*, which put into New Bedford for overhaul. After a few days at home, Captain Rathbun traveled to Boston with Trevett to settle with the Eastern Navy Board the status of the *Mary* as a prize. According to the latest ruling of Congress, proceeds from the sale of a ship of war went entirely to her captors, while in the case of a merchant vessel they were divided fifty-fifty with the Congress. Since Captain Johnson of the *Mary* held a Royal Navy commission, Rathbun and Trevett supposed that she qualified as a warship. Her cargo, therefore, need not be sent to a Continental agent for condemnation and sale. In recognition of his key role in the Nassau raid, on 27 February, Captain Trevett was appointed by Captain Rathbun and 48 crewmen as prize agent for all prizes taken on "the late New Providence cruise," including, of course, the *Mary*.[2] In the distribution of prize money, Trevett would be entitled to the usual 10 percent agent's commission.

Unfortunately for this plan, however, at the trial of the *Mary*'s status, held at Plymouth, Massachusetts, she was ruled a merchant vessel rather than a warship, and her cargo ordered handed over to the Continental agent, Leonard Jarvis. Captain Trevett's refusal to comply with this order pending an appeal to the Congress prompted some sharp comment from Jarvis, who wrote the Eastern Navy Board on 10 March,

It would have given me real pleasure to have found Mr. Agent Trivett and the Officers of the Sloop willing to send the Goods out of the Mary to Boston, but they have so long look'd upon them as their own that they cannot bring themselves to think of the delivering any part to the Continental Agent . . . .

I have not been wanting in my Endeavours to get the Goods lodgd with me to be sent to Boston, but without Effect. all that I can obtain, is, leave to take an Account of them.

The Goods Mr Casey [Vesey] tells me are all here, except a few Casks left at Marthas Vinyard to pay those who assisted in unlading &c. The Ship is strip'd and left at Woods Hole. If the Resolution of Congress should be constru'd in favour of the Captors, I shall be glad to hear that this Sloop is to be put out of Commission, being thoroughly persuaded that the Advantage arising to the States from her Distressing the Enemy is by no means adequate to the Expence . . . .[3]

Two days later Jarvis wrote again, adding to his complaints a threat to call on the militia to seize the *Mary*'s cargo by force. At the same time he was charged with the responsibility of paying off the *Providence*'s crew and getting her ready for another cruise—tasks which evoked noticeably less zeal on Jarvis' part than his cargo endeavors. Forwarding the sloop's muster roll with a request for money "if the Roll is to be paid off," he reported that, according to Lieutenant House, the *Providence*'s stern and quarters had to be rebuilt. "I shall engage Carpenters for the Purpose," he grudgingly told the Navy Board, "but I do assure you Gentlemen that nothing but a Desire of serving the Publick would induce me to have anything to do with the Sloop unless there should be a great Alteration in the Deportment of both Officers in General and the Men. There is no subordination on board, which is a little surprising considering the Number of Officers they have on board."[4]

Agent Jarvis' marked lack of enthusiasm for the *Providence* was fortunately not shared by the Navy Board, which called her "that lucky sloop" or by the Congress, which congratulated Captain Rathbun on his success. The Marine Committee, however, upheld the ruling of the prize court on the *Mary*, holding that "by the Resolves of Congress the Captors are only entitled to 1/2 of said vessel and Cargo."[5]

However bitter a pill this ruling was for Rathbun and his men to swallow, they accepted it with good grace. Not so Captain Trevett. Determined to put his case before the Marine Committee in person, he set off for Yorktown, where the Congress was sitting after fleeing from Philadelphia.

Trevett's action and his refusal to release either ship or cargo dismayed his captain. Rathbun assured Continental Agent John Bradford that Captain Trevett had "gone forward" against his advice and that because of Trevett's refusal to distribute their shares to the captors, fifteen of Rathbun's best men had left him. "Rathbun complains of him bitterly," wrote Bradford to Jarvis, "and says . . . he is content with the decree of the court and would have dissuaded him from going . . . ."[6] Captain Rathbun also expressed fears that great loss might occur from Trevett's management of the cargo—fears that in time would prove to be all too prophetic.

While Captain Trevett pursued his unauthorized journey southward (See Appendix E), the *Providence* lay at Bedford undergoing extensive repairs. Despite her agent's antipathy, the carpenters made good progress rebuilding the stern and quarters damaged by the *Mary,* and with the coming of spring, the work of provisioning and manning could be begun. Captain Rathbun divided his time between visits with his wife in South Kingstown and naval business in Boston and Bedford, occasionally acting as courier delivering Navy Board funds or messages. By the time he rejoined the sloop, he was anxious to take her to sea again and, with a crew that included many newcomers, to sail eastward for new adventure.

Unbeknownst to her captain, however, the Congress had made other plans for sloop *Providence.* She was one of six vessels "pitched upon" to carry secret despatches to France and, before official word had been sent to the Navy Board, it was advised by William Ellery to "forthwith send off an express to Bedford to Capt. Rathburn . . . if he shou'd not have sail'd, directing him not to proceed to Sea untill he shall have recd Orders from the Comee of foreign affairs wch will soon be transmitted to him, and he is most implicitly to obey . . . ."

"P.S. dont let the occation of the sloop Providence being detained be known to any one, no not even to the Capt. of her himself . . . ."[7]

With such instructions, Captain Rathbun had little difficulty in guessing the nature of his mission, but his impatience became increasingly harder to curb as week after week dragged on with no further orders. On 19 June 1778, the Marine Committee informed the Eastern Navy Board that Sloop *Providence* was to carry to France messages that the Committee for Foreign Affairs would "send up" in a few days. However, those few days passed without despatches; the *Providence*'s voyage to Europe was scrapped for some unknown reason, and after weeks of futile idleness in port, Rathbun finally received his sailing orders for a cruise to the eastward.

Heading for her familiar cruising grounds, on 7 August the *Providence* sighted a huge fleet of 30 heavily armed transports carrying British troops to Halifax, convoyed by the frigate *Aurora*. Another Captain would have quietly turned away, but not Rathbun. Undaunted by the formidable odds, Captain Rathbun ordered the drummer to beat to quarters and, the sloop cleared for action, at sunset attacked one of the transports.

A bitter action followed, during which the transport, which had 200 Highland troops aboard, gave a good account of herself. Although no casualty figures are available, at least one crewman aboard the *Providence* was wounded. Seamen Presbury Luce received a neck injury severe enough to incapacitate him for further service.[8] At midnight, her mast badly damaged, the *Providence* finally bore off under threat of approaching enemy reinforcements. It was one of the strongest convoys yet sent out from England, carrying some 5,000 troops, with each transport armed with from 10 to 14 guns.

With her mast temporarily fished, the *Providence* cruised for another three weeks until Captain Rathbun took her into Port Rosswell, 25 leagues west of Halifax, for more lasting repairs. There he heard that 5,000 British troops had landed at Halifax—a piece of intelligence that would be of vital interest to American forces.[9]

So it proved to be when, early on 12 September 1778, the *Providence* dropped her anchor in Boston Harbor. Captain Rathbun, imparting the bad news, learned some of his own. The disposition of the *Mary* had been settled by a quite different authority than the Congress—and one from which there was no appeal. A British firing party had burned the waterfront at Bedford, where her cargo was stored, and the ship herself at nearby Woods Hole.

The burning of Bedford and the *Mary* was a consequence of the failure of a second attempt to oust the British from Newport. When General Spencer's "Secret Expedition" of 1777 had come to

John Peck Rathbun's Deposition regarding the wounding of Seaman Presbury Luce, 7 August 1778. Courtesy, Massachusetts Archives.

nothing, a second assault was planned in 1778. General Sullivan was put in charge of local troops, assisted by two of Washington's ablest generals—the Marquis de Lafayette and Nathanael Greene. Naval support was to be provided by a huge French fleet under the Comte d'Estaing.

This time the success of the American operation seemed assured, and the position of the British garrison on Rhode Island looked nothing short of hopeless. Faced not only with superior land forces but, when d'Estaing's fleet sailed into Narragansett Bay on 28 July 1778, with overwhelming sea power, the British burned some small vessels to prevent their being taken, and on 5 August scuttled four frigates to forestall their capture. Among these were HMS *Cerberus,* old enemy of the Continental fleet, from whose jaws sloop *Providence* had snatched the *Hampden* two years earlier, as well as the *Juno* and *Orpheus,* two of the frigates that had recaptured the *Providence's* prize brig *Lucy,* taking her prize crew to Halifax prison.*

The only British deterrent to the speedy reconquest of Rhode Island by the Americans and their French allies appeared to be a hastily put-together squadron of Royal Navy vessels under the command of Admiral Lord Richard Howe. Howe's ships sailed up from New York to anchor off Point Judith on 9 August, the same day that General Sullivan landed his troops at the northern end of Rhode Island. D'Estaing decided it would be safer to confront the enemy at sea and, deaf to the urging of his American allies that he stay where he was, ordered his ships to sail out of the bay, cutting their cables in their haste.

During the next two days, both fleets maneuvered for advantage, the superiority of the French becoming ever more apparent. Then along toward evening of 11 August heavy rain squalls gave way to a screaming gale—the first hurricane of the season. It pounded both French and British vessels without letup until the morning of the fourteenth when d'Estaing's 90-gun flagship *Languedoc,* dismasted and rudderless, was attacked and damaged still further by enemy fire. His own ships came to his rescue, and both fleets, badly battered, limped off—the British for New York and the French into Narragansett Bay, where it anchored on 19 August.

---

*The Oceanographic Department of the University of Rhode Island has located these frigates, from which a diving program has already recovered a wealth of artifacts with many more to come.

Nine-pounder cannon from HMS Cerberus on replica mount. Courtesy, Underwater Bicentennial Expedition, University of Rhode Island.

Once again the British garrison at Newport seemed doomed. General Sullivan's land forces, despite the ravages of the same wild storm that had hit the ships at sea, had marched southward to lines just north of Newport, where they were prepared to attack with support from French marines and heavy cannon of the fleet. Once again, however, d'Estaing's decision saved the British garrison. He decided that prudence demanded that he repair at once to Boston with his fleet for refitting. The Marquis de Lafayette and General Nathanael Greene were rowed out to the flagship to plead for just two days of the promised support, which would surely be enough time to secure the surrender of the trapped British garrison. The French admiral listened politely, and at midnight on 21 August 1778, pulled up his anchor and sailed away.

The Americans were stunned, officers and men alike. General Sullivan determined to hold his lines, hoping for the return of the French, and did so until he learned that reinforcements were indeed on the way—but they were British, not French, coming up from New York. There was no alternative to retreat, and on 28 August under cover of darkness, the Americans began moving out their heavy equipment. The next morning the British set out to cut off the retreat and in several bloody encounters very nearly succeeded. Gallant American action saved the orderly withdrawal, however, and by the thirty-first General Sullivan's troops were once again back on the mainland. Not a moment too soon—on the first of September Lord Howe sailed with a big fleet into Narragansett Bay and landed some 4,000 troops on Rhode Island. The British occupation would continue uncontested after the abortive Battle of Rhode Island until the autumn of 1779, when ships and men were withdrawn to reinforce beleaguered troops to the southward.

Some of Lord Howe's ships, finding no French to fight, amused themselves with forays on Yankee shipping. On 5 September 1778, a flotilla sailed into the harbor at Bedford, Massachusetts, its object the destruction of the waterfront. As British troops systematically set fire to warehouses and shipping, up in flames went 80-odd vessels in the harbor and 26 storehouses filled with rum, sugar, molasses, coffee, and cotton.[10] With them went the precious cargo of the ship *Mary*—a good share of the *Providence's* prize money gone up in smoke. The *Mary* herself, having completed her repairs at Old Town, had got as far as Wood's Hole on her way to Bedford. There the British expedition touched the next day, on its way to a four-day occupation of Martha's Vineyard, long enough to do a little more burning—and up in smoke went the *Mary* as well.

Marine Captain Trevett learned this news upon his return from the Congress. Discouraged by the futility of his long journey southward as well as by the loss of both his prize money and the approval of his captain, he elected to leave the sloop *Providence*. Unfortunately the Marine lieutenant who took his place was no diarist, and with Trevett's departure came the end of the vivid eyewitness accounts of the sloop's activities.

In September, Captain Rathbun left the *Providence* in Boston taking on supplies, while he returned to his home in Rhode Island. His time ashore was extended by the difficulties the Navy Board was experiencing in supplying its ships. Inflation of the Congress' paper currency had caused prices to soar, and several vital provisions were in acutely short supply, among them flour, rice, butter, cheese, and, worst of all, rum.

Collecting these provisions and getting them loaded aboard took two months, and it was not until mid-November that the sloop was ready to put to sea again. She left port in company with the *Gen-*

eral Gates, an 18-gun brig recently acquired by the Continental Navy. The two vessels cruised to the eastward where, off Canso on 4 December, they took a Quebec schooner loaded with much-needed flour. The next day the *Providence* was battered by a howling winter gale. When it was over, there was no sign of the *General Gates,* and Captain Rathbun continued his cruise alone.

Christmas Day was celebrated by the sighting of a brigantine. When brought to after a brisk chase, she was found to be the *Chance,* carrying a cargo of rum and sugar, which ensured appropriate festivity aboard the *Providence.*

The luck of the sloop and her captain continued to hold. In the next two weeks they took three more good prizes, another brig with a cargo of rum, a ship laden with dry goods and provisions, and an Irish brigantine called the *Providence Increase,* full of coats. One of the prizes, ship *Nancy,* had had a rather hectic time. Captured first by an American privateer off Barbados, she had been retaken by a British ship before falling into Rathbun's hands.[11]

Manning her prizes left the *Providence* shorthanded, and the winter weather had battered her hull and rigging. In the middle of January 1779, she ran into New Bedford, whose waterfront had been somewhat restored, for needed repair. Captain Rathbun received congratulations from the Navy Board and instructions to get the necessary repairs completed with despatch "so that no time may be lost in following her good luck."[12]

Captain Rathbun had, however, come ashore ill and, wishing to spend some time with his family, he asked to be detached from the *Providence.* The Navy Board granted his request, characterizing him as a "very Active Spirited Officer" who had "sailed a long time in a small Sloop & by his Spirit and Success had made a great deal of money to the Continent."

It had indeed been a long time since 10 February 1776 when Lieutenant John Peck Rathbun had first mounted the quarterdeck of the *Providence* to take over his duties as second lieutenant. Acting as first lieutenant under John Paul Jones in both the *Providence* and the *Alfred* at the end of the year, he had commanded her himself since June of 1777.

The luck of the sloop and the valour of her captain had made their association a singularly happy one, and had brought glory to them both. Now three years after first coming aboard, Captain Rathbun said his farewells to a saddened crew and left the *Providence's* quarterdeck for the last time.

CHAPTER XII

Return of Captain Hacker and Action with the Diligent

FEBRUARY–JULY 1779

WHEN JOHN PECK RATHBUN left sloop *Providence* in February 1779, her command was given for the second time to Hoysteed Hacker. His naval career had begun rather inauspiciously when, in the *Fly*, he dismasted the *Hornet* in February 1776, and in October ran the *Hampden* onto a ledge. Transferred with his entire crew to sloop *Providence*, he had sailed eastward with Captain John Paul Jones on what was a highly successful cruise until a northeast snowstorm and the leaky condition of his sloop prompted Hacker to unceremoniously head for home, where he soon found himself caught behind the British blockade of Narragansett Bay. Commodore Hopkins ordered him to take Captain Whipple's berth on the *Columbus*, in which Hacker attempted to run the blockade in March 1778. John B. Hopkins had finally managed to get the *Warren* out a few weeks earlier, and Captain Whipple was about to make his successful bid for freedom in the ship *Providence*, but Hoysteed Hacker was not so lucky. The *Columbus* had been lightened and stripped of her heavy cannon in case of capture, and on a rough and windy night, Hacker took her down the river. There she was sighted by a patrol boat on the watch for a merchant brig; the signal guns brought out two British frigates. Cut off before he could round Point Judith, Hacker ran the ship hard aground. He kept the British at bay all night, and the next day, with reinforcements from Providence, completely emptied the *Columbus*, which was later burned by a British shore party.[1]

Now, nearly a year after the loss of the *Columbus*, Hoysteed Hacker had a command again. He joined sloop *Providence* at Bedford early in 1779 to find her still repairing. Her last stormy winter cruise under Captain Rathbun had damaged her false keel and ripped all the copper sheathing from her bottom, besides subjecting the sloop to the strain of crowding on sail when chasing prizes. Captain Hacker, like Rathbun before him, signed on what men he could at Bedford, but he had orders from the Eastern Navy Board to bring the *Providence* around to Boston for provisioning and final manning.

On 13 March the Navy Board expected the sloop "round from Bedford in a few days . . . don't think she will wait any time for men . . . . " Spring gales and high winds kept her in port for several more days, but late in March she sailed around Cape Cod to anchor in Boston Harbor.

There, true to the Board's prediction, her muster roll filled up rapidly. Her first lieutenant was Philip Brown, who had left that post in November 1776 to serve as prize master of the *Mellish*, which he had brought safely into Bedford. Second Lieutenant Nicholas Gardner had been aboard since the Nassau cruise under Captain Rathbun, whose late purser, James Rogers, had been promoted to sailing master. He had served on the *Providence* or her prizes longer than any other man aboard, having been Captain Jones' steward on the first Nova Scotia cruise. Surgeon James Cook was a carry-over from Rathbun's last cruise in the sloop, but nearly all the rest of the crew were newly signed on. Her total complement included 21 commissioned and petty officers, 7 seamen, and 16 marines.[2]

Sloop *Providence*'s luck might help the manning problem, but it couldn't do much about provisions. The Navy Board suffered from the same old shortages—"flour and rum are practically impossible to come by, and rice, butter, and cheese are not to be procured at any price." They despaired of getting bread. On 3 April they told the Marine Committee that the sloop was ready to sail except for bread, which they had decided to send her to Philadelphia to get.

This plan was modified by a request from the Massachusetts Council that some navy vessels be sent to scour Massachusetts Bay for some enemy ships reported there. With sloop *Providence* in Boston Harbor lay two frigates—the *Boston*, back from carrying John Adams to France in 1778, and Abraham Whipple's *Providence*. Shortly after the *Columbus'* abortive attempt to run the blockade, Captain Whipple, with Jonathan Pitcher (now recovered from his wounds) as first lieutenant, had managed to get the *Providence* out and, although severely damaged, to France. There he received John Paul Jones' congratulations on his escape, and early in 1779 returned to Boston.

On 13 April, both *Providences* and the *Boston* sailed for a ten-day search of Massachusetts Bay. When no enemy vessels were discovered, Captain Whipple returned to Boston, while frigate *Boston* and sloop *Providence* headed for the Delaware to look for bread.

The *Providence* never got there. On 7 May off Sandy Hook, New Jersey, not far from the spot where the *Providence* had fought her gallant action with the ill-fated *Mary*, she encountered HMS *Diligent*, the 12-gun brig that had given the Continental fleet trouble in Block Island Sound back in the spring of 1776. Captain Hacker ordered the sloop cleared for action, and as the drum beat to quarters, the men ran to their guns. The peace of the May morning was shattered as the two vessels hurled broadside after broadside at each other, the thunder of their cannon punctuated by musket shot at close range. Flying splinters flew across the *Prov-*

idence's deck as British balls plowed into her timbers, and more than one man fell bleeding at his post. It was the bloodiest action of the *Providence*'s whole career.

Thomas Hiller, a seaman aboard the *Providence*, gave this account of the engagement:

> Off Sandy Hook we fell in with his Britannic Majesty's brig *Diligence*, mounting fourteen guns, commanded by John Wallcroft [Walbeoff] and manned with 95 men. This vessel, as I heard her captain tell our captain, was sent out from New York with a picked gang, for the express purpose of taking the Sloop *Providence*. We engaged her about ten o'clock in the forenoon; and after a close fight of two hours and a half, during which we were not pistol shot off, indeed so near that the blaze of her guns several times set fire to our light sails with nettings; we conquered her at half past twelve o'clock. At the time she surrendered she had but six men on deck, and two of them were wounded. This I learned from her captain's conversation with our captain, after the fight.[3]

Hiller recalls six men killed aboard the *Providence* and thirteen wounded. Among the dead were the sloop's lieutenant of marines and Sailing Master James Rogers, whose steady rise in rank throughout his naval career thus came to an abrupt end.

Captain Hacker sent Lieutenant Philip Brown aboard the battered *Diligent* as prize master, and both vessels headed back for Bedford, pausing on the way only long enough to gather in another prize. It was a triumphant if damaged *Providence* that limped into Dartmouth Harbor in company with the *Diligent*, one of the few Royal Navy vessels captured by the Americans during the whole course of the war.

Two accounts of this action have survived in New Bedford history, both based on contemporary recollections. One quotes an old-timer aboard the *Providence* as saying, thumping his cane in his enthusiasm, "Why, It took three men to handle each gun when we went into action, but before the fight was finished one man did the same service."[4]. The other, handed down from "some of our folks of Revolutionary times," gives the nearly forgotten particulars of "a story about the old sloop *Providence*:"[5]

> The Providence was an armed sloop, commissioned as a privateer early in the Revolutionary contest. She was very successful in her cruising, and such was the extent of her depredations on British commerce it was determined by the enemy that a stop should be put to her career. Accordingly a brig of war of nearly double the force of the *Providence* was ordered to cruise for her. The two vessels met and

after an obstinate and bloody contest the Yankee sloop forced her powerful antagonist to strike and brought her into the port of Bedford. It was said that after the sloop had fired away all her shot her crew used some old iron spikes and bolts that were on board that belonged to a citizen of this town as substitutes, and that shocking havoc was made by them among the crew of the British brig. I can remember but two other particulars. So near to this port was the action fought that the blood of the killed and wounded seamen was running down the sides of the brig when she came into port. The wounded of the crews who died were brought on shore and interred on a small hillock that arose near the shore . . . . [6]

A rather pathetic, if distorted, British account of the action speaks of the "unequal contest," explaining that

. . . the *Diligent* cleared for action only on her larboard side and was attacked by her enemy on her starboard side; her timbers were so thin that musket shot came through; she lay very low in the water, and the seas washed on to her deck. When they realized the heavy odds against them, thirteen or fourteen of her crew skulked and went below. Nonetheless the heroic Walbeoff held out for three hours, when, with every officer but himself disabled, and with eleven dead and nineteen wounded, he struck. The *Providence*'s sides were proof to grape, yet she lost fourteen, of whom eleven were killed or died of their wounds. [7]

The pitiful frailty of the British brig was apparently not noticeable to the Americans. At her auction, bidding was so brisk that when she was finally knocked down to the Eastern Navy Board, it was at a price in excess of $26,000. Considering that John Brown's *Katy* had been valued at $1,250 back in 1775, it would seem that the brig must have been in pretty good condition, even allowing for the wild inflation of paper money.

Command of the *Diligent* was offered to Captain Hacker, but when he elected to stick with the *Providence* instead, it was given to Lieutenant Philip Brown, the oldest lieutenant in the fleet except Jonathan Pitcher, now first lieutenant of the ship *Providence* under Captain Whipple.

On 13 May the Eastern Navy Board sent congratulations to Hoysteed Hacker along with new orders. Intelligence had been received that seven British sail were lying in Tarpaulin Cove on Naushon Island, just off Martha's Vineyard. It was here in this cove that in November of 1776 John Paul Jones had sent boats under Lieutenants John P. Rathbun and Philip Brown to corral deserters and seamen from the privateer *Eagle*. This time a joint land-sea operation was hastily planned to take the enemy vessels. *Providence* and *Diligent* headed into Vineyard Sound where they were joined by two Massachusetts Navy brigs—the *Tyrannicide*, carrying 20 six-pounders and commanded by Captain Cathcart, and Captain Williams' 18-gun *Hazard*.[8]

In Hiller's words, "We heard of a number of the enemy's vessels being in the Vineyard Sound and sent over to Howland's Ferry [now Tiverton] for Capt. Barton who was stationed there. He came with his men . . . We pursued the enemy, but not being able to come up with them, they made their escape. We however retook several of their prizes and returned to New Bedford."

Seaman Hiller reports one further prize for the sloop that summer: "I also recollect that while in the *Providence* in June 1779 we took a little sloop coming from N.Y. as a flag that had obtained some prisoners; Capt. Simion Folger of Nantucket was one of the prisoners and was aboard of our vessel one night and part of a day."[9]

In the meantime, back in Boston Harbor, the frigate *Providence* had been joined by two other ships, the Rhode Island frigate *Warren*, commanded by John B. Hopkins, and the *Queen of France*, purchased abroad, under Joseph Olney. In mid-March, 1779, these two ships had sailed with the *Ranger*, which had been taken to France by John Paul Jones in 1777 and was now commanded by Thomas Simpson, on a cruise to the southward, where frequent British captures of Chesapeake Bay flour ships was creating the acute flour shortage in the north. After taking seven valuable merchant prizes and their escort, the 20-gun British ship *Jason*, the little squadron, in direct violation of orders to stay in southern waters, sailed northward again. Hopkins and Olney, coming into Boston, were suspended from their commands for disobedience of orders and irregularities in their handling of prize shares.

The question of who would be given command of the *Warren*, whose 18-pound cannon made her the strongest of all the American frigates, and the *Queen of France*, was weighed by the Marine Committee and the Navy Board. John Peck Rathbun, who had recovered his health but was now without a ship since his release from sloop *Providence*, was considered for command of first the *Jason*, then either the *Warren* or the *Queen*. In the end he received a commission to command the *Queen of France*. The *Warren* went to Dudley Saltonstall, who had gone from the *Alfred* to the Connecticut frigate *Trumbull*, which in two years he had never been able to get out of the Connecticut River. In light of future events, it is intriguing to speculate how the course of Continental Navy history might have been changed had command of the *Warren* been given to John Peck Rathbun instead.

However, it was to the *Queen* that Captain Rathbun was piped aboard with suitable ceremony in the spring of 1779. While his old command sloop *Providence* was still lying at Bedford, on 17 June, Rathbun in the *Queen of France* sailed, together with the *Ranger*, on a cruise under Captain Whipple in the frigate *Providence*. The little squadron headed eastward where, off Newfoundland, it came to anchor in dense fog. When the fog lifted in the morning, the Americans found themselves surrounded by a huge British merchant fleet. The *Queen of France* was practically alongside a big merchantman, and Captain Rathbun, playing the part of a British convoy captain, requested her master to come aboard. As soon as the British captain stepped through the entry port, he found himself a prisoner aboard the *Queen*, and his ship taken over by a prize crew. Captains Whipple and Simpson followed Rathbun's lead, and all day long the Americans quietly cut one vessel after another out of the British fleet. They took ten fat prizes in all, worth over a million dollars, adding to the Continent's stores of such badly needed items as rum, sugar, cotton, and spices, besides enjoying the fruits of what turned out to be the most lucrative cruise of the entire war.

Sloop *Providence* had missed a chance to sail on that Newfoundland cruise by being still at Bedford when the squadron left port— a lost opportunity that marked the end of her good luck. Late in June she came into Boston in company with the *Diligent*, to find the only Navy ship anchored there was the *Warren*, waiting for men. When Captains Hacker and Brown went ashore, they heard news of ominous events to the eastward that would profoundly affect their new orders.

On 16 June 1779, a British garrison under Brigadier General McLean had landed on Bagaduce Peninsula in Penobscot Bay, where Castine, Maine, now looks across to Islesboro. Guarded by three sloops of war, one mounting 16 guns, and the other two, 14, a force of some seven hundred enemy troops had at once begun construction of a fort on a rise commanding the harbor. The wilderness echoed with the ring of axes and the squeal of pulleys as supplies were laboriously hauled up the side of the peninsula. Work went slowly in the difficult terrain—the General called it a country fit only for wild beasts—and the fort was still in its early stages a month after the landing.

Massachusetts had been free of British occupation since 1776, and she viewed this invasion of her coast 175 miles to the eastward as the gravest of threats. From a base in the Penobscot, the British could not only bar the Americans from valuable timber supplies but they could swoop out and prey on colonial shipping. The Massachusetts Council began organizing an expedition to dislodge the British, and it intended to make sure that the force would be sufficient to do the job.

It was to be a joint land-sea operation. A call was issued for fifteen hundred militia under the command of General Solomon Lovell, with Lieutenant Colonel Paul Revere in charge of artillery. The Navy Board granted the Council's request that the three Continental vessels then in Boston Harbor—the 32-gun frigate *Warren,* sloop *Providence,* and brig *Diligent*—be sent along on the expedition. They would be accompanied by three Massachusetts naval brigs, the 20-gun *Tyrannicide* and 18-gun *Hazard,* which had already been cruising in Vineyard Sound with the *Providence* and *Diligent,* and a 16-gun brig, the *Active.* New Hampshire contributed a 20-gun ship, the *Hampden,* a privateer chartered by the state, to round out a total of seven naval vessels. Massachusetts had also chartered twelve privateers, all but one of which were both bigger and more heavily armed than the *Providence,* to make a really impressive force. In addition, a large number of merchant ships were chartered to transport supplies from Boston and troops from eastern counties.

As commodore of the naval part of the operation, the Council appointed Captain Dudley Saltonstall, who had been John Paul Jones' and Jonathan Pitcher's unloved commander aboard the *Alfred,* presently captain of the *Warren.* Under Captain Saltonstall's direction, the job of assembling, manning, and provisioning the array of ships went forward with maddening slowness. At the end of June, the exasperated Navy Board commented that the enemy must be stupid not to reinforce his outpost, "so much time has been taken up in preparing for this expedition that we doubt the success of it."[10]

However slowly, preparations were gradually completed. General Lovell's call for militia produced only about half the number of troops that had been anticipated, and many of the nine hundred that did respond were young boys or infirm old men. In order to waste no more time, he decided to set out with what men he had, leaving orders for more to join the expedition later.

Manning a fleet of this size, as might have been expected, took a considerable amount of time, but men signed aboard the *Providence* in surprising numbers. Missing from the new roster were the men who had been killed in the battle with the *Diligent* or transferred to her under Captain Philip Brown, and only ten of her former crew remained on board. These included Captain Hacker, Second Lieutenant Nicholas Gardner and Surgeon James Cook, besides the master's mate, carpenter, pilot, sailmaker, and three seamen, Thomas Hiller among them. In the ranks of the new crewmen were fifteen marines under Lieutenant Davis and Sergeant Thomas Philbrook, who left a vivid account of the forthcoming operation. Included in the names of twenty seamen were eleven whose "marks" and the obviously phonetic spelling of their names indicates that they probably spoke better French than English.[11]

With a crew of 63 all told safely aboard, the *Providence* was ready to sail earlier than the rest of the fleet. Captain Hacker was ordered to convoy ten transports to Falmouth (now Portland), and then to reconnoitre the coastline to the eastward. In mid-July, accompanied by the Massachusetts brig *Active*, sloop *Providence* shepherded her charges safely out of Boston Harbor and headed down the coast.

As the *Providence*'s little squadron left port, it may have passed some old friends coming in. At about the same time, the ships *Providence, Queen of France* and *Ranger* sailed triumphantly into Boston with the fat prizes taken on the Newfoundland cruise. It was too late for the three ships to join the Penobscot expedition, which, had Captains Whipple and Rathbun been there, would certainly have had a different outcome.

In the meantime, sloop *Providence,* having seen her charges safely into port, sailed again with the *Active* for Townsend (now Boothbay Harbor), where the Grand Fleet was to rendezvous and pick up the land forces. Somewhere along the way, Captain Hacker chased and brought to a sloop laden with rum, ordering a prize crew to take her into Casco Bay. He cannot have dreamed that it would be the *Providence*'s last prize.

CHAPTER XIII

Penobscot—The End of the Line

JULY–OCTOBER 1779

THE FLEET FOR the Penobscot expedition which sloop *Providence* had left manning Boston Harbor in mid-July was held in port by foul winds, but finally weighed anchor on 19 July 1779, reaching Townsend and the waiting *Providence* on the twenty-second. The militia were ferried aboard, and on the twenty-fourth the fleet sailed again. That evening the wind failed, forcing it to anchor off Fox Island (now Vinalhaven). On Sunday the twenty-fifth the ships sailed into Penobscot Bay, following the *Diligent, Tyrannicide,* and *Hazard,* which had been sent ahead to scout out the situation, and in the middle of the afternoon the fleet came to anchor off Bagaduce Peninsula.

The British, who were expecting them, had drawn their three sloops into a line protecting the transports, some of which had been readied as fire ships. In addition to their main fortification, they had set up an outpost farther down the peninsula, and had also sent a contingent ashore on Banks (now Nautilus) Island on the western side of Bagaduce. The battery on Banks covered the position of the British ships.

Late in the afternoon there was an ineffectual exchange of fire with the three English sloops and an abortive attempt at a landing on the peninsula. It was far less accessible than had originally been thought. Two sides were too steep to be scalable, the south face was protected by cannon in the fort and on Banks Island, and the western side, which offered the most likely approach, was itself a precipitous hill. Nonetheless an attempt was made to ferry troops ashore on the west side, but a stiff wind sprang up, forcing a recall of the boats.

All during the day of Monday, 26 July, the Americans probed the British defenses with intermittent, sometimes brisk, exchanges of cannonfire with both the sloops and the land installations. In the afternoon, according to Thomas Philbrook, marine sergeant aboard the *Providence*[1] (see Appendix F), Captain Hacker "thought to have a little diversion" and drive the British ships from their moorings. This he planned to do by setting up a battery on Banks Island, apparently unaware that the British had already had the same idea. Marines from the *Providence* and brigs *Pallas* and *Defence* climbed into boats and were rowed to the south shore of the island. At their approach, the British garrison quietly withdrew northward to the sloops. The American marines, some sixty in number, according to Philbrook, soon gained the summit of the island, which was thickly covered with wood and underbrush, and began building a breastwork. They were "very industrious

Scene of the disaster in Penobscot Bay and the retreat up the Penobscot River, 25 July—14 August 1779.

through the night, making as little noise as possible, that we might not be heard on board the ships." While the marines labored on the hill, three cannon, two 18-pounders and one 12-pounder, were sent ashore and manhandled up to the fortification. By dawn, all was ready. "We trimmed up a tall spruce tree on which we hoisted our flag and saluted our neighbors with the well loaded guns . . . and by the time it took them to get ready to return our morning call, a brisk fire was kept up from us and from the ships; we could frequently see our shot hull them, so that we must have done them considerable damage; they generally over-shot us, but unfortunately, one of their shot struck the top of our breastwork and killed two men and wounded three others." It was during this exchange of fire that the only casualties were inflicted on the British sloops, aboard which there were several killed and wounded. "After about three hours' firing the ships slipped their cables and moved up the river, out of the reach of our shot. We next went to work, cleared a piece of ground, and built us some comfortable huts to lodge in until further orders. Our little settlement we called Hacker's Island."[2]

Once "Hacker's Island" had been secured and the sloops moved out of range, the main body of the occupying marines were taken off. A small contingent remained to man the battery under the protection of the *Providence*.

Already there was trouble brewing in the top command. Commodore Saltonstall, despite overwhelming naval superiority, was dragging his feet. General Lovell, who was unwilling to attempt a landing on the peninsula with his motley assortment of troops until the British sloops were put out of commission, was disgusted at Saltonstall's refusal to attack. So were the naval captains who, on Thursday, 27 July, presented the Commodore with a petition. In it they urged that "the most spedy Exertions shou'd be used to Accomplish the design we came upon, We think Delays in the presant Case are extremely dangerous: as our Enemies are daily Fortifying and Strengthning themselves . . . being in daily Expectation of a Reinforcement . . . [we] intend only to express our desire . . . to go immediately into the Harbour, & Attack the Enemys Ships . . . ."[3]

Saltonstall remained unmoved, and a war council in the great cabin of the *Warren* on the same day resolved to go ahead with a landing even though the British sloops were not knocked out. On 28 July, the three Massachusetts brigs and a heavily armed priva-

teer were lined up offshore to fire broadside on the heights while
General Lovell landed three groups of troops—militia, artillery-
men, and marines—on the southwest side of the peninsula. It was
not an easy maneuver. As the boats pulled away from the fleet in an
early morning fog, they were showered with balls from British
muskets above. Once the men scrambled ashore on the narrow
shingle, they were faced with a steep hand-over-hand climb, pulling themselves up the face of the cliff by the brush and scrub,
unable to use their weapons until they reached the top. Resistance
on the landward end of the peninsula was relatively light, but the
outermost battery put up a stiff fight, and the Americans suffered
several casualties before driving the last of the retreating redcoats
into their main fort. One of those killed was Marine Captain John
Welch, who back in 1776 had sat on the court-martial of Captain
Hazard.

During the time that the British were occupied in repulsing
the assault on the heights, the American fleet could have made an
all-out attack on the three British sloops. Instead, only a half-
hearted attempt to engage them was made, and when the *Warren*
was hit in the mainmast and bowsprit, she backed off. It was a fatal
move. On the heights above, American troops waited to storm the
fort until the threat of cannonfire and reinforcement from the
British sloops was removed. The moment never came. Instead
they dug in on the edge of the peninsula and began strengthening
their defenses with supplies hauled up from below.

Now the stalemate began in earnest. The land forces on
Bagaduce were about evenly matched, though the British had the
advantage of their fortification. In the bay below, Saltonstall
enjoyed undisputable superiority, commanding a total of more
than 300 cannon against the 42 of the British. Had the Commodore elected to engage, it would seem a foregone conclusion that
the sloops could have quickly been put out of commission. Once
their protection were done away with, the capitulation of the fort
seemed certain.

At least so General Lovell believed, together with most of the
American captains, including the only other Continental Navy
captain present, Hoysteed Hacker. Not so Saltonstall. His only
possible danger lay in delaying long enough to permit reinforcements to be sent to aid the beleaguered sloops but, incredibly,
he refused to attack. Council after council of war held in the great
cabin of the *Warren* found him deaf to the urgings of General
Lovell and his own captains that he move at once. Day after pre-

cious day slipped by, and nothing happened. The bay, shimmering gently between its spruce-clad headlands, continued to look more like a yacht club rendezvous than a battle scene.

By 8 August Captain Hacker had had enough. He addressed to the "Gentlemen of the Navy and Army present" a letter outlining a plan to attack the enemy ships. In drawing up his plan, he had the cooperation and help of Lieutenant Brown and the three Massachusetts naval captains—Williams of the *Hazard*, Cathcart of the *Tyrannicide*, and Hallet of the *Active*. These five were to carry out the actual attack. The disposition of the other ships suggested in the plan seems largely designed to keep them out of the way of the *Providence*, *Diligent*, and the three brigs.

"Seeing we are come to this period of time without any Determined Resolution," Captain Hacker wrote, "I think it my duty to make my Sentiments known: That we attack the Enemy & in the following manner. That the *Warren* lead the way, the *Putnam* and *Hampden* to follow and anchor abreast the Enemies ships taking care at the same time to be a sufficient distance from the Enemies ships in case of an Explosion that they not be damaged by them"—a bit of irony inserted for Saltonstall's benefit. Eight privateers were to form a line against the British works on the heights and to keep up a "Moderate but a Continual Firing in order to Annoy them, so as to take their attention from the *Warren*, *Putnam*, etc." The battery on Banks Island was also to keep up a continual cannonade of the peninsula. A landing party of 100 marines and 300 militia was to be directed toward a recently erected British battery on low ground, in order to intercept any attempt at reinforcement by seamen and marines from the three sloops being attacked. The American fort was to fire cannister, grape or shells to confuse and annoy them "whilst we [the five naval vessels otherwise never mentioned in the plan] continue our attack on the shipping."

General Lovell was to use his own judgment as to the deployment of the rest of his army already on the peninsula. "The objection in our Last Council," the letter continues, "was that were we possessed of the Lower Battery we could not hold it, an impediment easily overcome by the men going under the Bank wich will be free from the Enemy, and will be Immediately under Cover of our Ships which of Course they must be in at the place above appointed or Else the Aforesaid plan will be Abortive." At the end of this "Can-

Major Bagaduce August 8th 1779

Gent:men

Seeing we are Come to this period of time without
any Determined Resolution, I think it my Duty
to make my Sentiments known, Which the
Subsequent lines are my full Oppinion,
That we Attack the Enemy and in the following
manner, That the Warren Lead the way, the
Putnam & Hamden to follow and Anchor Abreast
the Enemie's Ships taking Care at the Same
time to be a Sufficient Distance from the Enemies
Ships, In Case of an Explosion from them, that
they may not be Damaged by them (Furthermore)
That the Sally, Vengeance Black Prince Hector
Monmouth Sky Rocket, and Hunter, to form
a Line against their works on the Hill, and
to keep up a Moderate but a Continual Fireing
in order to Annoy them, so as to take their
Attention from the Warren, Putnam &c. The
Battery on the Island at the Same time to keep
up a Continual Cannonaeding on the Enemies
Works, The Ships to Acquire one Hundred Marines
to Land in order to Join three Hundred Militia
to act in Conjunction, to Make an Excursion on
their Lately Erected Battery on the Low ground,
In order to Intercept their Seamen & Marines in
Case they Should Attempt to Land, with a view
of Reinforceing their Grand works, at the same
time for our Capital Fort to keep up a fireing
of Cannister & Grape to heave Shels or any other
was Like Combustables they may think Necessary
to Confuse & Annoy them whilst we Continue

89 our Attack on the Shipping and Lower
works, takeing Care at the Same time that
they dont fire from our Foart Any Shot
that may Damage our Troops between the
Enemies upper and Lower Foart, The General
then at our fort to Conduct as he thinks proper
with the Remaining Part of his Army, which
According to my Calculation will Ammount
to Nine hundred men, I Look upon that part
of Cuting the Seamen & Marines of from Reinfor-
=ceeing Their Grand Fort to be an Important
part or piece of the Buisness, for they Certainly
Concist of one third part of their Foarce ——
The Objection in our Last Council was that were
we Posessed of the Lower Battery we Could not
hold it, But that Impediment in my Oppinion
is Easily Remideed as in the following manner
that our Men goe under the Bank wick will
be free from the Enemy, and will be Immedi:
=ately under Cover of our Ships which of Cource
they must be in at the place above Appointed
or Else the Aforesaid Plan will be Abortive

This Gentm is the Candid oppinion of your
friend and Humd Sert.
                          Hoystead Hacker
To
The Gentm of the Navy & Army
                    Present.
N.B. I desire you would Call a Council Immediately
To Know what Can be Done.

Captain Hoysteed Hacker's plan for attacking the British ships, Penobscot Bay, 8 August 1779. Courtesy, Massachusetts Archives.

did oppinion of your friend and Humb. Sert Hoysteed Hacker," the Captain added, "N. B. I desire you would Call a Council Immediately to Know What Can be Done."[4]

In response to this letter, the desired council was held aboard the *Warren* on 10 August, with both naval and military personnel attending. The Army people, including General Lovell and Lieutenant Colonel Paul Revere, were asked whether they could hold the ground to eastward of the fortress—the disputed "lower Ground." They answered in the affirmative. The question was then put to the captains in the Navy whether the ships should go in and destroy the enemy's shipping. Their answer was a unanimous "Yes."

Commodore Saltonstall's hand had finally been forced, and it looked as though the stalemate were over. Real action seemed in sight at last—until the next morning. Then the Army reneged. On 11 August, General Lovell held a conference that included no naval personnel. To the question, substantially the one agreed to the day before, Could they hold a post at the rear of the fort as well as the present ground, the answer was "No." One reason given was that they lacked enough force to *take* any new ground, let alone hold it. Another, with a ring of truth, confessed "The great want of Discipline and Subordination many of the Officers being so exceedingly slack in their duty the Soldiers so averse to the service and the wood in which we are encamped so very thick that on an alarm or any special occasion nearly one fourth part of the Army are skulked out of the way & conceal'd."[5]

Having been scuttled by the Army, the naval captains the next day debated whether or not the attack on the ships should be carried out anyway. The decision was negative, but not unanimous, and a committee, on which were Captains Hacker and Williams, was appointed to talk to the General.

On the same day, the Eastern Navy Board, which had lost all patience with Saltonstall, sent him an angry despatch. "We have for some time been at a loss to know why the enemy ships have not been attacked . . . It is agreed on all hands that they are at all times in your power . . . We think it our duty to direct you to attack and take or destroy them without delay: in doing which no time is to be lost as a reinforcement are probably on their passage at this time."[6]

The Board was right. British authorities in New York had learned of the American expedition on 18 July, and five days later a powerful naval squadron sailed for the Penobscot. Sir George Collier in his 64-gun flagship *Raisonable* commanded five frigates— two 32-gun, one 28, and two 20's—and a 14-gun sloop. It was an impressive display of Royal Navy strength and, if it could get there in time, it would outmatch the motley collection of American ships.

It could and did. On 13 August, the *Diligent* and *Active*, which had been patrolling outside the Bay since the 28th of July, sighted the sails of the British task force. Captain Hallet in the *Active* dashed into the harbor to alert the Commodore. The ship captains who gathered aboard the *Warren* for orders found Saltonstall unnerved. One final hasty war council, at which Hoysteed Hacker was not present, concluded not to stand and fight. In a unanimous vote, it decided to evacuate the troops and run up the Penobscot River.

The job of getting the men and ordnance from Bagaduce back onto the fleet was begun at once. In spite of squalls of rain, followed by fog, all night long the ships' boats plied back and forth, and by morning the troops and guns were all safely back aboard. On the morning of the fourteenth, the British garrison, unaware of the approach of their own fleet, were puzzled by the unnatural quiet of the American works. General McLean sent out a cautious scouting party, which brought back the astonishing news that the position had been evacuated and not an enemy soldier was to be found.

Except, that is, on "Hacker's Island." There the battery had been faithfully manned throughout the night, with the *Providence* standing by. It had been ready to cover the evacuation of the peninsula, should the enemy have opened fire, and was now, a British observer surmised, preparing to make a stand. With the peninsula abandoned and the fleet about to flee, there was no further hope of resisting, and the *Providence* began taking the men aboard. They had waited until the last possible moment. There was little enough time to get the marines safely off, and none for the heavy ordnance. The guns were left spiked, so that they could not be turned on the departing Americans by a British landing party that approached the island even as the marines left it.[7]

The movements of the American ships were hampered by the lack of wind that is common on the Maine coast on summer mornings. As the British ships lay outside the harbor, the American captains tried to form their ships into a defensive crescent protecting the transports, but there was not enough wind for them to hold their positions. The transports trying to make the run upriver on the flood tide were held back because what little wind there was was blowing downstream. Few of them could make any progress over the bottom. By the time a sea breeze sprang up early in the afternoon, it brought the British fleet into the harbor. Commodore Saltonstall hoisted the signal for every captain to shift for himself—and all hell broke loose. As the first of the British ships drew within range and opened fire, cannonballs rained around the fleeing Americans. Three vessels that tried to escape down the west side of Islesboro were cut off and caught, the *Hunter* and *Hampden* captured, and the privateer *Defence* blown up by her crew. The transports, which now had the wind in their favor but the tide on the ebb, were still unable to get up the river. They ran ashore and were set afire, the troops scattering into the woods. To the haze of powder from the British guns, now augmented by those of the three sloops, which had dashed out to join the fray, were added billows of smoke from the burning ships, and the din of cannonfire was periodically drowned out by the crash of falling spars and the boom of explosions as fire reached the powder magazines.

The rest of the fleet—naval vessels and some of the privateers—ran into the river. By cracking on all sail and using their boats for towing, they managed to make progress upstream. Those like the *Providence* that carried sweeps on deck were also helped by their oars, but others began to fall by the wayside. The *Warren* was one of them. The other naval vessels continued their struggle to make way, and with the *Providence*, the *Diligent*, *Hazard*, and *Tyrannicide* crept with painful slowness up the river, coming to anchor at midnight.

On Sunday morning, 15 August, they resumed their journey, now with the tide in their favor, and sailed still farther upriver, past what is now Bucksport to a couple of miles below the falls at Bangor.

For the four captains, Hacker, Williams, Cathcart, and Lieutenant Brown, this was no panicky flight from the enemy, but a strategic retreat. They had already agreed that if a suitable place could be found to fortify, they could stand off an enemy assault long enough for reinforcements to be brought overland or, at worst, inflict material damage on British ships coming up the river. In company with Army major William Todd, they were rowed ashore to look for a practicable spot. They found several. At this point, they had to report to the Commodore. Proceeding downstream, they came across the privateer *Vengeance,* whose captain agreed to carry them down to the *Warren.* On the way they passed several other privateers who were, on order from Captain Saltonstall, preparing to burn their ships. They also ran into Lieutenant Colonel Paul Revere, who was on his way home without orders. A few miles farther downstream, they spoke with a marine captain, who gave them awful news: the Commodore had determined to burn the *Warren,* and in preparation was already landing his men.[8]

After this blow, there seemed no reason to proceed, so they boarded the boat for the long row back to their ships. At the anchorage they found they had been joined by Captain Hallet in the *Active,* and four privateers getting ready for burning. The naval crews were waiting for their captains with mounting apprehension that was rapidly turning into panic. Rumor had it that only the privateers would be burned, while the naval vessels would try to make a fight of it. In this case, the men felt certain they they would be taken prisoner, a conviction that made them, as Captain Williams put it, "very uneasy." Captain Cathcart was forced to fire on his crew to get them back aboard the *Tyrannicide.* The people aboard *Providence* and *Diligent* must have shared the same fears, but as Continental Navy seamen were better disciplined.

At eleven o'clock that night, General Lovell appeared aboard the *Providence.* He had come from Commodore Saltonstall, he told Captain Hacker, with a request that the naval vessels send down some boats to tow the *Warren* upriver. The news that the Commodore might come up put new heart into the men, and boats were promptly manned and sent off downstream.

There can have been little sleep aboard any of the ships that night. The General elected to stay with the captains and all the officers must have stayed up to discuss their situation. It was by no means a comfortable one. Already fires were being set aboard the privateers, two of which were blazing away too close for safety. Flaming spars and rigging were dropping from the burning ships occasionally on the decks of the others, whose crews were kept busy putting out the fires. Still the captains hung on, hoping against hope for the appearance of the Commodore and a chance to save their ships.

At nine o'clock in the morning of 16 August, that hope died. A messenger arrived from downstream bringing word that the

Commodore had set fire to the *Warren*, which was already con-
sumed. It was his only decisive action. The privateers downstream
had likewise gone up in flames, including the *Vengeance*, aboard
which the four captains had gone downriver the day before.

Now the situation of the five naval vessels suddenly turned
desperate. Their boats were gone, the British imminent, their men
beginning to panic. Crackling flames aboard the drifting privateers
threatened to reach the magazines at any moment and blow all the
ships out of the water.

Fortunately the fleeing crews of the privateers had left a boat
or two grounded ashore. Lieutenant Brown was helped by his carpenter and General Lovell to get them floated, and as firing parties
began preparing to burn the ships, the crewmen were gradually ferried to the west bank of the river. On the *Providence*, Seaman Hiller
was one of the men charged with stacking anything burnable—old
canvas, rope, wood, wadding—at the foot of the mast, and soaking
the pile with oil once intended for the sloop's lanterns. After touching a match to it, the last man jumped into the boat for the final row
to shore.

Those officers and men who stood on the west bank of the
Penobscot to see their ships catch fire watched an awesome sight.
Of the nine vessels, some were smouldering hulks, some ablaze,
with flames licking up the tarred rigging to race up the masts and
spread outward along the yards. The river itself must have seemed
to be on fire, belching clouds of steam as flaring spars plunged into
the hissing water.

Hoysteed Hacker could not linger to watch the final agony of
sloop *Providence*, blazing like some giant crucifix against the eastern
sky. With the other captains, he was faced with taking his men on
a hundred-mile journey through the wilderness to the settlement
at Falmouth—a journey with agonies of its own. They would all
suffer from hunger, bramble scratches, mosquito bites, and blis-
tered feet before they saw civilization again. As they turned away
from their doomed ships for the last time, the acrid smoke that
filled their nostrils was less bitter than the resentment in their
hearts. They had held out until the last possible moment in the
face of desertion by the Army and the rest of the fleet, but beyond
the defection of their Commodore they could not go.

Seaman Hiller's account gives no hint of the perils of the
journey. "We then marched through the woods as far as the town
of Falmouth," he says, "where we were provided with provisions

until we were rested, and then we that belonged to the Continental service were transported to Boston by water."[9] Thomas Philbrook is more outspoken.

> Our retreat was as badly managed as the whole expedition had been. Here we were, landed in a wilderness, under no command; those belonging to the ships, unacquainted with the woods, and only knew that a west course would carry us across to Kennebec; whereas, there were hundreds of the militia that were old hunters, and knew the country. Some of these ought to have been detained as pilots, and we might all have got through in three days; but we had no one to direct, so every one shifted for himself. Some got to their homes in two days, while the most of us were six or seven days before we came to an inhabited country. I got through on the seventh day, after keeping a fast of three days. From Portland, I took passage in the frigate *Boston,* Capt. Tucker, was treated with much politeness by him and his officers.[10]

Not all the Americans fared so well. Nearly five hundred men were lost, together with all the ships. Some seven million dollars had gone for nothing. As word of the total disaster got back to Boston, disbelief gave way to dismay, and finally to searing indignation.

Repercussions were not long in coming. A Massachusetts committee of investigation was summoned to fix blame for the calamity. Testimony described those aimless meetings in the great cabin of the *Warren,* with Saltonstall's persistent refusal to move. It told of the acceptance of Captain Hacker's plan of attack—and the failure to put it into action. The Commodore's failure to give orders for the management of the fleet as it broke and ran, confronted by the oncoming British ships. The inferno that the mouth of the river became with the panic-stricken burning of transports and privateers.

There was testimony also by Captains Williams of the *Hazard,* Cathcart of the *Tyrannicide,* Hallet of the *Active,* and Lieutenant Brown of the *Diligent*—telling of the valiant struggle of the naval captains to make a stand and to save their ships. There is no deposition by Captain Hacker with the others filed in the Massachusetts Archives, but the testimony of each captain gives an account of the *Providence.* Their evidence was corroborated by Major William Todd, who had helped them search out a place to fortify, and who said simply that the navy captains, "seeing themselves deserted, burned their ships also."[11]

Saltonstall apparently never testified in his own behalf, and was found solely guilty of the fiasco. General Lovell was exonerated of responsibility, and Artillery Commander Paul Revere, accused of neglect of duty, refusal to obey orders, and leaving for Boston without orders, got off with a mild rebuke. It appears that the Massachusetts Investigating Committee was remarkably gentle with its own officers, probably hoping that, by laying all the blame on Saltonstall's shoulders, they could claim reimbursement from the Congress, which they ultimately got. Captain Saltonstall was subsequently court-martialed and dismissed from the Continental service.

Captain Hacker faced a naval court of inquiry into the loss of the *Providence*. Because he had consistently urged offensive action and drawn up his own plan to attack the British sloops, he was given a clean bill. The Navy Board wrote to the Marine Committee that "Captain Hacker has by his behavior at Penobscot established his Character as a good officer & we wish to see him again employed."[12]

The crewmen of sloop *Providence* had been detained in Boston by Captain Hacker, he, according to Hiller, "promising to obtain our wages so as to enable us to obtain clothing to go to sea again— But after trying his best for a great many days, he finally told us, we had better look up a ship and shift for ourselves as the government was too poor to pay us, but never to give up the cause for freedom as we certainly should obtain it notwithstanding the shameful expedition to the Penobscot."[13]

Epilogue

SLOOP PROVIDENCE'S SERVICE in the cause for freedom had ended in the chill waters of the Penobscot,[1] and her destruction marked the death of the early Continental navy. Of the eight vessels that had sailed so bravely from Cape Henlopen on the first fleet cruise in February 1776, not one now remained. The year 1777 had seen the loss of five of those vessels: the *Cabot*, driven ashore on Nova Scotia and captured by HMS *Milford*, and the *Andrew Doria*, *Hornet*, *Wasp*, and *Fly* burned in the Delaware in November to prevent their falling to the enemy. The first flagship, *Alfred*, had been captured in an inglorious action in March 1778, shortly before the *Columbus* was burned after an unsuccessful attempt to run the British blockade of Narragansett Bay.

The ranks of the early captains were thinned as well. Young Nicholas Biddle had died gallantly in action in the explosion of his frigate *Randolph* off Barbados early in 1778. Captain Hazard, Commodore Hopkins, his son John B. Hopkins, and now finally Dudley Saltonstall, had all been dismissed from the service. Of the original eight captains, only Abraham Whipple and Hoysteed Hacker still remained in the U.S. Navy.

In terms of actual accomplishment, neither the converted merchant fleet nor the more ambitious 13-frigate program would seem to have materially altered the course of the war. But the morale-building value of their successes was immeasurable, as was the extent to which their very existence diverted British naval forces to the American station or into convoy service. News of victory at sea, however slight, kept alive the conviction that the most powerful navy in the world was not invincible, and that it could not subjugate thirteen small colonies an ocean away.

The contribution of little sloop *Providence* to that conviction was in inverse proportion to her size. Between her impressive number of "firsts"—first colonial flagship, firing first broadside of the war at sea, first choice of both George Washington and the Continental Congress to perform naval service, first naval vessel to land the first marines, first to fly the Stars and Stripes over foreign territory—and her significant "last" as sole survivor of the early Continental fleet, she achieved two noteworthy distinctions. Her career total of 40-odd prizes was far in excess of that of any of the other vessels, and is the more extraordinary in view of her size and the weakness of her armament. Her most significant service, however, lay in her value as a proving ground for her officers, particularly her captains. From her broad quarterdeck were launched some of the proudest careers in the history of the early navy.

The contribution of the *Providence*'s first captain, John Hazard, to the service of his country was the negative one of getting himself cashiered, thus clearing the way for the advent of John Paul Jones. Captain Jones' exploits after leaving the sloop and the *Alfred* are too well known to need repetition here. (The interested reader will find Samuel Eliot Morison's *John Paul Jones—a Sailor's Biography* a fascinating and accurate account.) After parting from John Peck Rathbun to take command of the *Ranger* in 1777, he sailed her to France and glory, carrying the war into British ports and earning a decoration from King Louis XVI. Although he returned twice to America, in 1781 and 1787, he never again fought in Continental waters. In 1792 at age 45 he died and was buried in Paris; his body was brought to the United States in 1905 for ultimate interment in the Naval Academy chapel at Annapolis.

The other four captains of the late sloop *Katy-Providence* found themselves reunited shortly after her demise. Following the departure of the Penobscot fleet in July 1779, Captain Whipple had been ordered to take his squadron, fresh from its fruitful Newfoundland cruise, southward to help General Lincoln defend Charleston, South Carolina. The ships were not ready to sail until late fall, by which time Hoysteed Hacker had returned from the Penobscot, having sailed from Falmouth on the frigate *Boston,* which was then attached to Whipple's flotilla. Although the Navy Board wished to see Hacker "again employed," it had no command available, and he was ordered to join Jonathan Pitcher as first lieutenant aboard frigate *Providence.*

Commodore Whipple's little fleet included the two frigates, *Providence* and *Boston,* Rathbun's *Queen* of *France,* and sloop *Ranger.* It arrived at Charleston after a stormy voyage on 18 December 1779. The naval captains worked with General Lincoln planning the defense of the city, which the British intended to attack simultaneously by land and sea, but principally by water. On 20 March 1780, a powerful fleet under Admiral Arbuthnot passed over the bar and anchored in Charleston Harbor. To prevent its approach upriver, a line of eleven ships was sunk across the river entrance—among them John Peck Rathbun's decrepit *Queen of France.*

The unexpected collapse of land defenses and overwhelming British naval superiority spelled disaster for the Americans. In a protracted siege that slowly surrounded the city, the British forces finally accepted its surrender on 12 May 1780. All of the U.S. naval and marine officers were taken prisoner, but under parole were allowed to return to their homes until formal exchange with

British prisoners could be arranged. The American naval vessels, as part of the surrender terms, were turned over to the enemy.

The fall of Charleston and the loss of its last squadron was the death blow of the Continental navy. There were no commands available for the prisoner-captains, even had they been free to assume them, nor could they, at least for the time being, turn to the usual recourse of dispossessed captains—privateering. Some idea of the plight in which the captains found themselves is conveyed in an appeal made by Abraham Whipple to the Congress in 1786.

> . . . On the 20th of January 1780 by consent of General Lincoln, I sailed on a cruise of observation, fell in with the enemy's fleet from New York, and took 4 of them, being chased into harbor by 4 British ships of war. We then bent our whole force and strained every nerve for the defence of the town. The particulars of the siege with the struggles and sufferings of the army and navy need not be mentioned. They must be well known to Congress as they are to the world. I shall only observe that I faithfully exerted myself on this interesting occasion to promote the interest and honor of my company, and though the town was surrendered, America's honor was triumphant.
>
> My men having been shipped for a six months' cruise in a warm climate and my vessels destitute of clothing, these unfortunate fellows were reduced to the greatest distress from the severity of the memorable inclement winter of 1780. Feeling for their misery which I have not language to describe, I purchased clothing and necessary stores for their several ships and delivered the same to their respective pursers. The people were by this means relieved at my expense, and the full amount of what they received was stopped out of their wages, yet I have never been reimbursed a single farthing. On the 12th of May the capitulation took place and we all became prisoners of war. I agreed with the British Admiral for all our paroles, engaging that the seamen and marines should be exchanged. The last of June we arrived at Chester in Pennsylvania, great numbers of my people languishing under the smallpox and a variety of other diseases. I hired a house for their reception and accommodation at my own particular expense, whereby I am persuaded many useful lives were preserved to their country.
>
> I remained two years and seven months a prisoner, when I was at last exchanged for Capt. Gayton of the Romulus a 44 Gun ship,* during which time, as I was deprived of the power of doing business

---

* The reason for the long delay in exchanging Commodore Whipple was that the Americans held no British prisoners of equal rank. It was through the generosity of the French, who had captured the *Romulus*, that Captain Gayton was released in exchange for Whipple.

for my support, I suffered heavily in my finances, which, in addition to my disbursements for my country in the cause of justice and humanity, became very scanty and precarious, opening a gloomy prospect of their entire dissolution without leaving a wreck behind. Thus having exhausted the means of supporting myself and family, I was reduced to the sad necessity of mortgaging my little farm, the remnant I had left, to obtain money for a temporary support . . . . [2]

The justice of this complaint was not lost on the Congress, which ultimately did reimburse its faithful servant. Because of its acute shortage of cash, the Congress began to issue land grants to its petitioners, and Abraham Whipple accepted rights to a tract on the Ohio River. Settling on a farm in Marietta, Ohio, in 1796, he followed the soil instead of the sea until his death in 1809 at the age of 85.[3]

Captain Whipple was not unique in having his service prove financially disastrous. With mounting inflation in Continental currency, the Congress itself was nearly bankrupt, lacking funds to reimburse those captains and others, including Navy Board members, who had met many of their men's expenses out of their own pockets. In 1787, no longer able even to maintain its ships, it sold off the last U.S. naval vessel.

The other naval captains captured at Charleston were exchanged much more promptly than their Commodore. Hoysteed Hacker went aboard the frigate *Alliance* as first lieutenant under Captain John Barry, and early in 1781 sailed for France. After the return trip, which was enlivened by a mutiny and a vicious action with two British vessels, Hacker left the *Alliance* (in which Barry, unaware that the peace treaty had been signed in February 1783, fought the last engagement of the war the following March) and at the end of July 1781, took command of the Massachusetts privateer *Buccaneer*. How he fared in private service is a matter of conjecture; he died in New York in his seventy-first year.

Jonathan Pitcher remains a man of mystery, partly because records of his activities are few and partly because those that exist are confused by the fact that there was at least one other Revolutionary officer by the same name in the Rhode Island militia. Although not himself attached to the *Alliance,* he apparently sat on a court-martial held on one of her officers following a second mutiny, and in October 1784 signed a document relating to the sentence of the court. A gravestone in Cranston, Rhode Island, marked "Rachael, wife of Captain Jonathan Pitcher, died in 1798 in her 47th year" is possibly his wife's. For him there is no stone, and his epitaph remains Lieutenant Trevett's comment, "A better officer than Capt. Pitcher there cannot be."

And what of John Peck Rathbun, that "Spirited Officer" whose name was so long associated with the sloop, and to whose "Valour and Conduct" Commodore Hopkins attributed most of Captain Jones' success in the *Providence?*

Once released from his parole as a prisoner of war after the fall of Charleston, in the summer of 1781 Rathbun was commissioned by the Congress to command the Massachusetts privateer brig *Wexford,* armed with 20 guns and carrying 120 men. He took her out of Boston Harbor in mid-August, and set a course for the British Isles. Six weeks later, almost within sight of the Irish coast, his luck finally deserted him. At daybreak on Friday, 28 September 1781, the *Wexford* was sighted by HMS *Recovery,* a 32-gun frigate with a crew of 220. The Britisher promptly gave chase. Even Captain Rathbun's skill and strategy, without his lucky sloop, was not enough to effect the brig's escape from the faster frigate, and though he eluded her for an incredible 24 hours, having sustained her broadside after 4 hours, in mid-morning of the twenty-ninth, the *Wexford* struck.

Captain Rathbun, together with his officers and men, once again became a prisoner of war. This time, however, there was no parole—instead, prison in Ireland, followed by confinement aboard two prison ships, and finally transfer to Old Mill Prison in Plymouth, England. There, nine months after his surrender, he was taken ill and died on 20 June 1782, aged 36.

So ended too soon one of the most dashing and distinguished careers of the Revolutionary Navy. It was an end as inappropriate to his performance as sloop *Providence's* destruction in the Penobscot was to hers—almost as though the luck they had shared for three adventurous years began to run out when they were no longer together. Each had one signal success after their separation—Rathbun's fruitful Newfoundland cruise and *Providence's* capture of the *Diligent*—and then no more.

John Peck Rathbun's contribution to the cause for freedom went virtually unnoticed for more than a century and a half. Recognition finally came when the U.S. Navy named first a World War II destroyer and later an ocean escort vessel in his honor—both called *Rathburne.* A collateral descendant, Frank H. Rathbun, has nearly completed a book-length biography of his illustrious ancestor.

Sloop *Providence's* service to her country has been somewhat belatedly recognized by the U.S. Navy, which named a couple of vessels in her honor, the last a light missile cruiser decommis sioned in 1973.

In another way, perhaps inadvertently, the Navy has paid fitting tribute to the *Providence*. When it celebrates Navy Day on October 13, it commemorates the resolution passed on that day in 1775 in which the Continental Congress authorized two vessels to be sent to sea at Continental expense. The first of these, as contemporary documents unmistakably prove, was *Katy-Providence*, although history has pretty well obscured that fact. It is not likely to be again forgotten, thanks to the achievement of Seaport '76 in fitting out the reproduction of sloop *Providence*, which goes to sea as a constant reminder of the exploits of her valiant forebear, bringing living history to the citizens of her country.

It is neither easy nor inexpensive nowadays to build a unique sailing vessel of any sort, and when an 18th Century design must be brought into conformity with modern Coast Guard regula- tions, the problems are nearly—though fortunately not quite—in- surmountable. Seaport '76 has accomplished the formidable task of getting the *Providence* operational, ready to function as a dynamic symbol of the glorious maritime heritage of the United States. Generous support has come from many sources, but the vital force of Seaport '76 is its continuing and growing membership, a group of dedicated people from all parts of the country. It is these supporters who determine the functions and successes of the sloop, and it is they who thus will write the real epilogue to the career of America's first naval vessel.

Plans for Reproduction of USS Providence, built by Seaport '76 Foundation, Newport, Rhode Island. Courtesy, Charles W. Wittholz, Naval Architect.

Lines Plan

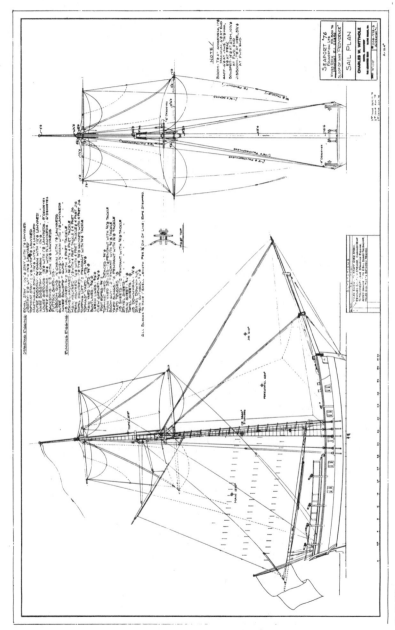

Sail Plan

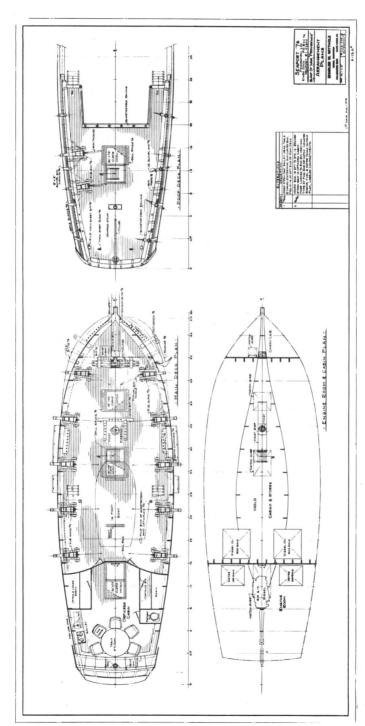

Arrangement Plan

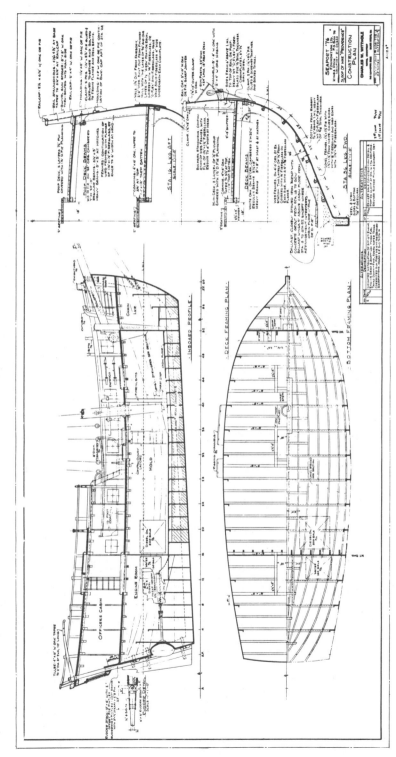

Construction Plan

Afterword

THE FRONTISPIECE PAINTING by Francis Holman, which was discovered in England by John Millar of Newport and later acquired by John Nicholas Brown of Providence, is signed by the artist, a British marine painter of some note, and dated 1777. It shows an armed American sloop, unidentified, attacking a British ship whose stern sports the portrait of a woman with "*Eliza*" writ large beneath it. It presents, besides a handsome marine battle scene, a series of problems.

First of these is the question of why a British painter should have done a canvas of an American naval vessel fighting an English ship. It seems safe to assume that Holman did the painting for Englishmen, probably on commission for the owner of the *Eliza*, which must, therefore, have escaped. The American sloop does not appear in the painting to be such a formidable foe to the much bigger *Eliza* that escape from her should be celebrated in oil—unless by some chance that sloop were already known, in England, as a very dangerous enemy.

So the search began for an American Continental Navy sloop that had both an international reputation and a hot engagement with an English ship before the end of 1777.

It was not hard to find the sloop with an overseas reputation. In the fall of 1776, John Paul Jones' cruise to Nova Scotia in the *Providence* had destroyed the British fishing industry there and left three hundred Jersey fishermen free to sail home to spread the news in England. At least one London newspaper carried the story, and a couple of Royal Navy frigates were ordered to capture the *Providence*.

The next step, to find an engagement between the *Providence* and a ship that got away, was easy too. Thanks to the journal kept by Marine Officer John Trevett, we have a detailed account of all the sloop's actions in 1777, when the engagement with *Eliza* must have taken place. We know that it did not occur earlier, and could not have later, in view of the date of the painting. In July 1777, off Sandy Hook, New Jersey, the *Providence*, then under the command of John Peck Rathbun, attacked a small flotilla of British vessels, a ship, brig, and schooner. The sloop immediately went after the ship. At the end of the battle, the ship and brig escaped, while the *Providence*, considerably damaged, had to settle for capturing the schooner.

This is certainly the engagement we are looking for. Not only is it a bitterly fought action between the *Providence* and a ship that got away, occurring at the right time of the right year, but details of the written account correspond remarkably closely to those in

Francis Holman's painting. The journal describes the action as taking place at sunset in light air, and Holman paints long light on a quiet sea. We have, we are sure, found the *Eliza*. Furthermore, detail in the painting strongly suggests that Holman was working with an eyewitness account of the affair, brought to *Eliza's* delighted owners in England. We know that the *Eliza* herself did not bring the news; it was surely carried by the brig that had joined in the action and also escaped.

There is just one trouble with our conviction that we have found *Eliza*. In actual fact, as Captain Rathbun discovered from the captain of the captured schooner, the name of the ship that got away was the *Mary*. We look further, but in vain, for any other encounter that might fill the bill within the right period, but there is no other engagement between the *Providence* and a ship, either earlier or later. The *Eliza* of Holman's painting simply must be the real-life *Mary*.

If this is indeed true, then we must find a reason for the change of name. Assuming that Holman himself was responsible for it, we ask what could possibly have made him do it. The first reason that springs to mind is that the *Mary's* owner, for whom the painting was done, for some reason refused to accept it. As we know, after Captain Rathbun's raid on Nassau that unknown shipowner had the best of all possible reasons for wanting nothing to do with the painting.

Early in 1778, not long after Holman had finished the canvas showing the *Mary's* triumphant escape from sloop *Providence*, the ship herself, laden with rich cargo from Jamaica, was expected back in England. What actually arrived for the owner of the *Mary* was, instead of his precious ship, some terrible news. The *Mary* had been captured by an American vessel. Worse still, that vessel was none other than the sloop *Providence*.

The rest is surmise, but must be close to what actually happened. The *Mary's* owner wanted no part of a picture of his ship under attack by the *Providence*. After his staggering loss, perhaps he no longer had enough money to pay for it. In any case, Francis Holman's market for the canvas had suddenly evaporated. Unwilling either to sell it as the *Mary* or to do much more work on it, he made the simplest possible alteration. Without touching the woman's portrait on the stern, he merely painted "*Mary*" out and "*Eliza*" in.

Why he chose "*Eliza*," except that it was a feminine name of an appropriate length, we do not know. Indeed, we have no information about the subsequent history of the painting—to whom it was sold, or what happened to it between 1778 and 1971 when John Millar discovered it in Greenwich, England. In view of the total mystery that surrounds the provenance of the canvas, it is remarkable that evidence collected two centuries after the event can both present and explain a striking anomaly—that a noted British painter should have immortalized an American engagement between the Continental Navy's most valiant sloop and her richest prize.

Appendices

Proclamation of King George III., relative to the Destruction of the Gaspee.

GEORGE R.
BY THE KING.

A PROCLAMATION:

For the discovering and apprehending the persons who plundered and burnt the Gaspee schooner, and barbarously wounded and ill-treated Lieutenant William Dudingston, commander of the said schooner.

Whereas, we have received information, that, upon the 10th day of June last, between the hours of twelve and one, in the morning, in the Providence or Narragansett River, in our colony of Rhode Island and Providence Plantations, a great number of persons, armed with guns and other offensive weapons, and led by two persons, who were called the captain and head sheriff, in several armed boats, attacked and boarded our vessel called the Gaspee schooner, then lying at single anchor in the said river, commanded by our Lieutenant William Dudingston, under the orders of our Rear Admiral John Montagu; and having dangerously wounded and barbarously treated the said William Dudingston, took, plundered and burnt the said schooner.

We, to the intent that said outrageous and heinous offenders may be discovered, and brought to condign punishment, have thought fit, with the advice of our Privy Council, to issue this our royal proclamation.

And we are hereby graciously pleased to promise, that if any person or persons shall discover any person or persons concerned in the said daring and heinous offences above mentioned, so that he or they may be apprehended and brought to justice, such discoverer shall have and receive, as a reward, for such discovery, upon conviction of each of the said offenders, the sum of *five hundred pounds.*

And if any person or persons shall discover either of the said persons who acted as, or called themselves, or were called by their said accomplices, the head sheriff, or the captain, so that they, or either of them, may be apprehended and brought to punishment, such discoverer shall have and receive, as a reward for such discovery, upon conviction of either of the said persons, the further sum of *five hundred pounds,* over and above the sum of *five hundred pounds,* herein before promised, for the discovery and apprehending any of the other common offenders above mentioned.

And if any person or persons concerned therein, except the two persons who were called the head sheriff and captain, and the person or persons who wounded said Lieutenant William Dudingston, shall discover any one or more of the said accomplices, so that he or they may be apprehended and brought to punishment, such discoverer shall have and receive the said reward or rewards of *five hundred pounds,* or *one thousand pounds,* as the case may be; and also our gracious pardon for his said offence; and the commissioners for executing the office of treasurer of our exchequer, are hereby required to make payment accordingly, of the said rewards.

And we do hereby strictly charge and command all our governors, deputy governors, magistrates officers and all other our loving subjects, that they do use their utmost diligence, in their several places and capacities, to find out, discover and apprehend the said offenders, in order to their being brought to justice.

And we do hereby command that this our proclamation be printed and published, in the usual form, and affixed in the principal places of our town of Newport, and other towns in our said colony, that none may pretend ignorance.

Given at our Court, at St. James, the twenty-sixth day of August, 1772, in the twelfth year of our reign.

God save the King.

APPENDIX B

DEPUTY GOVERNOR NICHOLAS COOKE
TO CAPTAIN JAMES WALLACE, R.N.[1]

Sir   East Greenwich, June 14th, 1775
    Long have the good people of this colony been oppressed by your conduct, in interrupting their lawful trade, and preventing the importation of the provisions necessary for their subsistence.
    The acts of the British Parliament, already filled with restrictions of trade, oppressive in the highest degree, seem by you, to be thought too lenient.
    Not controlled by those you affect to call your masters, you have detained the persons and taken away the properties of His Majesty's American subjects, without any warrant from the acts of trade; by which, you have greatly impeded the intercourse between this and the other colonies as well as between the different parts of this colony. The inhabitants expecting the interposition of the lawful authority of the colony, have borne these outrages with a patience almost criminal.
    The Legislature have heard their complaints, and in consequence of an act passed by the General Assembly this day, I demand of you the reason of your conduct towards the inhabitants of this Colony, in stopping and detaining their vessels. And I also demand of you, that you immediately restore the two packets, belonging to some inhabitants of the town of Providence; and all other vessels belonging to the inhabitants of this colony which you have taken and unjustly detained.
    So long as you remain in the colony, and demean yourself as becomes your office, you may depend upon the protection of the laws, and every assistance for promoting the public service, in my power. And you may also be assured that the whole power of this colony will be exerted to secure the persons and properties of the inhabitants against every lawless invader.
    An immediate answer is requested to this letter.
    I am, sir, your most humble servant

                                                    Nicholas Cooke

CAPTAIN JAMES WALLACE, R.N.
TO DEPUTY GOVERNOR NICHOLAS COOKE [2]

Sir,   His Majesty's Ship *Rose* Rhode Island, June 15, 1775
    I have received your letter of the 14th inst.; although I am unacquainted with you, or what station you act in; suppose you write in behalf of some body of people; therefore, previous to my giving an answer, I must desire to know *whether* or *not*, you, or the people on whose behalf you write, are not in open rebellion to your lawful sovereign, and the acts of the British legislature!
    I am, sir your most humble and most obedient servant.

                                                        Jas. Wallace

1. Barlett, ed., *Records of Rhode Island*, VII, 338.
2. Ibid.

Appendix C

Instructions to Captain Abraham Whipple
of the Armed Sloop *Katy* [1]

By the Honorable Nicholas Cooke Esq Deputy Governor, and Lieutenant General, of and over the English Colony of Rhode Island, and Providence Plantations, in New England, in America.

1. Instructions and Orders to be observed by Captain Abraham Whipple, Commander of the Sloop *Katy*, and Commodore of the armed Vessels employed by the Government for the Protection of the Trade of this Colony, in Pursuance of the Commission herewith given him

That it shall be lawful for the Said Abraham Whipple, and he is hereby required and enjoined in His Majesty's Name George the third King of Great Britain and So forth, for which his Commission and these Special Orders Shall be a full Warrant and Discharge to him, and all others on Board his Said Vessel and the or [other] Vessels fitted out and employed as aforesaid under his Command, to encounter expulse expel and resist by Force of Arms, as well by Land as Sea, and also to kill, Slay and Destroy, by all fitting Ways Enterprizes and Means, whatsoever, all and every such Person and Persons, as Shall attempt or enterprize the Destruction, Invasion Detriment or Annoyance of the Inhabitants of this Colony or Plantations: And to take and Surprize by all Ways and Means all and every Such Person and Persons, with their Ships Vessels, Armour, Ammunition, or other Goods, as Shall in hostile Manner invade or attempt the Hurt of this Plantation or the defeating thereof, or of the Inhabitants, or of any other Colony's lawfully joined and united with this Colony for mutual Defence and Safety against a common Enemy, in order to preserve the Interest of His Majesty and his Subjects in these Parts.

2. That all Ships and Vessels carrying Soldiers, Arms, Powder, Ammunition, Horses, Provisions, Cloathing, or any thing else for the Use [of] the Armies of Enemies of the united American Colonies Shall be Seized as Prizes.

3. That the Said Abraham Whipple Shall bring or Send into this Colony or Such other Ports or Places as the Exigency of affairs Shall make convenient and Suitable all Such Ships Vessels Goods and Men as he may Seize and take, with all Such Papers Writings and Documents as he may find on Board, to the End that Such Proceedings may be had thereupon as Law and the Necessity of the Case, may Require. And that Such Ship Vessel and Goods, Shall be kept and preserved, without Spoil or Diminution and the Bulk thereof not broken until legal Decision be given for the Forfeiture and Distribution thereof.

4. That no Person taken in any Ship or Vessel, tho known to be of the Enemy's Party Shall be killed in Cold Blood, wounded, hurt, or inhumanly

1. "Revolutionary Correspondence of Governor Nicholas Cooke," *Proceedings of the American Antiquarian Society,* New Series, XXXVI, 252–254.

treated, contrary to the just Permission of War, upon Pain of Severe Punishment. And that no female Prisoner Shall be in any manner abused under great and high Penalties.

5. That the Said Abraham Whipple Shall not do or Attempt anyThing against the Commerce or Trade of the United Colonies, or those who have commerce and Friendship with them, unless it be directed against their common Safety, and Such as is declared contraband by the Continental Congress.

6. That the said Abraham Whipple his Officers and Company, Shall endeavour to the utmost of their Power to give Aid and Succour to all Such Ships and Vessels as they may find trading for the Benefit and Advantage of these united Colonies, and labour to free them from every Distress.

7. That the Said Abraham Whipple Shall on bringing or Sending in any Prize immediately give or Cause to be given Notice to the Chief Authority of any Place where Such Prize Shall be brought in, every particular relating thereto, to the End that Justice may be done to all parties concerned.

8. That the Said Abraham Whipple Shall keep a Correspondence from Time to Time, and at all Conveniences, with the Commander in Chief of this Colony or the General Assembly, of all Prizes which he Shall take, and of every Thing Material which may occur; and observe Such further Orders as Shall be given him by the Assembly or his Superior Officers.

Given under my Hand and the Seal of the Col. afsd by and with the Consent and Approbation of the Committee of Safety the Day of [15 June] in the 15th Year of His Majesty's Reign A D 1775

By His Honor's Command

APPENDIX D

GEORGE WASHINGTON TO THE INHABITANTS OF BERMUDA [1]

Camp at Cambridge 3 Miles from Boston,
September 6, 1775.

Gentn: In the great Conflict, which agitates this Continent, I cannot doubt but the Assertors of Freedom and the Rights of the Constitution, are possessed of your most favorable Regards and Wishes for Success. As Descendents of Freemen and Heirs with us of the same Glorious Inheritance, we flatter ourselves that tho' divided by our Situation, we are firmly united in Sentiment; the Cause of Virtue and Liberty is Confined to no Continent or Climate, it comprehends within its capacious Limits, the Wise and good, however dispersed and seperated in Space or distance. You need not be informed, that Violence and Rapacity of a tyrannick Ministry, have forced the Citizens of America, your Brother Colonists, into Arms; We equally detest and lament the Prevalence of those Councils, which have led to the Effusion of so much human Blood and left us no Alternative but a Civil War or a base Submission. The wise disposer of all Events has hitherto smiled upon our virtuous Efforts; Those Mercenary Troops, a few of whom lately boasted of Subjugating this vast Continent, have been check'd in their earliest Ravages and are now actually encircled in a small Space; their Arms disgraced, and Suffering all the Calamities of a Siege. The Virtue, Spirit, and Union of the Provinces leave them nothing to fear, but the Want of Amunition, The applications of our Enemies to foreign States and their Vigilance upon our Coast, are the only Efforts they have made against us with Success. Under those Circumstances, and with these Sentiments we have turned our Eyes to you Gentlemen for Relief, We are informed there is a very large Magazine in your Island under a very feeble Guard; We would not wish to involve you in an Opposition, in which from your Situation, we should be unable to support you:—We knew not therefore to what Extent to sollicit your Assistance in availing ourselves of this Supply;—but if your Favor and Friendship to North America and its Liberties have not been misrepresented, I persuade myself you may, consistent with your own Safety, promote and further this Scheme, so as to give it the fairest prospect of Success. Be assured, that in this Case, the whole Power and Execution of my Influence will be made with the Honble. Continental Congress, that your Island may not only be Supplied with Provisions, but experience every other Mark of Affection and Friendship, which the grateful Citizens of a free Country can bestow on its Brethren and Benefactors. I am&c.

---

1. Fitzpatrick, ed., *Writings of Washington*, III, 475, 476.

APPENDIX E

EXCERPTS FROM THE DIARY OF JOHN TREVETT
MARINE OFFICER ABOARD SLOOP *PROVIDENCE*

1776: Cruise of the Alfred *and* Providence

I went on board the Sloop Providence Captain Histed [Hoysteed] Hacker, and I soon found we were to sail under command of John Paul Jones Esq. we sailed in a short time, we stopped at Tarpolin cove, where we found a small privateer belonging to Providence commanded I think by Capt. Rhodes. Com. Jones sent for me on board of his Ship late in the day, and gave me orders to arm and man our barge on board the Sloop, and he would have his barge manned and armed and sent along side our sloop, and then we were to go along side [the privateer], and while I was examining the Ships Articles, I was to give the barges crews order to press all we could, I did so, and we pressed 25 men out of 35 and carried them out on a cruise on board the Ship Alfred Com. Jones. We sailed to the eastward of Halifax, the first prize we took was a snow from England bound to Halifax her cargo dry goods, the next prize was a Ship called the Malech [*Mellish*] her cargo 10,000 suits of Soldiers Clothing ready made 1 set light horse accoutrements with carbines and a valuable invoice of Medicine chests! the Ship the most valuable out of 45 sail! the rest of her cargo trunks of Silk gowns and dry goods suitable for Gen. Burgoynes army at Quebec, the Ship haled down her colours to the Sloop Providence; she mounted 12 carriage guns and had between 60 & 70 men, the Alfred and the Snow coming down on us we then manned the Malech and ordered both for New Bedford, where they arrived safe. As soon as they arrived, without trial, for the Malech, she was onloaded and all the clothing taken out and waggons prepared to send them on to Gen. Washingtons army, at that time his army being in a distressed situation for clothing, and in this Ship was every article for a Soldier from the hat, to the shoes and at that time I can say with pleasure I had rather taken her, than a Spanish Gallion with hard money, although we took Continental money for our parts of all the prizes. We cruised off Halifax until we took 3 more Ships their cargoes seacoal &c when we had a violent snow storm, it being in the month of Nov. we [Providence] parted with Com. Jones and then we put away for Rhode Island and arrived the last of Nov. and the Alfred arrived safe at Boston. Shortly after (the 6th of Dec.) the British took possession of Newport. The ship Warren, Ship Providence & Sloop Providence, lay near Gould Island but we made the best of way to Providence, while the British fleet was running into Narriganset bay, the Sloop Providence had some men on shore on Gould Island cutting wood. I perceived a large quantity of hay stacked up there. I ordered one of the men to give me a brand of fire. I stepped into the barge and our sloop hove too, until I set fire to all the hay on the Island, as I well knew it would fall into the hands of the British, and all I received for this was the loss of silver knee buckle, and a Waistcoat, but had great contentment of mind which money cannot purchase. then we hauled our wind for the north end of Jamestown Island, the wind being S.W. as soon as we opened Narriganset bay, there was nothing to be seen but Ships, we under easy sail wishing some of them to give chase, we lay in the way until we gave them 3 shot, when immediately 3 of their ships with all sail they could pack gave us chase, which we wanted, we under easy sail stood up for Warwick neck; they finding we intended to get them a ground, signal was given from the Com. of the British Fleet and they gave up the chase, & then we went up for Providence. A short time after, one of our prize Ships running in for New Port was taken after receiving a number of shot, being cut off by one of their Ships near Prudence Island, and carried back to Newport, so ends this cruise.

1776–1777: Behind the Blockade

Dec. 6th 1776. This day my Father and Mother and a kinswomen and a young son of my Brothers went off for East Greenwich, they had but a few hours notice, they took with them some beds, and bedding, and a few trunks with clothing, and left there home with all the remainder of the furniture behind, with their wood, provisions, and every thing necessary for the Winter, and fortunate for them, the day they arrived at East Greenwich they fell in with Mr. Peleg Olden, who took them into his house, and treated them with every kindness that a good man could do, but to end this affair, all that he left behind, was lost partly by the British, but mostly by our own people. I will stop here, and now our Sloop Providence is at Providence fitting for another cruise and now it is Jan. 1777. we heard at Providence, that a British frigate called the Diamond had got a ground near Warwick neck, we went down with the Sloop, and one armed Galley, and we had 2. 18 pounders, which were [placed] on the point, at Warwick neck, which were played well on her during the night, but they started the water, and lighted her, that she floated before day, and went down for Newport, so that next day we returned to Providence, and soon after another ship took her station, not so near Warwick neck, at the same time we had a fire Brig, and Sloop fitting at Providence and soon was ready we went down the river with them, in the night waiting for a favorable time to chain them together. The time shortly came when we under took to chain them, but a sudden breeze of wind sprung up before we could chain, and the sloop-fire-vessel, got so near the ship she was obliged to run ashore, near East Greenwich, and we sat her on fire rather than she should fall into the hands of the enemy.

1777: Visit to Occupied Newport

The Brig and Sloop *Providence* returned to Providence. In a day or two after, I went over on a party to Capt. Nicholas Websters, to Rehobeth, while I was on this party Governor Hopkins & Com. Hopkins sent over Capt. Henry Dayton to me, for to come to Providence immediately, after they informed me that they contemplated fixing out a Cartel to send to Newport and for me to take out of the Sloop Providence 2 men to go with me, as there was some prisoners coming from Boston, and one Capt. Ayeres of Boston was to go Captain of the Cartel, as he was not to know who we were; that was a going his men, from that time I began to let my beard grow so as to disguise me, I took 2 of our midshipman from the Sloop Providence. The time soon arrived when the British prisoners came with Capt. Ayeres from Boston, we one and all disguised ourselves in the sailors dress, and made sail for Newport, and came to anchor near the long wharf, when Shortly—a barge come from the ship renown of 50 guns, laying outside—the fort. I informed Capt. Ayers and the British officer that our cable was so poor, we should be [here John Trevett's original diary begins] Apt to go ashore If we was to go out side of the fort Island, by that Meains the Barge went on Board and Brought A Midshipman and Some Men with him to take Charge of the Cartele and the British ALowed Capt. Ares to Gon on Shore When the Prisoners was Landed and he went to Mr. Thomas Townsends. Very Cold Wether and the Cove Froze over I had Plesher of a Veu of the Diment [Diamond] Friget laing on a Crene beLow the Long Wharfe stoping up her Bruzes we Gave her the Week before att Warrick Neck—and now I was Contriving how I Should Gett on Shore I Says nothing on My Tew Ship mates but noing we had but one Gang Cask of Warter on Board we had Plenty of Good Rum and Sugar noing that Sailors Liked a Sling or Can Hook in the Morning Such Bitter Could Wether; in the Night I stepe Down the Hole and Turnd the Gang Cask Bung Down So thatt in the Morning we had no Water on Board. You must think I went by the Name of Jack by My Ship Mates So as to Deseve Capt. Ares. Att Day Light as I Expected our British officer Wanted A Sling as Jack was Very Attentive he Says to Me have You Got any Good Spirits Aboard I informd as Good As Jamaca Could Afford then he Says Make a Good Sling well to to the Northward I Emeadely Told My Ship Mate Tom as that was the Name he went by then; to Gett the Warter While I would Gett the Rum and Sugar Redy Tom went into the Hole and Sune Returnd swearing; and Said by Some Axsident the Cask had Gott Bung Down and thare was no Warter on Board this was a Short Time After Day Light in the Morning the Officer Turns to Me and Says Jack Do You Know Whare You Can Gett Warter handy. I informed him that I had Sailed from this Place Some time before and told him there was some Good Warter Neair the Long Wharfe Jack Says this officer Step in the Boat with tew hands and that was our Tew Midship Man Tom & Bill that was the Names we Sailed by then Now the officer Gave us a Strick Charge Not be Gone More than Twenty Minets—This was Jest What I wanted I went into Mr. Philip Wantons Dock took out the Gang Cask and My Tew Mas Mates Carred itt up I went with them into Mr. Wantons Wash Room Whare tha had a Pump with Good Warter in the well [who] Should I See thare must Mr. George Lawton A Washing His Hands I Asked him to Len Me a funel to fill the Gang Cask he inform Me he had none but told Me Mrs Batte on the Long Wharfe had one I See Mr Lawton

Cast is Eye on Me hard butt made My Self Scase I gos to Mrs. Battes on the Long Wharfe finding She was ALone and Making a fire I new her well I asked Mrs. Battey to Le[nd] Me a Funel She Ansered Very Short no as no Soul was [near] I Goes up to her and Told her She Shou[ld] Lend Me one S[he] New My Mode of Speking and Says for God Sake Whare are You from I informed her from Providence She Says How Did You Leve My Son Mening Capt. Henry Dayton I informed her well now Says Mrs. Batte Speake Low for I Gott over head Severel of the officers of the British Transports Boards with Me and I Expect Mr. Batte a Shore this Morning as he is a pilot on Board of one of the Ships of War and iff he Sees You he May nowe You heair is the Funel will You Eat or Drink Any thing I told her no . . I must Remark fore or 5 Months before I took up this same Batte for a Torri. I had the Warter filled in a short time and Carred the Funel Back she had a Good Eole of Conversation and before I Left her she Said she was Affraid her Son and I should be Hanked for the British surtenly would Beait the Americans. I Larfed att her and said that Can never be; & I Never see no More of her I than went to the Longboat & Gott in the Gang Cask of Water and than the Tide was About Half Down I Says To Tom & Wm. them was My Shore Mates Leff the boat new Ground for I want to take A Cruse Around the Town Which thay Did I then went to Mr. Peleg Barkers Whare the Commander of the Hashens Quarterd I found Sentres att the Frunt Doors and Likewise Att the Wharf ware Sentres; I went Down Across Tew Wharfes Below and went into the Back Doors I found the Ketchen full of Hushens As I was well Acquainted with the House I shaped My Corse for the S West Rum thare I found Mr. Barkers Familey and Likewise Deacon Peckham from MedelTown Which I was Very Glad to see Alltho tha ware Very much Frited to see Me Thare I sune Got them Reaconsiled & told tthem to Make them Selves Ezea for I believed I new Whate I was Aboute we sune Got into Conversation I made All Inquira What and Whare and What Name of Trupes ware on the Island and Whare tha ware statined I was Much Plesed to Gett this Account I had no Expectation of; After I Got All the Information I could Gett thare I went to Mr. Waldrons thare tha had no Trupes Quarted thare I found a small family Dog My Farther had left behind Moving away in Such hast. I Lett him stay until I went to Capt. Lillebreges on the Parade then It was About Eleven A Clock AM he Kept A Tavern I went in & Called for a sling the Room was Crowded with Some British & some Heshan officers. I Emeadily went into the Kitchen Whare the Family ware Noing that Capt. Lillibrige had bene ill Treated by the British and had no Regard for them In a short time followed him out to the Barn and no one [being near] I made My self none to him he Emeadly Left the Barn . . . & went into the East Roome by our Selves he Gave Me what Refreshment I wanted and thare I Could see All the British officers & solgers & old Refege Torres Walking About the Parade but he Could not help Sheding Tears for My safty for feair of one of our Towns Men that visited his house all times in the Day of noing Me I was A Veuing the Parade When This one of the worst of Villians His Name Was William Crosen Came Rı ning up the

Steps Came Right to the East Door ware Capt. Lillibrige and I had been for some time he was not sune Anuf for I steped to the Door and I had My finger on the Lache and he suposed itt was fast went Emeadily thrue the Bar Room into the Ketchen I never bid My friend Capt. Lillibrige Good by steped out on the Parade and direct before Me Was Mr. John Wanton he spoke to Me and Called Me by My Name but I Did not Anser him and went Emeadetly Down the Long Wharf Quck Step I went Round the point and Came to Mr. Waldrons Whare My family Dog was thare I spent some time Got some Refreshment then itt was About 3 Aclock I thort by this time our boat would be Afloat I than bed Mrs. Waldron and the Family Good by took my faverite Dog and Went for the boat Jest as I Gott Neair Whare Mr. Jacob Richardson Leves on the Long Wharfe I mett the Midshipman Jest Goot on shore he handed Me out a Few Cuses & Dams I informed him that our boat had Gott Aground he told Me to go on Board Emeaditly for says he You Got some Dam Good frinds heair I said but Littel Made the Best of My way to the boat found her Afloat and My Comrades Waiting for Me we soone Roaed of but I must not forgett I saw Mr. Peleg Barker and his son Peleg Agoing Down the Long Wharfe And Eyeing our Boat and I well new the Antsiety tha had to see Me Gott on Board the Cartelle as she Lay of the head of the Long Wharfe we Very sune Goot Aboard and had not bene Long on Board Before Capt. Ares was orderd on board as itt had bene Reported that I was att Newport but Very Few would Beleve itt, Capt Ares said if itt had not bene for Me he Could have staid on shore I informed him I thort itt Must be A mistake but the Next Day we took in some Pasingers & some American Pisners and orderd for Providence the wind being Partly a head we ware obliged to beat some before we Goot by a British Ship of War that Lay off from Prudence but as sune as we Goot by the uper Ship I Left Tending the Jib Sheat and went Arft I says to Wm Come now take Your Turn forward so I took the Helm I see Capt. Areas Eyed Me; as I thort itt was not Long before we Got Abrest of Pertucksett Whare our sloop Providence Lay the Barge Emeadely Came ALong side I took one Man in My Rome to Work the Cartile up to Comadore Whipoles ship and I went on Board the sloop Providence I had then Anserd All and More than All My Expectations for I had in My head All thare Ships of War and Ware tha ware stained I Emeadely Shaved & Dresed My Self in My Sunday Dress I proseded Emeadely on Board Commadore Whipels Ship Whare I found Capt Ares; Arfter Capt Ares had Gone threu his Conversation the Comadore Turns to Me and asked Me What I had Descoverd Capt. Ares Looked Att Me and Did not now me; Arfter we had Gone Thru Capt Ares Turns to Me I Would not Run the Resk for the Cartele Loaded with Dollars I told him I had Anserd All My Expectations and More than I Expected.

1777: Escape frpm the Blockade, and a Cruise with Captain Pitcher

And now I am once More on Board the Sloop Providence and I find Johnathon Pitcher Esqr. is to Take the Command and we Only waiting for a Good Chance and now itt is Febuar and we Made sail Att sunset A Light Aind to the NE standing Down the River past one ship of Prudence and Went thrue Narraganset Bay And Run so Neair a 50 gun ship About 2 A M as to heair them A Talking on Board And Att sun Rize we ware becarmd About Tew Miles from the Light House and Could See Newport and the ships in the Harbor Abought Ten A M A small Breze sprunk from the S. West we standing to the East Ward We Arrived Att Bedford that Night we had but few Men on Boad as tha Could not Expect that we should Gett out of Providence River we Got Her Mandd and sailed on a Cruse to the Eastward Nothing Material Hapening untel we Arrived of Cape Bretton About 5 Legs. East Cape Breton in Sight; Saw several sail and herd a Number of Heve Cannon the Night before one Brigg Bore Down on us and began A fire Att Long Shot we Run from her About one Hour untell we Got in Good order for Action then we took in sail and Lett her Come up Close A Long Side and the Sea Very Smuth in forty Menets we Cut Away All her Cullers and tha began to be slak in a few Menets the began the fire as Brisk as Ever and Cut our sails and Riging Badly one 6 lb short we [   ] Lettel below the Hounds of the Mast itt Lasted About 40 Menets Longer When we Cut away her Main Top Mast and we Hailed them without A Trumpet being Close in on her Starboard Quarter and the Stoped Firing to no Wether tha give up or not And the Answer was Yes Capt. Petcher was badly Hert but Kept the Deck ontill she Gave Up but I can tell You itt was Dimon Cut Dimon Capt. Petcher sent me in the Barge first on board I found them a Vere Bloody Deck and Quarter Deck and her Spar's sailes & Riging Very Much Damaged I staied on Board untel I sent the Capt. on board our Sloop but a Going Down in the Cabin the Flouers was Spread as full of Wounded Men, as You Could scasley find Room to put You foot and I foun tha ware some of them Irish as tha Cry out for Jeses Sake to Spar's thare Lives tha ware Very Badly Wounded we found her to be A Brigg Directly from England she had Twenty fife Soldyers and Tew British officers and thare own Crew she was Loaded With Kings Stores, and Bound for Quebeck As sune as the Action was Over we found our Sloop so Wounded in the Marst & Spairs that we ware obliged to send Down her Top sail Yard & Top Mast and we Maned the Brigg and that Night the Wind Blew Hard with Squarls & Dark the Next Morning we found no More of Her Capt. Pitcher ordered her for Bedford and we ware Obliged to Give up our Cruse and put Away for Nantucket and in a short time we Arrived att Bedford Carring with us all our New Bergoine Soldyers and Officers and some sea Men we are now fixing our Vesel this is beginin of May 1777 and I find that Capt. John Peck Rathbun is to take Capt. Pitchers plase as he Went on to Congress and Got His Appointment one Werd More A Better officer then Capt. Petcher I think Can not be our Prisners ware sent to Boston only a few of them Run Away as tha Chose to stay in a frea Cuntry So Ends this short Cruse—

May 1777 We are Now fixing our Vesel for Capt. John P. Rathbun And I have Jest Recevd an Account of My Brother Constant Church Trevett being Taken. He Commanded a Mercht. Vesel Bound from the West Endeas to Carolina and was Taken by the British and sent for New York and put on Board A British Prison ship Called the Old Jersey I Emeadely sent on to Boston and Procurd a British Capt to send to New York and itt was Done in a short time but Tew Late; for before the British Capt. Arrived he was no More He Died with hared Treatment from the British Piruts as I May say & say the Truth, Black Bard the Notoris Pirut was A Christian to them Bilingate Villins that had the Command Att New York I shortly Arfter saw some Americans that was on Board the same Prison ship My Brother ware tha ware Exchanged and had Gott Home Butt tha Most of them lucked as if tha ware in a Deap Consumtion I herd a Nuff from My Poor Americans to Convince Me that iff I had My Choise I had Rather be Taken by Turks; but I must stop short Heair and say but Lettel Mark well Revenge is swiet.

1778: Voyage in the Mary, *from New Providence to Martha's Vineyard*

I had not Got on Board the ship for we saw a ship Bearing Down on us I Got on Board the ship and then we parted the ship standing for the sloop we Allterd our Course in the ship and the Next Morning we Gott by Abaco and see no More of ship Nor sloop and now we Making the Best of our way for Block Island I had the Log book Kept in the same Maner as If Capt. Henry Johnson had the Comand bound for New York this I had Dune in Case I had Come Acrors any British Cruser and I Did not intend to Run out of My Way from Any ship! We saw a Number of sails on our Pasage but never spoke with Any the first Land we Made was the Vinyard we are now Runing Down for Nantucket itt is now 18 Days since we Parted with the sloop Providence and we have had Very Cold Wither and hard Gailes out of thirty Men thare is not more than ten but Whos has thare Hands & feet froze one Man froze to Death his Name was James Dark. He informed Me When I took him att New Providence that he had bene taken by a British Privatear and that He belonged to Vergenea this Day we Ankerd under Nantucket the Wind still blowing Very heard so that we Can not Gett on shore we firing segnul guns the Next Day the Wind Continus Blowing so no boat Can Come on Board I thout itt Nesesere to bure James Dark and we Did itt in a Desent Maner the therd Day severel Boats from the shore Came on board being Very short of Provison sent on shore and Purchesed fife sheep so we ware well Provided with fresh Peck; the Wind Abates now A sail in sight Runing Down the south side of Nantucket; the Nantucket Men Not Less than Twenty on board our ship she stood Down for our ship these Men Agred one and All that itt was the Harlem Privatear from New York Now we Got under Way I Made the Nantucket Men an offer to sheair All Equal A Like for I should take her; out of the 20 I thing thare was Tew stood by us we stood for Each Other and before we Got up with her we Discoverd her to be the sloop Providence that we had parted with of Abaco As we Pased her we ware Rejoced to see them we had not time to Draw our shot and we Gave them A salute and tha Returnd in the same Maner we hove About and followed the sloop in; the Wind Modorrates Run and under Nantucket and we Came to Anker as the Wind would not Admit of Going over the Shoules this is the 20 of Feba. 1778 A Light are of Wind att N. Eeast and Lukes Like A storm Runing by the Round Shoule the snow begins to fly Quick & the blow Encreses; now a snow storm and so thik we can not see but a short Distanc Runing for Cape Poge About 12 Aclock our ship struck very hard on a shole Neair the Hors shue we had Very hard time A Considrabel of a sea we Kept. All sail on her until we Got Acrost the shole and Depened our warter and then we Lett go our Anker but Before we Goot of this shoul we Lost our Ruder and stove our Boat on Deck the Next Morning we found the sloop Providence Gott on shore Going into Old Town but sune Got of Again the Next Day by the Asistance of Boats we Got safe into Old Town thare we Discharged our Cargo Consisting of Rum Molases Sugers Corfea some Indego & Cotton a Valuable Cargo some part of our Cargo sent Down to the Hi anners [Hyannis] some to Boston but the Most sent to Bedford so Ends this Cruse

1778: Overland Trip to Yorktown

Now is March 1778 we are Arrived with the sloop Providence at Bedford the ship [Mary] we Left att Old Town Reparing and Getting a New Ruder then we are A going to Bring her to Bedford—Capt. Rathbun and My self sett out for Boston to Call on the Board of Warr [Navy Board of the Eastern Department] setting thare we spent part of Tew Days and Returnd to Tarnton [Taunton] Capt. Rathbun sett out for his Home and Left Me Att Tarnton to Go to Plimouth with Lawyer Paine of Tarnton to the Triall of the ship we had the Triall and itt Did not suite the Capters as she was a Commishon ship we Appeailed to a Hier Pope so that I Returnd to Tarnton with Lawyer Paine; Letters Rote to one Mr. Lewis Att Congress from Mr. Paine and a Number of Papers Lawyer Paine furnished Me with to send on to Congress then sett out for York Town [York, Pennsylvania] and in June [1778] I went on My Jurnea and I never Experenced so Hott Wether in America in My Life I Cripeled one Hors by the time I Arrived att A plase Called Crumpond Whare Col. Green and Majr. Flagg Lost thare Lives by the Refeges from New York Nothing Material Hapining till I Gott wel on to a Town Called Monmouth the Day before I Arrived thare fell in with a Grand Trupe of Light Hors Going Threw a Large an Loong Wood I was a Lone; I Drew My self a Lettel one side to see them parse Me and I was of a Pinyon that thare ware British Light Horse until I Rode fore Miles on My way and stoped to an inn and thare tha Informed Me that tha Ware Generul Washingtons Light Horse In thing I never wished to see Abutefule sight and so Grate a Number I had on a uniform Coat and a Coxade in My Hatt I thout tha ware no End to them tha pased Me on Acanter a Compliment by Hand not one Werd was said

by officers nor Men I then Proseded on My Jurne the Next Morning Early
I herd a Numer of smal Arms Discarged I sune Lernt that the British
Trupes had Left Philadelphia on thare Way to New York and the Ameri-
cans had Come up with A part of them this was as Hot Wether I think as
Ever I felt in the West indes the Next Day I parsed thru Whare I Came a
thart some Dead Bodeys that was not barred I was informed the Day
before that a Number Died with the Heait A Dringing Warter out of the
Broocks Nothing Material Hapening untill I Arrived att York Town, I saw
Governer [John] Collins & Wm. Ellery Esqr. was our Tew Dillegates att
the Time from the state of Rhodisland in Tew or thre Days Arfter I
Arived att York Town Congress Adjirned to Philadulphia, I then I sett out
for Philadeulphia Arfter I Arrived there I Called on Mr. Wm. Lewis An
Attorney and Employed him to Do My Buzness I Left Henry Johnsons
Comisson & the Log Book of the ship Mary with Mr. Lewis and so much
Money What he Agread to Do the Buzness for, Then I Made the Best of
My Way for Providence in the state of Rhodisland I Arrived att Provi-
dence in July When I Arrived att Providence I herd of Bedford being Burnt
I sett out for Tarnton & Bedford I found A Grate part of our Cargo Bunt
in the stores att Bedford and our ship Mary had got Feted att Old Town
Gott as far As Woodes Hole When the British burnt Bedford and Fare-
haven tha Burnt our ship att that time att Woodsis Hole so this Finished
My Jurne to York Town—

Trevett Leaves the Providence
        . . . as I have since the first of the War had no time to settel My own
besness I will take this Oppertunity and I sett out for East Grenwitch
Whare My Farther then Lived I had not bene att My farthers but A short
time before itt so hapened Early in A Morning Very fogge Morning I herd
the firing of Musketry I Emmeadtly Looked out of the Winder and saw
severel of Col. Greens Black Regment Making the Best of thare Way for
Portewume Directly Came by Lieut. Snow with A small fild pese I went
bacf of the House My Farther Lived in Whare was a small fort and put
some Musket Cartreges in My Pocket and then sett out for the shore the
fogg Breaking Away I saw the Remainder of Capt. John Alens House
Burning att the same time saw the Refege Fleet Comanded by one Leonard; one of his Tenders Aground Neair the shore Lieut Snow Gott His
field Pese Abrest of her and with the Help of some Muskets; we Kept the
Men from Getting her of and firing att the Remainder of the Fleet untill
tha bore Away and Run for Newport we Goot the Tender of and carried
her into Grenwitch and found the Refeges had not forgott Thare theving
buzness for thare was Plunder that tha had stole from Capt. Allen some
Life Calves and Other Afaires—All that I Did was Priming the field Pese
with the Carteriges I had in My Pocket and I had no Expectatoneither Did
I want any thing When the Prize was sold Col Green orderd Twenty fife
Dollars for My sheair—itt was Plesing [to me] for itt was not more then

fore or fife Hours that I was gone from Hone; that I Made Mone in fore or fife Hours att this time then I Did With Comadore Hopkins in Our Long Cruse of Take in New Providence the first time. So Ends this frakus—

APPENDIX F

THE NARRATIVE OF THOMAS PHILBROOK*

In the spring of this year, 1779, I engaged with Capt. [Hoysteed] Hacker, to go a cruise in the continental sloop Providence, but before we could get ready for sea, the Penobscot expedition was fitting out, and we were ordered to join that fleet. All the movements were slow and tardy, and it was not until near the last of June that the fleet could be got together. The armed force consisted of the Warren frigate, 36 guns, and Providence sloop, 14 guns; these were the only continental vessels, the rest were all private property belonging to Boston and Salem, and hired by the State of Massachusetts. They consisted of nine ships of from twenty-two to eighteen guns: six brigs of sixteen and eighteen guns, and forty coasting sloops of about one hundred tons each, employed as transports. The fleet was commanded by Commodore [Dudley] Saltonstall, of New London, and the land forces by Gen. [Solomon] Lovell, of Hingham. We sailed from Boston, (I think the last of June), the next day we anchored in Portland harbor to receive on board a part of the troops. We tarried here several days, and then sailed for Broad bay, where we were to receive the remainder of the militia. Hence we wasted several more days seemingly, for no other purpose, but to give the enemy sufficient time to prepare for us. We, however, got to Penobscot at last, having been twelve or fourteen days in making the passage, which we certainly might have done in four or five. We sailed up the bay, until abreast of the British garrison, where we anchored; taking special care to keep out of the reach of their guns. The fort is situated on a point of land formed by the junction of the Bagaduce and Penobscot Rivers, on a gently elevated piece of land which appears to have been cleared and cultivated for a number of years. The breast-work or fort was rather a rough looking concern, built with logs and dirt, and not more than three or three and a half feet high, which our long-legged militiamen would have straddled over without much difficulty. We expected that the troops would have been landed the next morning after our arrival, but the morning came and the day passed without any movement; some hard speeches were handed round at the expense of the General. The next passed as the former, but not without much grumbling. The British had two ships of twenty-eight and twenty-four guns, laying in the mouth of Bagaduce river, (this was all the naval force they had.) Our captain and the captain of one of the armed brigs, thought to have a little diversion and drive them from their moorings. This they got liberty to do. At sunset, I landed with thirty marines from the Providence, with as many more from the brig, all under the command of Capt. R.[obert] Davis, of the continental army. We landed on a small island of two or three acres lying in the mouth of the Bagaduce, about a

* Excerpted from Spirit of '76 in Rhode Island: or, Sketches of the Efforts of the Government and People in the War of the Revolution, by Benjamin Cowell, published in 1850.

mile below the ships. The island was thickly covered with wood and underbrush, we soon found our way to the summit (which was not very much elevated,) and commenced erecting a breast-work. We were very industrious through the night, making as little noise as possible, that we might not be heard on board the ships. Before the break of day, we had our works completed and received from one of the ordinance transports, three long 18 pounders, which we soon had mounted; as it began to grow light, we trimmed up a tall spruce tree on which we hoisted our flag and saluted our neighbors with the well loaded guns. This I believe, was the first they knew of our being so near them, as they appeared to be perfectly still and quiet; and by the time it took them to get ready to return our morning call, a brisk fire was kept up from us and from the ships; we could frequently see our shot hull them, so that we must have done them considerable damage; they generally over-shot us, but unfortunately, one of their shot struck the top of our breast-work and killed two men and wounded three others. After about three hours' firing the ships slipped their cables and moved up the river, out of the reach of our shot. We next went to work, cleared a piece of ground, and built us some comfortable huts to lodge in until further orders. Our little settlement we called Hacker's Island. We had now been here five or six days and the troops were not landed. A general uneasiness pervaded all ranks, both among the sailors and soldiers, something must be wrong. Our general was said to be a *very good sort of man,* but these good sort of men seldom make good Generals. I recollect that I thought then, and I still think that Mr. Lovell would have done more good, and made a much more respectable appearance in the deacon's seat of a country church, than at the head of an American army. It was, however, at last agreed upon to land the troops. (I think it was the morning of the seventh day after our arrival.) The place selected for landing was very injudiciously chosen, being a high bank covered with small trees and shrubs, with an ascent of at least forty-five degrees, whereas, about half a mile distant was a fine level cleared spot, sufficiently large to hold the whole army, where we might have landed under the cover of the guns of one or two of our ships without the loss of a man. This appeared very strange to us all, at the time, but I believe that all were of the opinion afterwards that the old General had agreed to go snacks with the Commodore in whatever they were to have for defeating the expedition. We were however, landed at the place appointed. The marines were first set on shore on the beach, some musket shot were fired at us from the brow of the hill, but we were at too great a distance from them to receive any damage. When the marines were all landed and about half the militia, we began our ascent, which was indeed a very difficult one; had it not been for the shrubs growing on the sides of the hill, we might have lost half our men before we gained the height. Though I was not encumbered with a musket, I found it difficult to keep my footing. When we had ascended about one third of the distance, the British from the brow, began a brisk fire upon us, which they kept up till we were within a few rods of the top; they then courageously fled and left the ground to us. In this ascent we had forty men killed and Capt. [John] Welch, of the marines on board the Warren frigate, a very amiable young gentleman, and a brave officer. Our brave General did not lead the van in their ascent, neither did he bring up the rear, probably he and the Commodore were walking the Warren's quarter deck with their spyglasses to see the fun. I saw him two hours after on the hill, giving orders about building huts, for which he probably was well calculated. With the marines belonging to the Providence and brig Tryall, we returned to our little isle, where we found good cheer and comfortable quarters. In three or four days the militia were comfortably housed as if we had come to spend the summer with our English neighbors, when everybody knew, that knew any thing, that an express had been sent to Halifax, and that they would be prompt in sending a reinforcement which might be expected in a very short time. Councils of war were held every day on board the Commodore's ship; the result commonly was, the Commodore and General could not agree, probably they had agreed in one point, and engaged not to agree in any other. Thus, day after day passed away without any thing being done. Some of the captains of the fleet frequently landed on the Bagaduce shore, either to amuse themselves by rambling in the woods, or to reconnoiter the enemy. In one of these excursions, the Commodore being with them, they spent the most of an afternoon; towards evening they were discovered from one of the English ships, and immediately a boat with a company of soldiers was sent on shore. On seeing the boat put off from the ship, they each made the best of their way for their boat which they had left waiting for them. They all reached the boat nearly at the same time, but the Commodore was missing. They waited, but he came not; it began to grow dark, the British boat had returned to the ship; finally, at 9 o'clock, they concluded to leave him to his fate and take care of themselves. The next morning at sunrise, he was seen on the beach, and a boat immediately sent to take him off. He said he was closely pursued, and in making his escape he had got so far into the woods, that he could not find the way out in the dark, but it was generally believed that he found a very good berth on board one of the British ships. Tumults now ran high, the General was hissed and hooted at wherever he made his appearance, and the Commodore cursed and execrated by all hands. Capt. Hacker offered, with the Providence and the six brigs that if the General would attack the fort, all the men from the ships would gladly join him; he, (Capt. Hacker) would enter the river with the small vessels and engage to bring out the English ships. But no, it was not feasible;—according to the best accounts we could get, the British had only five hundred effective men in their garrison. Their naval force we knew was only two small ships. We had between three and four thousand militia, with sixteen ships and brigs well armed and manned. It is strange that these spirited fellows were kept peaceable so long; the sailors indeed, talked hard of leaving their ships, and under a commander of their own choice, pushing forward and storming the fort. A single word of encouragement from any of the captains in the fleet, would have set them in rapid motion, and I have no doubt but they would have succeeded, but we had dallied away our time too long: more than thirty days had been spent in idleness since our first anchoring, and not a single movement made to annoy the enemy. On a fine summer's morning, five lofty ships were discovered in the offing. All knew who they were, for all had expected them for some time; it was now all hilter skilter. The men from the shore were ordered to embark as soon as possible, and the fleet to weigh anchor or slip their cables and proceed up the river. We were soon under sail with a fair wind. The English ships were not more than three miles from us, but the wind so favored us, that we kept clear from their shot. As we came towards the head of navigation, the Warren frigate grounded, was immediately cleared of her men and blown up. The other ships soon followed her example, and as fast as they could land their men and some stores, set fire to their vessels and left them. Our retreat was as badly managed as the whole expedition had been. Here we were, landed in a wilderness, under no command; those belonging to the ships, unacquainted with the woods, and only knew that a west course would carry us across to Kennebec; whereas, there were hundreds of the militia that were old hunters, and knew the country. Some of these ought to have been detained as pilots, and we might have got through in three days; but we had no one to direct; so every one shifted for himself. Some got to their homes in two days, while the most of us were six or seven days before we came to an inhabited country. I got through on the seventh day, after keeping a fast of three days. From Portland, I took passage in the frigate Boston, Capt. [Samuel] Tucker, was treated with much politeness by him and his officers.

Notes

Chapter I

1. John Russell Bartlett, *The Destruction of the Gaspee*, 116.
2. Ibid., 16–21.
3. Captain James Wallace to Vice Admiral Samuel Graves, 12 Dec. 1774, PRO Admiralty 1/485, LC transcript.
4. Remarks &c on board His Majesty's Ship *Rose*, 26 April 1775, PRO Admiralty 1/485, LC transcript.
5. Simon Pease to Nicholas Brown & Co., Nicholas Brown Papers, JCBL.
6. Gage Papers, CL.
7. Mass. Archives, vol. 143, 80.
8. Bulletin, Fort Ticonderoga Museum, IV 3: 65.
9. *Newport Mercury*, May 8, 1775.
10. Dr. Ezra Stiles Literary Diary, Force transcript, LC. Hereinafter referred to as Stiles Diary.
11. John Brown to Ambrose Page and Nicholas Cooke, 12 June 1775, Misc. Mss., RIHS.
12. Bartlett, *Colonial Records of Rhode Island*, vol. VII, 346–347.
13. *Proceedings*, American Antiquarian Society, XXXVI, 252–254.
14. Samuel Green Arnold, *History of the State of Rhode Island*, 350–351, n.

Chapter II

1. PRO Admiralty 1/485.
2. Ibid.
3. Stiles Diary, June 15, 1775.
4. Captain James Wallace to Vice Admiral Samuel Graves, 19 June 1775, PRO Admiralty 1/485.
5. Abraham Whipple, Message to Congress, June 10, 1786, Whipple Papers, RIHS.
6. Nicholas Cooke Correspondence, AAS *Proceedings*, New Series XXXVI, 256.
7. Whipple Papers, RIHS.
8. PRO Admiralty 1/485.
9. *Newport Mercury*, August 14, 1775.
10. *Providence Gazette*, August 5, 1775.
11. Stiles Diary, August 10, 1775.
12. *New York Journal*, August 31, 1775.
13. PRO Admiralty, 51/804.
14. Bartlett, *Colonial Records of Rhode Island*, VII, 368–374.
15. PRO Admiralty 1/485.
16. John C. Fitzpatrick, ed., *The Writings of George Washington*, III, 385–388.
17. Washington Papers, LC.
18. Fitzpatrick, III, 420.
19. Collections, RIHS, VI, 119, 120.
20. Ibid, 123, 124.
21. Fitzpatrick, 476–478.
22. Collections, RIHS.
23. Nicholas Cooke to George Washington, September 15, 1775, Washington Papers, LC.

24. *Autograph Letters of George Washington, from the Collection of Frederick S. Peck, Barrington, R. I.*
25. Collections, RIHS, V, 133.

Chapter III

1. Graves Conduct, British Museum, 128–129.
2. R. I. Mss., vol. XII, RIHS, 121.
3. Bartlett, *Colonial Rrecords of Rhode Island*, VII, 368–374.
4. John Adams, *The Works of John Adams*, III, 6–8.
5. W. C. Ford, *Journals of the Continental Congress*, III, 278–279.
6. Nicholas Cooke Correspondence, AAS *Proceedings*, New Series, XXXVI, 277–278.
7. Nicholas Cooke Papers, RIHS, vol. I.
8. Ford, JCC III, 293–294.
9. Ford, ed., Webb Papers, I, 107–110.
10. Ford, ed., JCC III 311–312.
11. PRO Admiralty 1/485.
12. *Newport Mercury*, Nov. 13, 1775.
13. Cooke Mss., RIHS.
14. Collections, RIHS, VI, 135, 136.
15. *Providence Gazette*, Dec. 2, 1775.
16. The supposition that Rathbun was prizemaster of the schooner is based on the fact that, although his navy pay dated from 20 Nov. 1775, like the others who sailed in the *Katy*, he did not report aboard the fleet until 10 Feb. 1776.

Chapter IV

1. Nicholas Brown Papers, JCBL.
2. Ford, ed., JCC III, 395–402.
3. Ibid., 402.
4. Simon Gratz Autograph Collection, HSP.
5. Knollenberg, ed., Ward Papers, RIHS.
6. Nicholas Cooke to Samuel Ward and Stephen Hopkins, Dec. 12, 1775. Morristown National Historical Park, Morristown, N. J.
7. Nicholas Cooke Papers, RIHS.
8. Joshua Humphrey Ship Yard Accounts, Ledger D, HSP.
9. James Wharton Day Book, HSP.
10. Charles Roberts Autograph Collection, HCL, 723.
11. Nicholas Brown Papers, JCBL.
12. Ibid.
13. Ford, ed., JCC III, 378–387.
14. PRO Admiralty 1/484, 3, 613.
15. Papers, Continental Congress (Letters of John Hancock and Miscellaneous Papers), 58, 239–240, NA.
16. Hopkins Papers II, 41, RIHS.
17. Harbeck Collection, HUL.
18. Esek Hopkins to John Hancock, 9 April 1776, Papers, CC, 78, XI, 33–35, NA.

19. PRO Admiralty 1/240; enclosed in Barkley to Gayton, March 21, 1776.
20. *Andrew Doria* Journal, PRO Admiralty 1/484.
21. "Journal of John Trevett, USN," *Rhode Island Historical Magazine*, vol. VI & VII, hereinafter referred to as Trevett's Journal.
22. Journal of H. M. Schooner *St. John*. PRO Admiralty 51/4330.
23. *Andrew Doria* Journal, PRO Admiralty 1/484.

Chapter V

1. Hopkins Letter Book, RIHS.
2. Force, comp., *American Archives*, 4th, V, 846–847.
3. PRO Admiralty 1/484.
4. Force, AA 4th, V, 846–847.
5. *Connecticut Courant*, May 20, 1775.
6. Hopkins Papers, RIHS.
7. Fitzpatrick, ed., *Writings of Washington*, IV, 476.
8. Hopkins Papers, RIHS.
9. Papers, CC, 58, 259, NA. An attested copy.
10. Ibid, 263–265.
11. Hopkins Papers, RIHS.
12. Hopkins Letter Book, RIHS.
13. Ibid.
14. Papers, CC, 58, 149, NA.
15. Captain John Paul Jones to Joseph Hewes, Hayes Mss, NCDAH.
16. Whipple Papers, RIHS.

Chapter VI

1. Nicholas Biddle to Charles Biddle, Capt. Nicholas Biddle Papers 1771–1778, on deposit, HSP.
2. John Paul Jones to Daniel Tillinghast, Harbeck Collection, HM 21666, HUL.
3. Simon Gratz Autograph Collection, Case 5, Box 28, HSP.
4. Etting Autograph Collection, HSP.
5. Papers, CC, 58, 161–162, NA.
6. Muster Roll, sloop *Providence*, MassHS.
7. Papers, CC, 58, 81–82, NA.
8. Ibid.
9. Ibid. 85, NA.
10. Ibid, 89, 92.
11. Ibid.
12. George L. Miner, Notebook, RIHS.
13. Jones Papers, LC.
14. Papers, CC, 58, 91–92, NA.
15. Force, AA 5th II, 443.
16. John Manley's Account Book, NHS.
17. Hopkins to John Bradford, Oct. 19, 1776. John Bradford's Letter Book, LC.

Chapter VII

1. "List of Officers & Men belonging to the Ship Alfred who are entitled to a Share of the Ship *Mellish* & Brig *Active*," *Revolutionary War Rolls*, vol. 52, p. 84, Mass. Archives.
2. Hopkins Papers, RIHS.
3. Ibid.
4. Deposition of Justin Jacobs, MSS, vol. 16, RIHS.
5. Trevett's Journal.
6. Jones Papers, LC.
7. Ibid.
8. Ibid.
9. Ibid.
10. Morison, *John Paul Jones*, p. 78.
11. Bartlett, *Colonial Records of R. I.*, vol. VIII, 112.

Chapter VIII

1. Hopkins Papers, RIHS.
2. Ibid.
3. Jones Papers, LC.
4. Field, *Esek Hopkins*, 207.
5. Morison, *John Paul Jones*, 97.
6. Trevett's Journal.
7. Cooke Correspondence, R. I. Archives.
8. Hopkins Papers, RIHS.
9. Jones Papers, LC.
10. Paullin, ed., *Out-letters of Continental Marine Committee I*, 65–71.
11. Hopkins Papers, RIHS.
12. No direct documentary evidence of Jones' and Rathbun's activities during the early months of 1777 is presently available. Deduction as to their traveling together to Philadelphia is based on their simultaneous presence there and the timing of Rathbun's journey to Boston.
13. Hopkins Papers, RIHS.
14. Cooke Correspondence, R. I. Arch.
15. Hopkins Papers, RIHS.
16. Cowell, *Spirit of R. I. in '76*, 145.
17. Hopkins Papers, RIHS.
18. Vice Admiralty Court Records, Halifax, N.S.
19. Cooke Correspondence, R. I. Arch.
20. Esek Hopkins, Jr., is, in several Hopkins' histories and a Brown University catalogue, reported as having died in Halifax prison in March 1777. However, he signed a request to go into private service in 1778, and the *Providence Gazette* on October 2 and 30, 1779, reports him sending in prizes as captain of the privateer *Lively*.

Chapter IX

1. Papers, CC, M332, R6, NA.
2. Sloop *Providence*, Muster Roll, RIHS.

3. G. S. A. Pension Application of Andrew Burnett, NA.
4. List of Officers & Men entitled to prize shares in Loyalty, etc., *Revolutionary War Rolls,* vol. 52, 15–17, Mass. Archives
5. Votes and Resolutions of the Eastern Navy Board, LC.
6. Trevett's Journal.
7. South Carolina *American & General Gazette,* Dec. 25, 1777.

CHAPTER X

Chief Source, Trevett's Journal.
1. *North Carolina Gazette,* Feb. 13, 1778.
2. Papers, CC, M247, NA.
3. Rathbun, "Rathbun's Raid on Nassau," *U. S. Naval Institute Proceedings,* Nov., 1970.

CHAPTER XI

1. Rathbun, "Rathbun's Raid on Nassau," *U. S. Naval Institute Proceedings,* Nov., 1970.
2. Papers, CC, A7, M625, NA.
3. Papers of William Vernon and the Navy Board, Publications, RIHS, 217, hereinafter referred to as Vernon Papers.
4. Ibid., 219–220.
5. Papers, CC, M332, R6, NA.
6. John Bradford's Letter Book, LC. June 17, 1778.
7. Vernon Papers, RIHS, 241.
8. Revolutionary War Petitions, Vol. 185, Mass. Archives.
9. Papers, CC, M625, R67, NA.
10. Ellis, *History of New Bedford,* 117–118.
11. Eastern Navy Board Out-letters, MassHS.
12. Ibid.

CHAPTER XII

1. *Independent Chronicle,* Boston, April 16, 1778.
2. Muster Roll, Sloop *Providence,* NHS.
3. G. S. A., Pension Application, Thomas Hiller, NA.
4. Ellis, *History of New Bedford,* 101–2.
5. Ricketson, *The History of New Bedford,* 302–3.
6. According to Ellis, op.cit., n. 102, this mound was leveled in 1830 and the skeletons reburied. In 1841 and 1889 they were again moved, finally to Oak Grove Cemetery. The medical examiner pronounced them the bones of white men.
7. Clowes, *The Royal Navy,* IV, 26.
8. Eastern Navy Board Out-letters, MassHS.
9. G. S. A., Pension Application, Thomas Hiller, NA.
10. Eastern Navy Board Out-letters, MassHS.
11. Muster Roll, Sloop *Providence,* NHS.

CHAPTER XIII

1. Cowell, *Spirit of '76 in Rhode Island*, 317.
2. Ibid., 317.
3. Papers Relating to the Penobscot Expedition, Mass. Archives, vol. 145, 88–89. (Hereinafter referred to as Penobscot Papers.)
4. Ibid.
5. Baxter, ed., *Documentary History of the State of Maine*, XVI.
6. Eastern Navy Board Out-letters, MassHS.
7. Penobscot Papers, Maine Archives.
8. Penobscot Papers, Mass. Archives, vol. 145.
9. G. S. A., Pension Application, Thomas Hiller, NA.
10. Cowell, *Spirit of '76 in Rhode Island*, 320–321.
11. Penobscot Papers, Mass. Archives, vol. 145.
12. Eastern Navy Board Out-letters, MassHS.
13. G. S. A., Pension Application, Thomas Hiller, NA.

EPILOGUE

1. Both Laird Clowes' *The Royal Navy, 1899*, and J. J. Colledge's *Ships of the Royal Navy* (Newton Abbot, 1969) list sloop *Providence*, 12 guns, Captain Hacker, captured by Sir George Collier in the Penobscot on 14 August 1779, and taken into the Royal Navy. N.A.M. Rodger of the Public Record Office, London, after extensive investigation, in a 25 June 1975 letter to the author points out that Clowes' list, which contains several errors and omissions, appears to confuse the sloop *Providence* and the ship *Providence*. The ship *Providence* is listed as destroyed, although she was certainly taken at Charlestown on 12 May 1780, commissioned in the Royal Navy, and sold in 1784. Colledge apparently repeats Clowes' error.
2. Whipple Papers, RIHS.
3. Whipple Genealogy, RIHS.

Bibliography

Manuscript Sources

British Museum, London, England (BM)
    Graves Conduct
John Carter Brown Library, Providence, Rhode Island (JCBL)
    Brown Papers
Clements Library, University of Michigan, Ann Arbor, Michigan (CL)
    Gage Papers
Haverford College Library, Haverford, Pennsylvania (HCL)
    Charles Roberts Autograph Collection
Historical Society of Pennsylvania, Philadelphia, Pennsylvania (HSP)
    Captain Nicholas Biddle Papers, 1771–1778
    Etting Autograph Collection
    Simon Gratz Collection
    Joshua Humphrey Shipyard Accounts
    James Wharton Day Book
Henry E. Huntington Library, San Marino, California (HUL)
    Harbeck Collection
Library of Congress, Washington, D.C. Manuscript Division (LC)
    John Bradford's Letter Book
    John Paul Jones Papers
    Public Record Office, London, England, Admiralty Transcripts.
    Votes and Resolutions of the Navy Board, Eastern Department,
    1777–1782
    Washington Papers
Maine Historical Society, Portland, Maine (MeHS)
    Papers Relating to the Penobscot Expedition
Massachusetts Archives, Boston, Massachusetts (Mass. Arch.)
    Papers Relating to the Penobscot Expedition
    Revolutionary War Rolls
Massachusetts Historical Society, Boston, Massachusetts (MassHS)
    Letter Book, Navy Board Eastern Department, October 23, 1778–
    October 29, 1779, New York Public Library Photostats
    Muster Roll, Sloop *Providence*
Morristown National Historic Park, Morristown, New Jersey (MNHP)
    Papers
National Archives, Washington, D.C. (NA)
    General Services Administration, Pension Applications
    Papers of the Continental Congress (Letters of John Hancock and
    Miscellaneous Papers)
Newport Historical Society, Newport, Rhode Island (NHS)
    John Manley Account Book
    Muster Rolls, Sloop *Providence*
    Journal of Lt. John Trevett, USN
North Carolina Department of Archives and History, Raleigh, North
    Carolina (NCDAH)
    Hayes Manuscripts
Public Record Office, London, England (PRO)
    Andrew Doria Journal

Rhode Island Archives, Providence, Rhode Island (RIArch.)
   Governor Nicholas Cooke Papers
   Muster Rolls, Revolutionary War Vessels
Rhode Island Historical Society, Providence, Rhode Island (RIHS)
   Moses Brown Papers
   Collections
   Hopkins Papers
   Miner, George L., Notes, Sloop *Katy*
   Miscellaneous Manuscripts
   Muster Roll, Sloop *Providence*
   Rhode Island Manuscripts
   Vernon Papers (Papers of William Vernon and the Eastern Navy Board)
   Abraham Whipple Papers

PRINTED SOURCES

Adams, John. *The Works of John Adams*. With notes by Charles Francis Adams. Boston: Little, Brown, 1865. vol. III.

Bartlett, John Russell. *Colonial Records of Rhode Island*. Providence: A. Crawford Greene, 1862.

Bartlett, John Russell. *The Destruction of the* Gaspee. Providence: A. Crawford Greene, 1861.

Baxter, James P., ed. *Documentary History of the State of Maine*. Portland: Lefaser and Tower, 1910. vols. XVI, XVII.

Beck, Alverda S., ed. *The Correspondence of Esek Hopkins Commander in Chief of the United States Navy*. Providence: Rhode Island Historical Society, 1933. 101 pp.

——————. *The Letter Book of Esek Hopkins Commander in Chief of the United States Navy*. Providence: Rhode Island Historical Society, 1932. 151 pp.

Clark, William B. and Morgan, William J., eds. *Naval Documents of the American Revolution*. Washington: Naval History Division, Department of the Navy, 1964–1972. vols. I–VI.

Fitzpatrick, John C., ed. *The Writings of George Washington,* from the Original Manuscript Sources, 1745–1799. Washington: Government Printing Office, 1931–1938.

Force, Peter, ed. *American Archives*. Washington: M. St. Clair Clarke and Peter Force, 1837–1853. 4th ser., 6 vols. (Mar. 7, 1774 to Aug. 21, 1776); 5th ser., 3 vols. (May 3, 1776 to Dec. 31, 1776). No more published.

Ford, Worthington C., ed. *Correspondence and Journals of Samuel Blachley Webb*. New York: The Wickersham Press, 1893–1894. 3 vols.

Ford, Worthington C. et al, eds. *Journals of the Continental Congress,* 1774–1789. Washington: Government Printing Office, 1904–1937. 34 vols.

Fort Ticonderoga Museum Bulletin. Fort Ticonderoga, N.Y.

Knollenberg, Bernhard, ed. *Correspondence of Governor Samuel Ward, May 1775–March 1776*. With a biographical introduction based chiefly on the Ward Papers, covering the period 1725–1776. Providence: Rhode Island Historical Society, 1952. 254 pp.

Massachusetts Soldiers and Sailors of the Revolutionary War. A compilation from the archives prepared by the Secretary of the Commonwealth. Boston: Wright and Potter, 1896. 17 vols.

Nash, Gilbert. *The Original Journal of General Solomon Lovell, Kept During the Penobscot Expedition, 1779, with a Sketch of His Life.* Boston: Weymouth Historical Society, 1881. 127 pp.

Paullin, Charles O. *Out-Letters of the Continental Marine Committee and Board of Admiralty August, 1776–September, 1780.* New York: De Vinne Press, 1914. 2 vols.

"Records of the Vice-Admiralty Court at Halifax, Nova Scotia: The Condemnation of Prizes and Recaptures of the Revolution and the War of 1812." *Historical Collections of the Essex Institute.*

Revolutionary Correspondence of Governor Nicholas Cooke. *Proceedings of the American Antiquarian Society,* New Series, XXXVI.

Stiles, Ezra. *Dr. Ezra Stiles Literary Diary.* Force Transcript. Washington: Library of Congress.

Trevett, John. "Journal of Lieutenant John Trevett, USN." *Rhode Island Historical Magazine,* Newport: Newport Historical Publishing Company, 1885–1886. vols. 6 and 7.

"Papers of William Vernon and the Navy Board." *Publications of the Rhode Island Historical Society,* vol. VIII, no. 4. Providence: Rhode Island Historical Society, 1901, pp. 197–277.

Washington, George. *Autograph Letters of George Washington, from the Collection of Frederick S. Peck, Belton Court, Barrington, Rhode Island.* Providence: Rhode Island State Bureau of Information, 1932. 32 pp.

NEWSPAPERS

Boston Independent Chronicle
Connecticut Courant
Newport Mercury
New York Journal
North Carolina Gazette
Providence Gazette and Country Journal
South Carolina American and General Gazette

SECONDARY SOURCES

Allen, Gardner W. *A Naval History of the American Revolution.* Boston: Houghton Mifflin, 1913. 2 vols.

Arnold, Samuel Green. *History of the State of Rhode Island.* D. Appleton and Co., N. Y.: 1860. 2 vols.

Atkinson, Amalia I. *Captain Rathbun's Last Voyage.* New England Historical and Genealogical Register. Boston, Mass. vol. CXV.

Chapelle, Howard I. *The History of the American Sailing Navy.* New York: Norton, 1949.

Clowes, William L. *The Royal Navy, a History from the Earliest Times to the Present.* Boston: Little, Brown, 1899. 7 vols.

Cooper, J. Fenimore. *The History of the Navy of the United States of America.* Philadelphia: Thomas Cowperthwait and Co., 1841.

Cowell, Benjamin. *Spirit of '76 in Rhode Island.* Boston: A. J. Wright, Printer, 1850.

Ellis, Leonard B. *History of New Bedford and Its Vicinity, 1602–1892.* Syracuse: D. Mason & Co., 1892.

Emerson, Amelia F. *Early History of Naushon Island.* Boston: Thomas Todd Co., 1935.

Emmons, George F. *The Navy of the United States, from the Commencement 1775 to 1852; with a Brief History of Each Vessel's Service and Fate as Appears upon Record.* Washington: Gideon and Co., 1853.

Field, Edward. *Esek Hopkins Commander in Chief of the Continental Navy During the American Revolution 1775 to 1778.* Providence: Preston and Rounds Co., 1898.

Hedges, James B. *The Browns of Providence Plantations—The Colonial Years.* Providence: Brown University Press, 1968.

Lorenz, Lincoln. *John Paul Jones, Fighter for Freedom and Glory.* Annapolis: United States Naval Institute, 1943.

Morgan, William James. *Captains to the Northward.* Barre, Mass.: Barre Gazette, 1959.

Morison, Samuel Eliot. *John Paul Jones—A Sailor's Biography.* Boston: Little, Brown, 1959.

Neeser, Robert W. *Statistical and Chronological History of the United States Navy, 1775–1907.* New York: Macmillan, 1909. 2 vols.

Rathbun, Frank H. "Rathbun's Raid on Nassau." *United States Naval Institute Proceedings,* Vol. XCVI (November, 1970), 40–47.

Ricketson, Daniel, *The History of New Bedford.* New Bedford: Privately Printed, 1858.

Roelker, William Greene. "The Patrol of Narragansett Bay (1774–76)," *Rhode Island History,* VIII, 45–63.

Smith, Charles R. *Marines in the Revolution.* Washington: History and Museums Division, U. S. Marine Corps, 1975.

Index

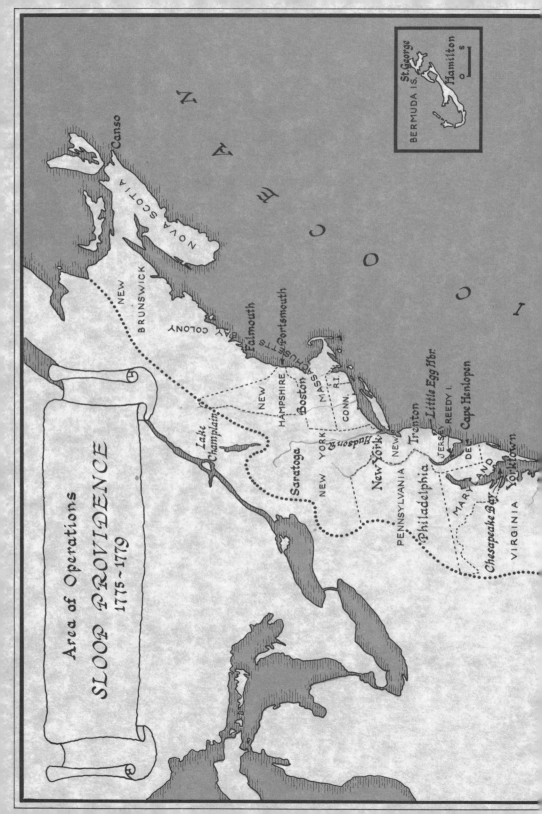

Area of Operations
SLOOP PROVIDENCE
1775 ~ 1779

Canso

NOVA SCOTIA

NEW BRUNSWICK

ATLANTIC OCEAN

MASSACHUSETTS BAY COLONY

Falmouth
Portsmouth

Lake Champlain

NEW HAMPSHIRE

Boston

MASS.

R.I.

CONN.

Saratoga

NEW YORK

Hudson

NEW YORK

Trenton

Little Egg Hbr.

REEDY I.

Cape Henlopen

PENNSYLVANIA

NEW JERSEY

Philadelphia

DEL.

MARYLAND

Chesapeake Bay

Yorktown

VIRGINIA

BERMUDA IS.

St. George

Hamilton

0   5

BERMUDA IS.

Dorothy deFontaine

A T L A N T I C

N

NORTH
CAROLINA

New Bern

SOUTH
CAROLINA

Georgetown

Charleston

GEORGIA

Savannah

St. Augustine

Gulf of
Mexico

ABACO

BAHAMA IS.
NEW PROVIDENCE

0   150   300
Miles